A TASTE OF
PARIS

ALSO BY DAVID DOWNIE

A Passion for Paris:
Romanticism and Romance in the City of Light

Paris to the Pyrenees:
A Skeptic Pilgrim Walks the Way of Saint James

Paris, Paris: Journey into the City of Light

Quiet Corners of Rome

Paris City of Night

Food Wine Burgundy

Food Wine Rome

Food Wine Italian Riviera & Genoa

Cooking the Roman Way:
Authentic Recipes from the Home Cooks and
Trattorias of Rome

Enchanted Liguria:
A Celebration of the Culture, Lifestyle and
Food of the Italian Riviera

La Tour de l'Immonde

The Irreverent Guide to Amsterdam

Un'altra Parigi
(with Ulderico Munzi)

A TASTE OF PARIS

A History of the Parisian Love Affair with Food

DAVID DOWNIE

ST. MARTIN'S PRESS
New York

Printed in the United States of America. For information, address St. Martin's Press, 175 Fifth Avenue, New York, N.Y. 10010.

www.stmartins.com

Library of Congress Cataloging-in-Publication Data

Names: Downie, David, author.
Title: A taste of Paris : a history of the Parisian love affair with food / David Downie.
Description: First edition. | New York : St. Martin's Press, [2017]
Identifiers: LCCN 2017018869 | ISBN 9781250082930 (hardcover) | ISBN 9781250082954 (ebook)
Subjects: LCSH: Food—France—Paris—History. | Gastronomy—France. | Paris (France)—Description and travel.
Classification: LCC TX637 .D657 2017 | DDC 394.1/20944361—dc23
LC record available at https://lccn.loc.gov/2017018869

10 9 8 7 6 5 4 3 2

To the courageous, life-loving Parisians
who know Paris will always be Paris
despite demagoguery and terror

Thought is entirely dependent on the stomach nonetheless those with the best stomachs are not the best thinkers.

—*Voltaire writing to Jean le Rond d'Alembert,* 1770

CONTENTS

PART FIVE

ENTRÉES, *TROISIÈME* SERVICE: VERSAILLES *À LA ROYALE,* 1638–1715

PART SIX

ENTRÉES, *QUATRIÈME* SERVICE: *ANCIENNE* NOUVELLE, 1700S

PART SEVEN

ENTREMETS, *CINQUIÈME* SERVICE: REGIME CHANGE, LATE 1700S–EARLY 1800S

PART EIGHT

HORS D'OEUVRES: DINING OUT, 1800S

PART NINE

DESSERT: MODERN TIMES, MID-1800S–LATE 1900S

PART TEN

DIGESTIF: NEO-RETRO-POST-POSTMODERN *NOUVELLE D'AUTEUR,* 1970S–THE PRESENT

THANKS AND ACKNOWLEDGMENTS

A huge *merci* to my wonderful and talented editor, Charles Spicer, and *magnifique* agent, Alice Martell, for their viral enthusiasm, skill, and friendship; my wife, Alison Harris, for her research and incisive suggestions; and David Malone, for once again providing a retreat where I was able to do much of the research for this book.

Many thanks to friends Alice Brinton, Catherine Healey, and Mia Monasterli for logistical help; to Andrew Dalby for his wisdom regarding ancient Lutetia; to Jorge Zelaya and Alan Perry, caterers extraordinaire, for explorations of Paris' food supply chain; to friends, relatives, and colleagues including Jean Kahn, Russ Schleipmann, Lou and Dan Jordan, Stacy and Marianne Pagos and Keith Haller, Janet Hulstrand, Elatia Harris, Jonell Galloway and Peter White, Adrienne Kimball, the Horne family, the Labadie and Kuhl families, Jamie DeMent and Richard Holcomb, Everett and Shirlene Harris, Paul and Amy Taylor, Jay Smith, Don George, Linda Watanabe McFerrin and Joanne Biggar of Left Coast Writers, Karen West of Book Passage, Diane Downie and Paul Shelley, Janet and Chapin Day (and Laurie, Evie, Susan, Elaine and Larry), Margo MacTaggert and Chris Oram, Sheila Fischman and Don Winkler, Sandra Gilbert, Adrien Leeds, Charles Trueheart and Grant Rosenberg, who by their generosity have made our book tours and events possible.

Official thanks to the researchers, librarians, and historians at the Bibliothèque Mazarine (Patrick Latour, Christophe Vellet, and Florine Levecque),

Marie-Laure Deschamps and Sylvie Robin at the Musée Carnavalet, Catherine Brut of DHAAP, Marie-France Noël-Waldteufel and Jérémie Benoit (Le Petit Trianon) at the Château de Versailles, Steven Wright of UCL Special Collections, and Jeffrey H. Jackson of Rhodes College, and to April Osborn at St. Martin's Press.

A TASTE OF PARIS

PART ONE

Aperitif

"Garçon, a taste of Paris, s'il vous plait!"

A CONSPIRACY OF PLEASURE

Imagine a gastronomic romp through Paris weaving the living past into the lively present, the story of the great Parisian conspiracy to enjoy life—the city's centuries-old passion for food, wine, dining out, and entertaining. That's what this book is about.

Long ago this love affair with food and wine earned Paris the title of the world's capital of fine dining. I had a foretaste of the fun as a young man during my first visit to the city in 1976. A decade later in the spring of 1986 I became a full-time conspirator, taking possession of a seventh-floor, cold-water walk-up maid's room in the 17th arrondissement near the Arc de Triomphe. As soon as I unpacked I began mapping out Paris' gastronomic topography—the markets, stores, restaurants, and cafés that became my second home.

As a lover of edibles, potables, and urban exploration, my goal was to transform my life into an endless treasure hunt through the City of Light's historical layers, from the roughshod days of ancient Gaul and Julius Caesar to the multicultural, molecular present and its superstar chefs. That joyful, sometimes irreverent, unapologetically personal treasure hunt is the object of these pages.

On that first chill day in November over forty years ago I sensed the sublime Parisian conjunction of things contemporary marinated in yesteryear. But I was only eighteen and could not understand how or why the intersection of physical, historical, and cultural ingredients had come together, placing Paris above other great food cities like Rome, Madrid, London, New York, and Shanghai.

My first sit-down lunch in Paris in 1976 was anything but gourmet. I chose a vintage bistro on the lateral heights of Montmartre far from the scrum at Sacré-Coeur, a church that still looks to me like a lumpy white wedding cake topped with scaly octopus-head cupolas. The bistro had a tobacco burnish. It also smelled of wine, stale beer, toasted cheese, and sweat with an overlay of talcum powder and perfume: Parisians at the time seemed allergic to soap and water. An unusual wire rack on the bar displayed hard-boiled eggs. I watched fascinated as grizzled men peeled the eggs and wolfed them while gulping glassfuls of white wine and joking at someone's expense, possibly mine.

Alone on the outdoor terrace I studied my foot-long baguette sandwich. It sat on a white saucer on a round table tilted above the drizzly city. Peeking inside I saw ham, cheese, and cornichons. Beyond, through the misty keyhole view, were the tin-covered gabled roofs and distant spires of the city bathing in native sepia. I devoured the atmosphere. The sandwich seemed secondary.

Most of all I remember the eye-stinging mustard, presumably from Dijon. It came in a white porcelain jar with a wooden paddle. The waitress showed me how to apply it not with a spoon to the ham and cheese, but rather on the doughy inside of the bread using the paddle. It was the first of many corrections.

In retrospect the baguette was probably baked from frozen dough and the ham, cheese, mustard, and pickles pulled out of cold cases and off dusty shelves. I didn't know and wouldn't have cared. I was in love.

CALIFORNIAN CUISINE

In the mid-twentieth century when I came of age in enlightened Northern California, even in a gourmet household the zeitgeist was not yet organic, free range, fair trade, locally grown, or homebrewed. Sourcing was limited. The farmers' markets and mom-and-pops were gone. For the boomer children of the 1950s and '60s, like me, supermarkets were playgrounds. My mother, a European transplant, adored them.

Paris was different. No matter what they looked like or where they lived Parisians shopped and ate with glee. Unlike me they were thin amid indescribable bounty. If I flipped a franc, it would land on something worth swallowing. Shoehorned between the bistros and cafés, restaurants and brasseries, chocolate shops and wine shops were groceries of the kind we no longer had. The butcher shops were decorated with flocks of farmyard animals and wild game, the real thing but now very dead, staring at passersby from hooks, fur, head, feathers, tusks, and horns trickling. Whole lambs' heads roasted along with the chickens in giant rotisseries. You had to love food to gaze at the offerings with rapture as the Parisians did. The displays reminded me of still-life paintings in the Louvre, masterpieces of gore.

I learned to say "fishmonger" in French and stood mesmerized before the stands where live crabs and lobsters wrestled. Back home the same entertainments were staged at Fisherman's Wharf for tourists. Here normal customers bought live sea creatures, dragging them away in caddies with squeaky wheels or slung into premodern string bags. The oysters came in a variety of shapes and sizes, on the half shell or whole. I wondered if each tasted different. What work to cook them, I thought, until I saw diners gulping them raw like the seals gobbling sardines at Fleishhacker Zoo in San Francisco.

The vegetable end of the spectrum was no less astonishing. Pyramids of bumpy, contorted squashes and lopsided orange pumpkins, anemic apples, and suggestively shaped pears tumbled from fruit stands. Nowhere had I seen or smelled so many cheeses: mold-pocked blue or green Roquefort, runny Vacherin, and giant wheels of aged hard Comté or floppy Brie oozed and rolled and crept across counters and sidewalk tables. They seemed eager to escape, like the lobsters and crabs. On street corners charcoal-dusted men wearing berets yodeled and hawked blackened chestnuts. I burned my fingers and palate on a paper cone brimming with them hot off a brazier.

Burned, blistered, and puckered my mouth would not stop watering. Drowning by hunger seemed a real possibility. Cold intensified the sensation. The chattering of my teeth could not erase the red wine stains on them renewed daily at lunch and dinner. Thanksgiving was upon us. But the streets of Paris were a permanent party, the city laid out like overstocked supermarket aisles and banqueting tables. Maybe every day was Thanksgiving in Paris. Hadn't I read somewhere about a movable feast? The relish for life spread across the sidewalks, giving everything, even the smoggy yellow atmosphere, a special flavor, a tasty tang.

That first taste of Paris was one reason I relocated to the city ten years later. In the interim, I had slimmed down from an obese youth into an average-sized late twenty-something. By reading Sartre, Camus, and others I had also caught an incurable disease: romantic existentialism. The binomial seemed contradictory, but was really a paradox. Where else could I live and write but Paris?

DELICIOUS AND SOMETIMES NUTRITIOUS

Beyond the low rent, an unforeseen dividend of my windowless garret was the lack of kitchen facilities. Eating was an adventure. The cafés, bistros, and brasseries offered cheap, often delicious, and sometimes nutritious fare. No proper bohemian novelist had a kitchen. Never did Balzac, Hugo, Flaubert, Musset, or Maupassant, let alone their female counterparts think of preparing food or shopping and cleaning.

Regularly scheduled escapes from my room were essential. I got busy drawing up a roster of favorite places for watching the world sup and swill. They exuded an attainable past, a flavorful, redolent history to be studied and consumed. The choice seemed limitless.

In the existentialist enclave of Saint-Germain, for example, I skipped the haute touristy Les Deux Magots, Café de Flore, and Brasserie Lipp, and went several times a week to Le Petit Saint-Benoit, unchanged then and still in business now, a Left Bank landmark. Unchanged meant the menu, bread and tooth-staining wines had presumably been around in similar form since the restaurant's founding in the Belle Époque. The requisite cloth-draped wooden tables for two lined the sidewalk. They were crammed side by side indoors, where a chalkboard hung, a cabinet with numbered pigeonholes held the napkins of regulars, and the waitstaff snapped dishcloths at crumbs and shouted after spiking your scrawled order for crunchy crudités, green pepper steak, and a carafe of white or red. The dining room was scented by garlic and sautéed onions, boiled fish and beefy pot-au-feu, roasted pork and cigarette smoke. The firm-boiled potatoes and herrings came bathed in seed oil, not in Ernest Hemingway's bread-mopped olive oil from *A Moveable Feast* but that seemed alright. Maybe things were different in the 1920s, I reasoned, and anyway who cared if Hemingway preferred remembering olive oil.

The Right Bank was also rife with romantic dives. One particularly dark and seedy street, a contemporary Court of Miracles in the still-unfashionable, smog-blackened Marais was home to Le P'tit Gavroche. The food was less memorable than the adhesive quality of this shadowy old bistro's tile floor. But the tawny interior and the literary moniker made up for it. Gavroche evoked the heroic street urchin of Victor Hugo's *Les Misérables,* a ragamuffin who would have gladly sunk his baby teeth into anything including the bistro's veal blanquette thickened with fistfuls of flour. I loved it, lumps and all.

Both Gavroche and Hugo had lived nearby: Hugo in a lavish mansion on Place des Vosges, Gavroche at Place de la Bastille inside a giant papier-mâché elephant, as told in a remarkable work of fiction. Hugo's favorite part of Paris for many years was the Marais, and it soon became mine, and my new home, in the shape of a tiny apartment complete with an electric hot plate and indoor plumbing. New digs and mod cons didn't stop my culinary explorations.

Also on my growing list of restaurants, places glowing with the brand of yesteryear that fed my gaudy imagination, was the venerable Trumilou on Quai de l'Hôtel de Ville. A hundred yards east of city hall, this was one of those joints we used to call "greasy spoons" where white and blue collars slid their backsides on oxblood-red vinyl banquettes. Trumilou has improved to the point of unrecognizability, but in the mid-1980s was known for its yellowish walls, a palimpsest of insect-capturing layers. The kitchen supplied the tacky grease. Generations of clients layered on the cigarette, pipe, and cigar fumes that made swirls on the walls when grazed by stray fingers. The food seemed succulent enough, though everything including the celery root salad, braised rabbit, Normandy apple tart, and house wine had a smoked quality, still the case in many Paris eateries today, where tobacco addiction is a prerequisite for hiring. Performance art—an unrecognized native specialty—reached paroxysms if a fly or hair was found in the onion soup or a member of the scarab family scurried along the wainscoting.

Farther inland on the Right Bank, with lighting from some long-ago World's Fair, linear miles of brass, and ranges of napkin nooks for regulars, Bouillon Chartier served the working classes, package tourists, and ladies of the night of the Faubourg Montmartre and Grands Boulevards. I long suspected that Émile Zola and the real-life doppelgänger of his prostitute-heroine Nana, as well as the sexually repressed Symbolist painter Gustave Moreau and his equivocal partners were habitués at Chartier a century or so before I became one. This appetizing, speculative condiment helped send down the mounds of oven-roasted potatoes and chicken of admittedly indifferent texture and fleeting flavor.

The Latin Quarter was even lousier with atmospheric dives, more than could be counted, largely because they were hidden in banks of smoldering tobacco. Coughing, my eyes filled with tears, I sometimes joined the hordes of college kids crowded into the single, airless dining room of Polidor on rue Monsieur le Prince, later glorified in Woody Allen's nostalgic *Midnight in Paris*.

Did Allen know that pioneering Romantic Age photographer Félix Nadar had lived four buildings up the street at number 45, and may well have procured the oysters he famously swallowed for months on end from the eatery that was here before the founding of Polidor?

I don't recall ever seeing oysters on the menu of student places like Polidor thirty or forty years ago. Then again especially in the days before 2007 when

Bistro in the rue Mouffetard, 19th century

smoking was allowed indoors it was easy not to see, and even easier not to pay attention to what was on your plate in Paris. What anyone ate or drank was not what the restaurant experience was about. The unappetizing term "foodie" and the nauseating "foodista" had not yet been coined. Wine bores were still rarely seen outside Michelin-starred temples of haute cuisine, and I had neither the means nor the desire to enter them.

Each distinctive quarter of the city boasted several nonesuch eateries of iffy repute, only-in-Paris locales with handwritten, mimeographed menus generally bearing dates of foundation reaching into the nineteenth century, the golden age of Paris restaurants and a coveted pedigree.

Though I did not patronize them I mapped out the upper scale from centuries past and sometimes stood before the city's gastronomic pilgrimage sites at dinnertime, fantasizing about what I would eat and who I might meet. Le Taillevent, named for France's first celebrity chef and cookbook writer, was so exclusive you could not even approach it if improperly attired. I didn't eat there until I'd lived in Paris for over a decade.

Given the location on the quay of another famous luxury restaurant, I could not help speculating whether the supreme Romantic seducer, the poet, playwright, and novelist Alfred de Musset had held George Sand's famously small hands at a table in the dark recesses of Le Voltaire. This velvety establishment was and remains in the building where Voltaire, a fussy eater, having finished *Candide* and several other masterpieces, died in the dying days of the Ancien Régime. It was plausible. If not Le Voltaire, then Musset and Sand might have been habitués at the even older and more beautiful Lapérouse a few blocks upstream. Sand, among the world's unrepentant lushes, lived in an attic apartment between the two establishments. Only once in my bachelor days did I enter either restaurant and then only to glance around before being

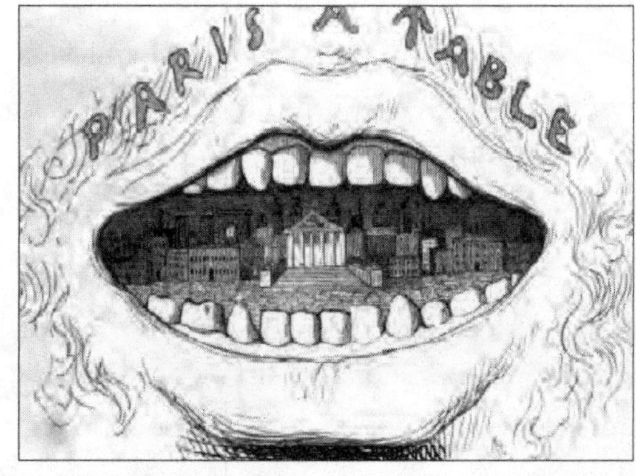

Paris as Temple of Gastronomy, from Eugène Briffault's 1846 Paris à table

escorted out. A single meal at such a place would have cost more than my monthly rent, ruining me the way his first meal in Paris at Véry ruined Balzac's tragic hero Lucien de Rubempré.

A RECIPE FOR CULINARY SEDUCTION

Le P'tit Gavroche is no longer in business. The longevity and apparent changelessness of the others I knew over a quarter-century ago is like that of Paris itself—tenacious and little short of miraculous. So it is not surprising, not to me, that decades after my early explorations these and scores of similar revamped evergreen establishments still thrive. The theatricality of the experience is intact despite the digital age and is, I have long suspected, one of the ingredients in the Parisian recipe for culinary seduction: atmosphere, *atmosphere*! Courtship, love, romance, sex, and food are intimately linked in the City of Light.

Ironically, given my love of history and the past, in the late 1980s I was contracted by Paris' hip, sassy, modernist Gault & Millau guides to edit, translate, adapt, and contribute to various European guidebooks for the American market. Through my labors I soon discovered the cookbooks and revolutionary writings of the classic Napoleonic-era chef Antonin Carême and his contemporaries the proto-food theorists Grimod de la Reynière and Jean Anthelme Brillat-Savarin. They piqued my curiosity about the rise of French cuisine. Luckily Gault & Millau also championed "terroir," a newfangled concept it seemed to me but one I embraced with gusto, especially when I found that the term was coined in the early 1800s. Eventually I began writing restaurant reviews and travel articles for publications worldwide and in the 1990s added my own guidebooks and cookbooks to the mix, then histories, crime novels, and essay collections. As a correspondent or contributing editor to an array of glossy magazines, my assignments often came with all expenses paid.

I navigated the galaxy of the Michelin-starred temples of gastronomy, savoring their sous vide, *chaudfroid*, vertically constructed, molecular, intoxicatingly complex cuisine. It often left me feeling dazed, queasy, and baffled.

Food and wine had become a livelihood and a way of life. I poked new holes in my belts then bought new, longer belts and an elasticized wardrobe. As the years turned into decades and I realized I was a Paris lifer I became increasingly fascinated by the Who, Where, When, Why, and How of the city, especially its culinary past.

Where and how had the Parisian love affair with food and wine started? Was it genetic or a myth, like the French Paradox? Had the Gallic tribespeople and their Roman conquerors loved eating and drinking and handed the tradition to their successors, or had it all begun in the Middle Ages, the Renaissance, or in Versailles during the reigns of the gourmandizing Bourbon kings such as Louis XIV? The nineteenth century seemed like yesterday in Paris so I guessed that's when modern tastes were formed.

The past was endlessly engrossing, but it eventually became clear to me that it was equally urgent to ask some hard questions: Was Paris, the birthplace of the restaurant and haute cuisine, still the greatest of food cities and if so why? Had French cooking died, as some pundits claimed, including brash Americans parachuted behind the lines with expense accounts and attitude?

To find at least a few of the answers to these questions and place them in something like chronological order I decided to begin at the beginning, in the bull's-eye of the city, where Paris was born more than two thousand years ago, the Île de la Cité and Latin Quarter, and share my findings in book form. Voilà: *A Taste of Paris.*

Paris, edible Panthéon, Eugène Briffault, Paris à table, *1846*

PART TWO

For Starters

Antiquity *à la Parisienne*, c. 53 BC–c. AD 500

A medieval vision of ancient Lutetia Parisiorum, 13th-century map

CRYPTIC CULTURE

It was ordained that the Île de la Cité should be shaped like a ship and anchored midstream in the Seine, a floating Holy of Holies in the flow of Paris history. In its glory days the island gave modern vocabularies like our own the word and notion of "city"—and much else. Despite the ravages of rebuilding in the mid-1800s and the blight of contemporary mass tourism, the isle still provides a fine backdrop, not to grab, but rather to sip a coffee or tea or linger over something spirited. When the mood moves me, and my gastronomic balance of priorities places atmosphere over food, as it did in my early days in Paris, I sometimes indulge in an unambitious meal at a café or restaurant that was once the haunt of aristocrats, clergymen, or my favorite fictional police commissioner, Jules Amedée François Maigret.

Ungenerous critics consider the Île de la Cité a culinary wasteland with nary a gourmet food or wine emporium, no outdoor markets except those selling songbirds and potted palms, and not a single remarkable place to eat. Certainly they're right. But they also miss the perennial intangible attraction: This is ground zero in the edible and drinkable epic of Paris. Squint and salivate and you might discover that the monument-studded island is a stony *mille-feuille,* a luscious layer cake of mixed metaphor, mongrel civilization, and dubious lore.

Before digging for buried treasure, to whet my appetite I usually give a nod to Notre Dame, the current, 850-year-old iteration of the city's prime place of worship, a worthy successor to the Temple of Jupiter secreted, it's claimed, in bits and pieces somewhere under the cathedral. Then I descend into the archaeological crypt fronting this hallowed shrine of the Gothic and get down to speculative business.

All distances in France are measured from a brass circle set into the paving of the square above the crypt. Metaphorically, distances in style, technique, and fashion in French cooking, eating, and entertaining might also be measured from here.

Making up the *mille-feuille* are alternating layers of limestone, sandstone, and brick, crumbled foundation walls, broken paving stones, hewn blocks, column bases, streets and wells from late antiquity or the Middle Ages, a section of nineteenth-century sewer, and prodigious quantities of dust. What has the crypt to do with anyone's passion for food and wine? The answer is fairly simple: by reading the rubble like a recipe your imagination can reconstruct a lost world that isn't as lost as all that. Traces and remnants of Rome are easy enough to identify in the streets and on the menus of the city today, and in the culinary preferences of Parisians.

The most telling vestige is the ancient rampart of Lutetia Parisiorum, the "mud city" or "city near the swamps" of the Celtic Parisii tribe, a place subsumed into the Roman Empire's maw almost 2,100 years ago by Julius Caesar and his legions.

After nearly three centuries of prosperity and security the stones for building this massive wall were quarried in the late third century AD from the arena and amphitheater by the Romans themselves—to keep the barbarians at bay. The rampart is the first of many rings of city walls, an old-growth tree or a halved onion if you prefer. Like their ancestors, certain contemporary Parisians cultivate a siege mentality: the 1970s beltway around the glittering City of Light separating it from the benighted suburbs and the rest of the world is the latest rampart, an objective correlative of socioeconomic, ethnic, and culinary isolationism. The center of town is still officially called Paris *intra muros*: intramural Paris, meaning "within the walls."

Skeptics, culinary nationalists, and incorrigible optimists may wriggle, but French gastronomy is more like the rampart, city walls, and beltway of Paris than you might at first imagine. It's an edifice built with a dash of originality from the inventively recycled, resized, and repurposed past, a bulwark of national identity against what's widely perceived nowadays as barbarian globalization, gastronomic and otherwise. This attitude isn't new: Louis XIV began instituting French culinary nationalism over three hundred years ago.

See what happens when you try telling French chefs—especially the coven of militant star chefs who have lobbied UNESCO to list the French way of cooking and eating among the world's intangible treasures—that French cuisine, language, and culture are a hodgepodge. You're likely to be throttled by a sous-vide tube if you point out that culinary protectionism goes against everything history teaches about this nation and its cuisine.

Nationalists enjoy oysters as much as the next guy but they're unlikely to swallow suggestions that the city of Paris itself grew like an oyster shell, in layers, built from the intermingling of imported styles, merging the Mediterranean and Northern Europe, and so did the culture that produced the often-complicated delicacies and refined nectars Parisians and visitors adore today or prefer to fashionably disdain as unworthy of past greatness. The culinary continuum reaches from the Celts and Romans to the contemporary practitioners of haute and molecular. No rampart or beltway can protect it, and it's worth asking the big question of whether any should.

The crypt's dizzying historical vortex and especially its dust are guaranteed to impart upon visitors a mighty thirst. They always leave me eager for fresh air, sunlight, and drink. Where? A creature of habit I take a turn around the buttressed back of the cathedral before following rue Chanoinesse, one of the only old streets left on the island, curved like a jawbone with teeth as crooked as my own. Narrow and scarred, the street was traced in the time of the food-and-wine-loving Charlemagne along the inside of the Ancient Roman rampart that girded the island like a pudding mold.

If ever the carriage doors stand open when I pass, I brave the wrath of concierges and sneak into the courtyards behind. Some harbor mossy medieval wells, half-timbered buildings, and sculpted wooden banisters on steep, openwork staircases. Others are paved with tombstones snatched from erstwhile places of worship, and incorporate sections of a chapel and a fortified tower destroyed a century or more ago. Several of the buildings' foundations and cellars date from the city's remotest days. One scenic slumping landmark houses what is among Paris' longest-lived hostelries, Au Vieux Paris d'Arcole.

Depending on whose wisdom you consult and which way your tastes lie, Au Vieux Paris is either the prototypical honeypot for those who can't spell "gastronomy" in a spelling bee or it's a rare slice of living history. You won't be crowded by locals in the dining rooms, that's for sure, but the same can be said of the city's internationally revered temples of gastronomy and its hot spots and "bistronomie" gastro-bistros, too. No French spoken.

Unsurprisingly given the proximity of the cathedral the property was originally owned by the church and dates to about 1512. It's been a tavern or similar since either 1594 or 1723, the record isn't clear. Either way few establishments in Paris have been around longer. "Quaint" is writ large. Blacked wrought-iron bars on the windows attest to the pre-Revolutionary presence of a wine seller's shop and watering hole. The wisteria-draped façade and wantonly romantic faux-medieval décor; the old prints, rough stone walls, and exposed timbers; the wall sconces, chandeliers, and miles of scarlet upholstery and wallpaper, not to mention the boudoir-like salons upstairs in what were bedrooms, set the scene. In the vaulted cellar, patrons may select a bottle—some of them very good—to accompany a meal and, while at it, are free to imagine the prelates of old doing the same. Few ate better in medieval and Renaissance Paris than churchmen and women.

Guests are plied not with ersatz re-creations of Parisian fare from the Renaissance, but with edible specialties from the Aveyron region of the Massif Central, the cradle of at least half the city's crabby café and restaurant owners—grumpiness like tobacco addiction being a prerequisite in the business. Subtract some of the overabundant sauces and pause for thought before you raise your fork: In a slightly different guise the foie gras, duck, or beef on your plate might have appeared on Caesar's or Charlemagne's table. But I am getting ahead of myself.

'TIS MEAT

There's another reason to follow this roundabout route. A savory, sacrilegious story clings to rue Chanoinesse—or perhaps another nearby street renamed or no longer in existence, under the city's main hospital across the way, for instance. It's the true story that inspired the ghoulish tale of *Sweeney Todd,* the one in which the barber and the meat pie maker next door carry on a gruesome trade. Books, movies, and musicals have refashioned the yarn. It's a fascinating early lesson in the dangers of iffy provenance. The actual cannibalistic events took place not in London, but here, in 1387, when the street bore the name rue des Marmousets.

"A murderous pastry-maker," wrote the ecclesiastical chronicler Jacques Du Breul in 1639, recalling the events, "aided by his neighbor, a barber, who pretended to give a man a shave, killed the man in his house and used his flesh to make meat pies which were found to be more delicious than others, given that the flesh of humans is more delicate than that of other animals because of the foods man eats."

One wonders how Jacques Du Breul knew.

I'm told the best cuts of homo sapiens are sweet, like horseflesh, but I couldn't swear to it. Like venison, horsemeat isn't to my liking though I've eaten it several times. Out of curiosity or professional necessity and sometimes unwittingly I have eaten many things in many places, from the rotten, long-buried shark fin of Greenland to the *garum* fermented fish sauce of Rome or the worm-filled wriggling cheeses of Sardinia; the roasted eyeballs of sheep and heads of calf or kid to the teats of cows and the milk-filled intestines of their offspring; the lungs, esophagus, and brains of suckling lambs; tons of tripe and bowels and blubber; lard and pig-blood sausages, pig's trotters and marrow-filled long-cooked trotter bones; guinea pig, cockscombs, ostrich, cat, dog, crocodile, snake, eel; the caviar of snails and spawn of river fish and the eggs of too many species to count; frog legs and sea urchins and sea cucumbers and oysters and cockles and mussels or octopus and squid carpaccio, too. But of all the things I've ingested I have not tasted human flesh. Not to my knowledge, at least. Perhaps my favorite Parisian pâté or terrine was sourced from a barber shop?

Anthropophagy has a long and noble pedigree in France: Caesar remarked upon the cannibalism of the Celts of Gaul who considered the practice an act of courage, the ultimate siege food at Alesia, for instance, where the courageous Vercingétorix and his Gallic tribesmen resisted. It did not, alas, save them from Rome. In antiquity, cannibalistic barbarism was fairly common: Certain Romans of the decadence delighted in supping on giant moray eels fed with the flesh of butchered slaves. As Voltaire noted, "The same crimes are committed everywhere: to eat your enemies is but an extra ceremonial. The wrong does not consist in roasting, but in killing them."

Charlemagne, salad-lover, from a 15th-century stained-glass window, Moulins cathedral

By rounding the corner from rue Chanoinesse into rue de la Colombe you soon come across a cobbled pattern on the street marking the path of the Roman rampart. Following the quays west and downstream from there you pass alongside the Conciergerie, a fortress and prison from the 1200s poised atop remnants of the Royal Palace. Here the kings and queens of France lived, on and off, from late antiquity until the reign of Charles V in the second half of the 1300s. You can't exactly cup your hands and peer into the windows. If you could, you would see one of the only medieval refectories and kitchens left in Paris. The imposing stone fireplaces and chimneys in each of the four corners of the semi-subterranean Guards Room are where the victuals were prepared.

CORE SAMPLES

Where are we headed? To the Place Dauphine on the island's downstream end: I go there when I want to take a core sample, a cross section, of Paris' culinary history, starting with the first years. The reason is not merely that the kitchen gardens, orchard, and vineyard of the ancient and medieval royal palaces once stood here. Charlemagne adored lettuce, watercress, arugula, and chicory, by the way. The real reason is that the island's most appealing, least compromised cafés and restaurants line this handsome, triangular square built more than four hundred years ago by Henri IV, a king nicknamed "the evergreen gallivanting geezer." A hearty eater, formidable drinker, and unrivaled philanderer Henri IV is therefore among Parisians' favorite kings to this day.

Before you choose a roost, pause to nose the breeze. The gallant monarch's airborne equestrian statue facing the square on the Pont Neuf broadcasts, metaphorically, a winey scent of raw garlic, and perhaps stewed chicken and partridge, too. Parisian legend has it that in Henri's baptismal water floated a clove of garlic. When fully grown he munched whole heads of it, washed down with a liter or so of crisp, white Jurançon wine from his native Navarre. Henri is the ruler who ordained "a chicken in every pot" for the peasantry and, when his nagging confessor scolded him for his extravagant marital infidelities, ordered the confessor be served his favorite food, partridge, for an entire month. When at last the prelate objected "But sire, partridge again?" the king retorted "Queen again?" This is one of many reasons Henri IV is a national hero, at least among men who don't know the meaning of political correctness.

Though Place Dauphine was savaged in the 1800s and 1970s by vandal-modernizers, many of the brick-and-stone pavilions have survived at least in part. No visit is complete without an exploration of the basements. They often house the kitchens as they did in the early 1600s and now also discreetly accommodate the essential modern conveniences.

Paris' Palais de Justice and main courthouse face the quiet tree-lined enclave. It's great sport to watch which way the magistrates and lawyers waddle. Follow them. They are and always have been a reliable gastric barometer. France's twosome of celebrated writer-gourmets of the turn of the nineteenth century, the fathers of restaurant criticism Grimod de la Reynière and the epicurean philosopher Brillat-Savarin were both magistrates. To this day the legal profession is what keeps the Place Dauphine alive and real.

Sitting on the terrace of Le Bar du Caveau or perhaps Restaurant Paul, or within the thick old walls of Les Voyelles, Sequana, or La Taverne Henri IV where novelist Georges Simenon's fictional Inspecteur Maigret hung out,

I enjoy watching the waitstaff scrawl their daily culinary poetry on chalkboards while pondering what lies beneath each menu item and each paving or foundation stone. Sometimes the food is surprisingly fresh, tasty, and satisfying at these largely interchangeable eateries. But here as elsewhere in Paris sometimes I am reminded of the quip by the famous nineteenth-century food writer Charles Monselet. When a restaurateur slipped gold coins into his pocket and later complained that no review was forthcoming, Monselet exclaimed "I thought you were bribing me to *not* write about you."

CAESAR SALAD

Rewind 2,069 years give or take. In all probability the one item Julius Caesar and his lieutenant Titus Labienus did not eat was salad, at least not upon their armed entry into Lutetia Parisiorum in or around 52 BC. Episodes of battle in Lutetia are recounted in Caesar's unputdownable *The Conquest of Gaul* and it is known Caesar called a meeting of the Gallic tribes in the island-city in 53 BC, before the Parisii unwisely plumped for Vercingétorix. But it's unclear whether Rome's legions stayed long enough to have more than a picnic following the Battle of Lutetia or whether they merely watched the stronghold burn, decamped, and returned later to impose permanent rule.

Much to the chagrin of French culinary chauvinists, the written record and archaeology so far have failed to yield anything allowing investigators to affirm that Lutetia, the Parisii's capital, was notably different from other colonial Roman cities in Gaul. The imperial-era lifestyle—meaning the religious rites, arts, crafts, industries, and architecture; city planning, farming, hunting, fishing, trading, and cooking; eating, drinking, riotous banqueting, feasting, and carrying on—was remarkably similar throughout the Roman territories in Gaul. Lutetia was strategic enough and sizable enough, sited amid forests and rich farmland on navigable rivers where Bronze Age trading routes and Roman consular highways met. But it was neither extraordinarily large or populous or essential to the Roman conquest, not, at least, compared to Lyon, five times its size, or Reims, twice the size of Lyon.

Perhaps Paris had one distinct advantage: It was a relay station on the oyster run from Boulogne-sur-Mer to points south. A researcher might someday prove that an oyster shell found on the Palatine or under the Coliseum, an oyster gobbled by Cicero or Apicius or Lucullus or Emperor Nero, if you prefer, came from Boulogne and reposed for a spell in one of Lutetia's refreshing saltwater tanks—a kind of proto-aquarium apparently engineered by the greatest of Roman gourmets, the genial Marcus Gavius Apicius. Saltwater tanks were found in many cities and built to keep oysters and probably also crabs and lobsters alive far from the sea.

The modest spread of ancient Paris is well documented. It corresponds, roughly, to the Left Bank's Latin Quarter and Île de la Cité with a beachhead opposite on the Right Bank centered on today's Châtelet neighborhood. A Gallic citadel stood where the Panthéon stands today. The Romans built their forum abutting it. The record is destined to remain partial though finds continue to be made in archives and underground, in the basements and subsoil of the city and its outskirts. Who knows what will turn up next among the sewer pipes and lost car keys? Recent work on a freeway downstream from Paris at suburban Nanterre suggests the real Lutetia was sited there. Nanterre and Paris may have been parts of a sprawling settlement with multiple fortified units, probably built about two hundred years before the Romans arrived.

This is also bad news for culinary nationalists. Like the Romans, the Celts of Gaul were newcomers, a warlike Iron Age nation from the Steppes that exterminated or ingested or otherwise subsumed the Neolithic tribes residing on the Seine's banks since at least 4,000 BC. Mercenaries, headhunters, and sometime-cannibals the Celts did not decorate Lascaux or erect the dolmens and menhirs that populate the pages of *Astérix* cult comic books today. It is curious, don't you think, that modern Parisians never speak of their indigenous artistic Stone Age forebears and persist in referring sometimes in jest but often with deadening seriousness to *Nos ancêtres les Gaulois,* not a brand of cigarette.

The Battle of Lutetia must have been a muddy mess. It took place in the swampy plain of Grenelle outside the Gallic city near today's Les Invalides, where the Corsican known as Napoléon lies in his tomb. Whether Lutetia was torched by the Celts, the Romans, both, or neither, and whether the arson and surrender took place in 52 or 51 BC is a bone historians will continue to pick for another few centuries. The conquerors started building or rebuilding and reshaping the Gallic city around 30 BC—a hiatus long enough to allow the embers to cool. They chose the same site, enlarging it to about 180 acres and filling it with 10,000 imported Romans plus Celts and other "barbarians."

FIGS AND FOIE GRAS

At the height of the empire, from the first to third century AD, the swaggering Romans thought they had tamed the barbarians for good and did not bother to build a wall around Lutetia. "Rash" is a kind assessment of their forward planning.

Thanks to a century or more of digging, the sites of Lutetia's amphitheater, arena, bathhouses, main streets, river ports, and temples are known. More importantly for the earthy gastronome, so are the locations of the ancient city's slaughterhouses, dumps, and latrines. Two imperial-era butcher shops have been unearthed, one in rue de la Harpe, site of a McDonald's franchise; the other in rue Monsieur le Prince, near Polidor. It is in these underground repositories that the refuse, waste, and butchered carcasses of ages past are consulted, like the frail manuscripts and flaky tomes in the famous Mazarin Library nearby on the Seine, a trove of things culinary from the late Middle Ages to the Modern Age, where I am often to be found working up an appetite.

One unusual fact remains a mystery: Despite the millennia-old Parisian passion for salad, and despite the Romans' mania for arugula and other flavorful lettuces, none have been found among digested or dumped local specialties two thousand years ago.

"Tell me why lettuce, which used to close the repasts of our forefathers, now commences our feasts?" asked the grumpy first-century poet Martial. Other than cabbage, no trace of leaf vegetables has cropped up and no root vegetables, either; not even the ubiquitous turnip. Then again the potato, so revered in the form of frites, had not yet crossed the Atlantic and turnips are admittedly pretty boring.

The evidence suggests the Celts and first Roman colonists alike fed on fava beans and lentils; peas, leeks, celery, and squash; polenta-like gruel, bread, eggs, cheeses, pork, or wild boar; mutton, beef, or river fish such as perch, pike, zander, eel, and bream. Much of the above was enlivened or at least made tolerable with copious splashes of salty *garum* or dabs of crushed garlic paste washed down with cold river water, imported Roman wine, goat's or ewe's milk, or Celtic *cervoise,* known nowadays as beer.

If this sounds limiting, stay seated, the Romans hung around for about five hundred years, creating what the French call Gallo-Roman civilization, with the "Gallo" first. They are the only conquered nation I know using a hyphen to defeat the former oppressors who gave them a language, culture, and cuisine, not to mention a gene bank constituting probably 95 percent of who they are.

By the time Julian was crowned emperor in Paris in AD 360 in the bathhouse at Cluny, the city's oldest standing structure, things were looking up. Amid the monuments and mansions, the bathhouses and theaters, a multitude of taverns, fry shops, and bakeries sprang up. On the menu was abundant local wine; large, flat oysters and shellfish from the coast; exotic fruit like figs, peaches, cherries, and pears; and game, especially boar and hare, most of it no longer wild but raised in enclosures.

This was a brief golden or perhaps a gilded age. Ironically after the first Germanic incursions of the AD 280s, Lutetia shrank back onto the Île de la Cité and in the time of Julian had morphed into what some have termed a resort or leisure community. It certainly was a lively, lawless place with plenty of entertainment, music, and revelry. The young yet serious-minded Julian was the first to call Lutetia by its modern name, Paris, and was clearly besotted by the place, not its inhabitants.

"I happened to be in winter quarters at my beloved Lutetia, for that is how the Celts call the capital of the Parisians," Julian wrote in the oldest surviving document that describes aspects of daily life in the city. "It is a small island lying in the river. A wall entirely surrounds it, and wooden bridges lead to it on both sides. The river seldom rises and falls, but usually is the same depth in the winter as in the summer, and it provides clear water which is very pleasant to drink."

From his breezy rooms in the royal palace Julian could look across the Seine upon gentle hills cloaked in vines, vineyards ringing Paris from the third to nineteenth century—for well over 1,500 years. "A good variety of grapevine grows here," Julian noted, "and some people have even managed to make fig-trees grow by covering them in winter."

Why would an emperor bother mentioning figs? Historians of antiquity know the answer. Figs were essential to Roman happiness, not only because they are delicious fresh. Dried figs ground and mixed into flour flavored fancy breads. More important, dried figs were the fattening food of the farmers who raised pigs and geese, producing imperial-era foie gras. So important was it that the vulgate Latin word for fig, *figa,* and fig-fattened, *ficatum,* evolved into the Italian *fegato* and French *foie,* meaning liver, not fig.

It was not the French, but the ancient Egyptians and Greeks before the Romans who pioneered the fattening of waterfowl livers. In Rome devouring the marbled hepatic organs of geese and pigs became the rage. The plutocrat-gastronome Apicius perfected the technique during the reign of Tiberius. The mania spread throughout the empire and might explain why figs were transplanted and coddled in distant, chilly Paris. The most common avian carcasses found in the city's archaeological digs are those of the noble goose, the best of birds for making foie gras.

You can tell that Emperor Julian wasn't a native Parisian. Neither a gourmand nor a party boy, he hated banquets and functions, subjecting himself to moral and physical rigors unpopular among the high-living Roman colonists. "The boorish Celts put up with these ways of mine," he remarked, "but they are naturally resented by a prosperous and gay and crowded city full of dancers and flute players and more mimes than ordinary citizens, people with no respect at all for those who govern. For the blush of modesty befits the unmanly, but manly fellows it befits to begin your revels at dawn, to spend your nights in pleasure, and to show not only by your words but by your deeds also that you despise the laws."

To a denizen of Paris today this sounds disconcertingly familiar. The imperial party pooper complained that Parisian hedonism was at its wildest in "the marketplaces and theaters." Surely if cafés and restaurants with high-tech sound systems had existed in Julian's time, the wicked revelers would have carried on then as they do now into the night, every night, gobbling oysters and foie gras and swallowing rivers of wine as they puff Gaulois luxuriantly on the terraces and sidewalks of the city.

TRIMALCHIO'S FÊTE

So you say you'd like the historical perspective on Parisian entertaining today? Look no further than Rome.

Emperor Domitian famously called the Roman Senate into special session to discuss the best way to cook a giant turbot. To the Roman mind, accustomed to the feasting of the gourmet politician-warrior Lucius Licinius Lucullus, the bulimic gluttony of obese Emperor Vitellius, who gobbled offerings off the altars of the gods, the extravagance of oligarchic Apicius, and the gross pleasures and ungoverned appetites of the most notorious emperor of all, Elagabalus, who fed his dogs foie gras, it's no wonder the Celts appeared to Emperor Julian to behave like "boorish" barbarians in the mid-300s AD.

Despite the Mediterranean influence many Parisii continued to squat on the ground or sit on hay bales when they dined. They used their pocketknives to carve then wolf rustic food on the hoof or—when getting fancy—off wooden plates. Roman food was sliced and minced and devised to be eaten with the fingers in a recumbent position. The Celts disdained it and the Romans' fine tableware, cloths, tables, chairs, and triclinium couches, not to mention the kind of complicated cuisine codified by Apicius in the first known collection of recipes *De re coquinaria*. The Apician style of gluttonous overeating was satirized by the wickedly humorous Petronius, and though the events didn't take place in Paris they might have.

"An excellent choice of hors d'oeuvres was brought in," says the fictional narrator of *Trimalchio's Feast*, Petronius' send-up of a nouveau-riche freedman with gourmet pretentions, the kind Emperor Julian may well have encountered in Lutetia. Green and black olives were served out of the saddlebags of a bronze donkey then came the dormice seasoned with honey and poppy seeds. "Smoking sausages were arranged on a silver grill," Petronius adds, "underneath it dark Syrian plums were made to look like black coals, scarlet pomegranate seeds red-hot ones."

Fat and sassy, Trimalchio is carried into the banquet hall to the sound of music and propped on overstuffed cushions. Just like a modern nouveau or fashionista, around his neck he tucks in a long napkin. On his left pinkie he wears a huge gilt ring and on the last joint of the next finger a ring apparently of solid gold, spangled with tiny iron stars. "Moreover, lest we should fail to take in all his magnificence, he had bared his right arm, adorned with a golden bracelet and an ivory circle fastened by a glittering clasp."

As Trimalchio sits picking his teeth with a silver toothpick a tray is brought in with a basket holding a sculpted wooden fowl, its wings fanned like a hen laying eggs. "Slaves approached and amid a burst of music began to poke through the straw, and having discovered some eggs they distributed them among the guests," the narrator continues. "So we took our spoons, which weighed not less than half a pound each, and broke the eggshells made of flour paste. I was tempted to throw my egg to the floor—it looked like a chick had been formed inside—but an old hand on the dining circuit next to me said 'There's bound to be something good inside.' I stuck my finger through the shell and pulled out a plump reed-bird surrounded by egg yolk nicely seasoned with pepper."

Note that pepper was extortionately expensive in antiquity, featuring in nearly all of Apicius' recipes.

The paired wine for the banquet was honeyed mulsum, parenthetically essential for making foie gras, at least according to Pliny, who chronicled how Apicius drowned his fattened pigs with it.

Between courses the guests washed their hands with wine, water not being good enough for Trimalchio's table.

But it's the main course and dessert readers remember best. The pièce de résistance was served on a double tray bearing the twelve signs of the zodiac arranged in a circle. Over each the maître d' had placed an appropriate delicacy.

> An Egyptian slave served bread on a silver bread plate while Trimalchio croaked out a popular song from the musical farce "The Garlic Eater." As he sang, four slaves stepped forward in solemn dance-steps to the sound of music and removed the cover from the upper part of the tray. Underneath we saw capons and sows' breasts and a hare with feathers stuck in its back to represent Pegasus.

In the corner of the tray a figure of the satyr Marsyas held a wineskin "from which peppery fish sauce flowed over fish swimming in it as if they were in a stream." The best was yet to come. "The servants hung pieces of tapestry along the front of our couches, with hunting nets embroidered on them and huntsmen armed with spears, and all the paraphernalia of the hunt." From outside the dining room came confused sounds, dogs rushed around the table and another tray followed bearing a huge wild boar. Hanging from his tusks were small baskets of dates. Scattered around the boar were pastry piglets.

A bearded gargantuan barbarian appeared, slashed the side of the boar with a hunting knife and out of the gash live thrushes flew. "Bird-catchers were at hand with long rods, and they caught the birds quickly as they were fluttering around the dining-room," the narrator tells us. A bird was handed to each guest and the dates were served to the accompaniment of music.

Did such a feast ever take place in Lutetia? If so, there is no record of it.

Granted there isn't much of the boorish Parisii left in contemporary Parisians except, perhaps, the obsession with fancy pocketknives. A certain kind of neo-Trimalchio, preferring the pricey Laguiole brand, will wield his knife even in polite company. Dine at some of the self-consciously swank *grandes tables* I know, including one named for Apicius, and you'll see there's plenty left over from imperial Rome, starting with the gold-draped clients, the décor, and the theatricality worthy of Petronius. Some years ago at historic Ledoyen, a multiple-starred temple of gastronomy, I saw a member of the sleeve-dog set slip nibbles of foie gras to his pets in the style of Elagabalus.

What also lingers from this seemingly remote period is the teeter-totter opposition of rustic simplicity to innovative sophistication and elaborate or scientific "new" cuisine, a struggle usually referred to as "the ancients versus the moderns." As you'll see in these pages it's also reminiscent of Nietzsche's "eternal return," a repetition that to the unobservant looks different each time.

WAITING FOR THE BARBARIANS

As you wait for your drink or food to be served at Place Dauphine—and wait you will almost everywhere in modern Lutetia—you might be amused to recall that it was the Greeks who called the Romans barbarians. The Romans called everyone else barbarians including the Celts of Gaul. The Celts called the Franks and Germans and others from even farther north or east barbarians—and many French still do, adding Englishmen and Americans into the mix despite the advantages of NATO and the great brotherhood of Europe.

Sooner or later the Roman party had to end. "The luxury of Rome continued growing until the end of the 4th century," wrote Alexandre Dumas in *Le Grand Dictionnaire de Cuisine,* one of my favorite food books. "A great noise was heard in the distant, unknown countries of the north, the east, the south, and countless hordes of barbarians arose with a great ruckus and rolled across the Earth.

"Some came on foot, some on horseback others on camels others still on chariots pulled by reindeer," Dumas thunders with biblical intonations, his telescopic rendition of the Fall of Rome more gripping than most academic histories. "Rivers washed them along atop their shields. The sea carried them along in boats. They sent the populace fleeing before them with the steel of their swords, as shepherds drive their flocks with wooden crooks. They overthrew nation upon nation, as if the word of God had ordained: 'I shall mix and spin the peoples of the world as the hurricane spins the dust.'

"They were unfamiliar, insatiable dinner guests at the table where the Romans devoured the world."

According to Dumas' colorful narrative Alaric the Goth tells a monk who tries to halt him, "'Something pushes me to overturn Rome.'" Alaric arrives and "three times surrounds the Eternal City and three times withdraws like an ebbing tide."

At last Alaric agrees to lift the siege if Rome gives him all its gold, all its silver, all its precious jewels, and all the barbarian slaves within its walls. "'What is left for the inhabitants?'" he is asked. "'Their lives,'" answers Alaric.

As Dumas tells it, the Romans handed over five thousand pounds of gold, thirty thousand pounds of silver, four thousand silk tunics, three thousand scarlet hides, and, most important, three thousand pounds of pepper—worth its weight in gold, silver, and jewels. "To save themselves," adds Dumas, "the Romans even melted down the statue of Courage."

Next on the roster to rage and rape come the Vandals, but events get really dramatic for Paris when Attila the Hun gallops up to overrun Gaul. With hundreds of thousands of barbarians in his train, Attila's encampments covered an area of three miles. "Disdainful of the golden or silver vases of Greece, he eats bloody meat off wooden plates," remarks Dumas with disgust. Forget the carpaccio and tartare, for Rome and, evidently, Dumas, uncooked meat was the ultimate measure of barbarism.

Five hundred cities are burned and destroyed, countless thousands tortured and murdered with unimaginable cruelty, seemingly directed by the wrath of God. "So passed these men, driven by a savage instinct, into the midst of the Roman orgy they extinguished in blood."

By a miracle, Paris was spared.

The historical truth is that Attila avoided Paris to concentrate his forces on Cenabum—today's Orléans—and couldn't be bothered to circle back for the kill. But miracles being miracles the lucky event was attributed to the prayerful intervention of the militant Christian nun Saint Genovefa, alias Sainte Geneviève, protector and patron saint of Paris from the sixth to seventeenth century when she was retired in favor of the Virgin.

Sainte Geneviève soon came to the rescue again, supplying food to besieged Paris when in AD 464 the next wave of barbarians attacked, led by the Frankish king Childeric. Again Paris was preserved yet it fell to the sword of Childeric's son Clovis who defeated the last Roman legion under Syagrius in 486 and ushered in the Merovingian dynasty of "French" kings. According to the hagiographies what transformed the barbaric Merovingian Franks into good civilized Frenchmen was, of course, Latin, cuisine, and Holy Communion wine—in other words Rome on three counts. Sainte Geneviève before dying in AD 511 or 512 performed her last miracle in 508 by converting Clovis into a man of the book.

When the bloody dust and smoke had settled the only people left standing were a handful of old men holding the Gospel and a cross, according to Dumas. The power of the emperor and pontifex of Rome passed into the person of the pope, the center of the world shifted to the Vatican, and its monasteries, refuges, and churches carried the civilization of Rome, purged of its orgiastic elements, into an age of darkness.

"The scent of the banquets of Trimalchio, Lucullus, Domitian and Elagabalus which had awakened the appetite of the barbarians was no longer," writes Dumas, winding up his historical survey. In a final salvo he quotes his contemporary, the heroic chef Carême who in the early 1800s said, "When there was no more cooking in the world, there was no literature, no high and quick-witted intelligence, no inspiration, no notion of a social ideal."

Dumas and Carême were products of a day when little was known of the so-called Dark Ages largely because so many documents had been lost. They did not fully comprehend how Rome, its cooking and winemaking had lived on in the hearts, minds, and stomachs of many, preserved in the parchments, papyruses, and tablets that recorded the words and deeds of the notable or notorious, including Marcus Gavius Apicius. His collection of recipes survived in manuscript form, a late fourth- or early fifth-century compilation of Apicius' writings and those of anonymous contributors, copied and recopied on scrolls by monks in scriptoria. The earliest surviving complete manuscripts date to the 800s or early 900s AD. They were rediscovered in the Renaissance and finally published in book form in Milan in 1498.

Ironically enough like many Romans of distinction, Apicius wrote equally well in Greek—parts of his memoir are in that language, which was preferred by sophisticates over the Latin of soldiers and Christians. It may well be that this celebrated Roman was of Greek parentage. That was the strength of Rome: It was the first multicultural, multiethnic, globalized melting pot, able to absorb the peoples, languages, building techniques, and cuisines it subsumed and grow stronger from them. Sound familiar?

THE LEFTOVERS

What is thrilling at least to me is to speculate on how in modified and sometimes hard-to-recognize forms many foods and food-related habits have survived the ravages of time, the invasions and massacres and floods and fires, the plagues and changes in religion or political and economic systems, and live on in Paris today. Why this should surprise anyone I'm not sure given that the Indians and Chinese among other great civilized nations have been eating many of the same dishes for millennia.

My mental list of survivor or remnant edibles and eating habits reads like one of those indigestible nineteenth-century banquet menus you find in old books. But indulge me and consider a favorite few because they are quintessentially Parisian today.

For one thing, there may not be many wooden plates in use in Paris households but there's plenty of raw or bloody beef and veal and other meats on tables. Also served underdone are lamb and mutton, bloody squab and undercooked fish, eaten the way the boors and barbarians preferred it, *à la Vercingétorix* or *à la Attila* if you prefer.

The Ancient Roman obsession with raw live oysters on the half shell, frogs, snails, and foie gras lives on in Paris with bells and whistles tied on. The inhumane treatment of oysters then and now has barely changed: They're caught wild or cultivated, shipped to Paris, and eaten squirming under a painful rain of vinegar with shallots or lemon juice (admittedly citrus is a medieval novelty). The Ancient Romans sometimes cooked them, but the French rarely do. Voltaire was an exception. He boasted he'd eaten as many oysters as Samson had killed Philistines, and he may have been the first enlightened soul to plead against the cruel practice of live ingestion.

Frog legs are French, you think? Certainly! But they were also beloved of the centurions and gourmets of antiquity: Recipes for preparing them are not for the squeamish. They involve skinning the creatures and eating more than the legs. As to snails, Apicius dedicated an entire though short chapter of his recipe-memoir to them. The Romans prepared gastropods in countless ways (and still do), while the descendants of the Celts have narrowed the field to the same holy trinity of ingredients applied to frog legs: garlic, butter, and parsley. Always larger than life dear old Apicius fattened his snails until they could no longer retract into their shells. This curious fact allows me to segue naturally into foie gras, a delicacy that speaks volumes and will no doubt make me many enemies.

FAT, LIVERISH, AND WINEY

Reportedly the ancient technique of fattening goose liver was preserved above all among the sequestered populations of Mediterranean Jews forbidden to eat pork and adept at cooking with schmaltz—i.e., poultry fat. What better source of tasty kosher fat than a foie gras? Like so many skills and arts it was rediscovered in the Renaissance, in Germany and Italy, most notably in the Jewish ghetto of Rome. Eventually it made its way back to France, possibly in the saddlebags of Leonardo da Vinci or another Italian artist, engineer, architect, artisan, or cook imported by King François I and his mixed-blood Franco-Italian successors in the 1500s to transform Paris into the "New Rome." The great papal chef of Rome Bartolomeo Scappi mentions the Jewish connection in his 1570 cookbook *Opera*. Despite years of searching I have found no reliable reference in French texts to foie gras before the 1500s.

Who knows, the much-maligned Medici of Florence who in the sixteenth and seventeenth century provided France with two queens and at least four kings may have packed some Italian-Jewish *fegato grasso* along with the silver forks, which they and their descendants browbeat their Gallic hosts to adopt. The process required several centuries. Even the voracious Sun King in his best imperial Roman style disdained this novelty and preferred his bejeweled fingers to a pronged implement.

However it made its way over the Alps, foie gras was promptly ordained a French specialty and so it has remained, *parbleu*! As the gourmet Curnonsky wrote nearly a century ago, "Foie gras will always be one of the culinary marvels garnering and maintaining the global glory of French cuisine." Maybe that's why it now garnishes hamburgers at certain establishments. Foie gras is unquestionably at its best in France today. The Italians make only trace quantities of *fegato grasso* serving it in their usually ludicrous, pseudo-French temples of *cucina nuova* or *cucina creativa*, which in my experience are neither new nor particularly creative.

In the early 2000s my gastronomic overindulgence led me to develop steatosis—meaning an enlarged, fat-veined liver. French doctors told me that, technically speaking, I was a walking, talking foie gras. That may be why I am particularly intrigued by this controversial delicacy. When I savor it as I sometimes do on Place Dauphine at Restaurant Paul—housemade, sprinkled with coarse salt, and flanked by rhubarb chutney—I feel as cannibalistic as Vercingétorix besieged at Alésia, or the *Sweeney Todd* pastry maker of the Île de la Cité.

Wicked Apicius used honeyed mulsum wine to suffocate his foie-gras-bearing pigs and though roughshod and primitive in comparison, when properly made, mulsum is surprisingly similar in spirit to its present-day descendants, the Sauternes or Rives-Hautes and other fortified wines of the south of France, then as now the perfect accompaniment to foie gras.

As to Paris and wine, given the climate and soil the *vinum* of Lutetia was probably always rough, acidic, and low in alcohol as it is today: Small quantities of wine are still produced atop Montmartre and by a handful of eccentrics, some of them bistro owners. Others are employed by the city of Paris and charged with the pocket-sized vineyard at Bercy on the eastern edge of town. I remember Bercy as one of two historic wine-warehousing districts. The other was Jussieu, destroyed in the 1960s by modernizers and replaced with a university campus of egregiously awful design.

In antiquity Parisian wines were not known for traveling. Other regions of France have historically been better suited for winegrowing. That did not stop the Abbey of Saint-Germain-des-Prés on the Left Bank from maintaining vast vineyards around Jussieu and several other outlying and Latin Quarter districts, and making wine in huge quantities for its monks, sharecroppers, and indentured servants. They had something on the order of 25,000 acres under their charge, much of the land given over to the growing of Communion wines. It's hard to imagine, but the Latin Quarter's lively, landmark-lined rue Saint-André-des-Arts linking Jussieu to Place Saint-Michel and Saint-Germain-des-Prés was built to give winemaker-monks access to their vineyards. The gentle slope behind the hulking church of Saint-Sulpice edging the Luxembourg Garden was also one of the abbey's prized inner-city winegrowing plots.

Stepping out from the Prefecture of Police, a block away from Place Dauphine, Simenon's Inspector Maigret enjoyed many a balloon-shaped glassful of non-Parisian wine at the archly traditional, atmosphere-soaked wine bar Taverne Henri IV and so occasionally do I. There are hipper spots and better-stocked, more professional ones, too, but if you fancy a platter of Gallic ham and a quaffable bottle from Alsace, Beaujolais, or perhaps the Loire Valley, you could do worse.

At some hard-to-pinpoint moment in the Middle Ages or Renaissance the French were able to enjoy sweet revenge by teaching their former colonial masters how to make decent wine. The great wines of Piedmont, Tuscany, and other Northern and Central Italian regions bear the French trademark to this day. Paris may have produced only plonk for 1,600 years or so but became the great wine city of France for a number of reasons. It was the main market for Burgundies, Champagnes, and Bordeaux, thanks to royalty and riches. It is still among the great wine cities of the world, with scores of outstanding wine merchants.

HAM, MUSTARD, AND FRITES

Both the Romans and Celts especially the Sequani tribe were experts at making ham, the biggest single export item from Gaul to Rome and a kind of cultural identity card of the French to this day. "The Sequani are bounded on the east by the Rhine and on the opposite side by the Saône River," noted Strabo at the beginning of the Christian era. "It is from them that the Romans procure the finest salted-pork."

Rarely used raw, the ham of antiquity was often salted and/or smoked and/or air-dried. Before use it was boiled in milk or water then devoured. Boiling was a favorite cooking method not just for ham. Many meats cured or fresh were cooked twice, to purge them of their salty, gamy, or less-than-fresh taste and—though ancient cooks did not know how this happened or why—to sterilize them of mysterious unpleasantness that caused stomachaches or worse, what we nowadays call harmful bacteria.

That condiment I spread on my very first ham-and-cheese baguette sandwich was none other than *vinum mustum ardens,* i.e., "burning new wine" alias *moutarde* or mustard. Yes, *moutarde* from Dijon and everywhere else in France also springs from remote Roman origins. A favorite of Apicius he records many recipes calling for mustard and gives a variety of complicated versions for making the spread. Basic mustard is still a blend of crushed naturally spicy mustard seeds, salt, and wine or vinegar.

Here's Apicius' formula for *vinum mustum ardens*: "Crushed mustard seed, honey, nuts, rue, cumin, vinegar." It's actually quite delicious. I'm surprised it isn't made today.

Reaching Paris in antiquity, mustard presumably disappeared for a time but in any case was revived and improved by the monks of the Abbey of Saint-Germain-des-Prés in the 900s AD. Unlike the ancient and medieval vineyards, or the twentieth-century bohemian clubs and literary hangouts of that celebrated neighborhood, mustard has never gone out of fashion. It is, you might say, ubiquitous though perhaps not in the heady realm of haute cuisine. Peppy mustard is the French condiment par excellence for fries and, if you ask me, beats ketchup or Belgian mayonnaise by several imperial miles.

THEY'VE GOT ATTITUDE

Beyond the foods and wines themselves it's the attitudes, habits, and penchants of the past that thrive today in modified forms that can be elusive to spot. Salad, for instance: Parisians often eat salad as a starter, an imperial-era tradition, as Martial remarked in the first century AD, unless of course they have it to clean the palate before or with the cheese course, an older, republican-era habit that may have died with Julius Caesar and only reappeared in the nineteenth century.

Speaking of cheese, the same year Vesuvius erupted and covered Pompeii in lava, AD 79, Pliny the Elder mentioned the mold-pocked cheese of France that now goes by the name Roquefort, recipient of the nation's first appellation of controlled origin or AOC. What the French usually forget to mention is Pliny complained because the cheese tasted medicinal—all that good penicillin in the stinky mold. Thousands of years before the Celts or Romans showed up, the Neolithic peoples of France—and just about every other European country—were making cheeses. The French word *fromage* comes from the Latin *forma*—i.e., the round wheel Italians call *formaggio.* De Gaulle's famous quip about the ungovernable nature of a country with hundreds of rival curds has become a commonplace. Equally celebrated and quoted though lacking in politically correct sensitivity is the quintessential French aphorism of Brillat-Savarin: "A meal without cheese is like a beautiful woman with only one eye." It was a daring claim for an upper-class gourmet to make in the early 1800s, when cheese was still considered the food of the poor. The separate cheese course sometimes presented nowadays on a platter or trundled out on a cart in stellar hostelries is a thing of the last few hundred years. Before that a single perfect wheel or lump of cheese was generally served among the entremets or desserts.

Despite the irresistible Parisian pastries, mousses, and *mille-feuilles,* a selection of pungent, ripe cheeses often trumps dessert to this day. A meal without *fromage* whether eaten at home or in a fine restaurant in Paris is indeed incomplete, at least to the Gallic soul and palate.

From Roquefort the AOC scheme, invented in 1925, was extended to other foods and above all wines. That was barely ninety years ago. But sourcing and provenance have always been an obsession with the French and especially the Parisians, who produce nothing of their own, not even champignons de Paris, yet seem always to have the finest produce and ingredients on their tables.

Is this interest in appellations and origins recent, say, a matter of the last two or three hundred years? No. I'm afraid not. It's another leftover from the Greco-Roman world.

The importance of provenance to a Greek or Roman gastronome can't be exaggerated, at least I haven't figured out how to tell taller tales. The lengths to which Archestratos, Montanus, Athaneus, Martial, Lucullus, and Apicius went in procuring or praising the best of the best make the efforts of the most exigent or pretentious contemporary Parisian chefs, foodistas, and other varieties of gourmet seem laughable.

Exigent, you say? The fourth-century-BC-poet-gourmet Archestratos coveted the sturgeon from Rhodes and the mullets farmed in freshwater ponds pinpointed between Priene and Miletus, disdaining others and especially the inferior saltwater mullets from the Ionian Sea. Montanus could tell in an instant exactly where his oysters and sea urchins came from, right down to the rock or stretch of coast, according to Juvenal. Athaneus clamored for bacon made by the Cerretans, a tribe in Spain. Martial urged "Let epicures devour ham!" and wanted his from the Menapii in Westphalia on the Rhine. Lucullus hauled sweet cherry and apricot trees—roots and all—from Pontus back to Rome, coddling them in his orchards because their luscious fruit was better than that produced by native Italian trees.

But, as ever, it is Apicius who beats all comers. The story of his gastronomic travels and suicide is too well-known to repeat—the plutocratic glutton's last, ruinous, failed expedition from Campania to Libya to seek the perfect, plump prawn, his bitter disappointment, and, after a particularly lavish feast and a reality check with his accountant, the deadly realization he was too poor, a mere multimillionaire, to continue spending seven figures on each of his private banquets. Better to die than skimp!

Much to the regret of French culinary chauvinists, the great gourmands of antiquity make no mention of anything delicious coming specifically from Lutetia or its environs. That isn't surprising given the remoteness of the island-city relative to Rome and the Mediterranean *caput mundi*—or *stomachus mundi* if you prefer.

Likewise if there was an Apicius or Lucullus of Paris, he hasn't been discovered or recovered. But the decadent, end-of-empire food-mad spirit of the Greco-Roman world reappeared at some point in the Middle Ages everywhere in Europe certainly in time for the wine- and salad-loving Charlemagne's coronation as Holy Roman Emperor in AD 800. This love of food, wine, and entertaining has animated royalty and the rich in Paris ever since. Over the centuries it seeped down through layers of old-money families into the parvenu bourgeoisie. In the last hundred years or so it has penetrated to the formerly famished roots of society: Even the most modest wage earner today enjoys something of the city's culinary bounty.

PART THREE

Entrées, Premier Service: Medieval Renaissance, c. AD 500–c. 1600

DARK OR LIGHT?

For a thousand years or more, from the implosion of Rome to the Renaissance, evolution in what and how Parisians and other Europeans ate progressed at the pace of a fatted escargot.

Other than the obligatory geographical, climatic, and predictable social class variants, peasants in Burgundy and Bavaria, and aristocrats in Prague, Paris, and Padua, continued largely in the hybrid Roman-barbarian mode of late antiquity. As a geographical and political entity, Gaul disappeared and France came into being during this long period but there was no French cuisine per se only certain national preferences.

Boiling, roasting, and frying were the top-three typically French-cooking techniques. Then as now Parisians and their countrymen enjoyed foods undercooked, rare, or raw, and favored the acidic to the sweet-and-sour beloved by medieval Italians, Germans, and the English. A compound called *verjus* so acidic it doesn't tickle but rather removes the skin from the palate became the rage. It's easy to make: take the juice of unripe grapes—*raisins verts*—mix with salt, voilà you have verjuice. When grapes are not available, substitute anything lethally sour and acidic: unripe gooseberries or currants will do, elderberries, pomegranates, crab apples, sloeberries, pears, and so forth. Sometimes raw sorrel was added to make sure it parched the throat. Startlingly verjuice lives on as the name of the chic Franco-American Verjus restaurant on rue de Richelieu in Paris, and in a number of rustic French recipes today and is even produced and sold by an artisan in the Périgord region. Lemon juice or vinegar are the modern equivalent but are nowhere as acidic.

Spice was nice and the nicer the spice, the higher the price. Anyone who could afford spices used them abundantly in sauces to jazz up a meal. They were too expensive to be a cloaking device and no one would have wasted them on tainted meat. It's hard to imagine today but ginger became the French spice par excellence, followed in popularity by cinnamon. Eventually more and cheaper spices from the south and salt cod from the frozen north began moving along European trade routes finding their way into aristocratic and bourgeois kitchens in the late medieval period coincidentally stimulating, it is claimed, the beginnings of modern capitalism.

As a general rule though, in Paris and everywhere in the West, the sand got stuck in the hourglass of the centuries. The nobility favored wild game and winged creatures whose claws never touched the grubby soil. Peasant food was down to earth. The beef, mutton, and root vegetables boiled in cauldrons; the suckling pig, chicken, and pheasant roasted on the spit; and the hare and rabbit stewed in earthenware pots atop the embers. Anything cooked in a pot was called a potage, by the way, not just vegetables or soup. Over time kitchen gardens and a kind of primitive stove conceived specifically for pots both came to be known as *potagers*. Atop such ranges the sacred French pot-au-feu bubbled away—and bubbles on today, a late antique or medieval survivor.

Relative stasis doesn't mean medieval Parisians and others elsewhere didn't rejoice in their food and drink—when they had it. Famine followed feast, a roller-coaster ride of war, plague, crop failure, drought, flooding, and occasional bounty, most of which the rapacious clergy and feudal lords creamed off for themselves. Comfortably seated by roaring fireplaces, no doubt the peripatetic abbots of Cluny and Saint-Germain-des-Prés in Paris, and equally migratory kings Clovis, Charlemagne, and Charles V ate very well. By most accounts impoverished city dwellers suffered even more than peasants. There were no middle classes to speak of; therefore, little ferment or social mobility, and not much inventiveness around the cooking hearth. It's something to keep in mind as the middle classes of the world shrink away today.

Physically the city of Paris mirrored this stasis, remaining largely within its Ancient Roman limits from the 300s to 800s AD and only gradually inching outward with new lopsided growth rings of wall from the late ninth, late twelfth, and most imposingly the late fourteenth centuries. That's when finally France's first homegrown cookbooks and proto-celebrity chef Guillaume Tirel alias Taillevent appeared atop the city's bastions. Why would Tirel stand on the ramparts? One set of them happened to curl along the Seine to protect the new royal palace of Charles V in the Marais where Taillevent worked his culinary magic.

This darkling picture needs straightening and lightening, because it leaves out the simple, luminous joys of breaking bread—literally breaking it, since dinner rolls and loaves were usually joined at the hip, made to be snapped apart at table. The word "companion"—*cum panis*—hints at this. The dining scene was vibrant in its own small, gritty way. Medieval Paris was one of the world's biggest and most populous cities, with scores of *auberges,* taverns, cabarets, estaminets, hostels, and traiteurs—those caterer-delis still so popular today. The streets were filled with the cries of hawkers selling fresh-baked savory or sweet tarts, meat pies of surprising flavor, as we know, plus fruits, vegetables, and more. Beyond the bedroom or blood sports, entertainment in the medieval world was limited, making the conviviality of shared meals and libations all the more essential.

SCALLOPS AND ABBOTS

Leaving your roost at Place Dauphine and exiting the Île de la Cité by the Petit Pont, where the wooden bridge Emperor Julian described stood, and following the Ancient Roman road, now called rue Saint-Jacques, a few blocks south to the Hôtel de Cluny you enter one of those only-in-Paris time tunnels. The Hôtel de Cluny was the Paris town house of the Abbey of Cluny, a town in southern Burgundy. In all probability the rubble core of the complex was built in the second century at the height of the Roman Empire, though it may have arisen a hundred years earlier, at the same time as the now-buried Temple of Jupiter under Notre Dame. For the last century and a half the Hôtel de Cluny has housed the National Museum of the Middle Ages, one of my favorite cultural repositories.

Like the cathedral's crypt the former Roman bath complex at Cluny is an objective correlative of Paris history and a compendium of architectural styles *à la Parisienne.* The charming jumble looks like a mouthful of broken molars repaired with elaborate fretwork crowns. It features the brick-and-stone *frigidarium* or ancient cold baths, where Julian was lifted on shields by his boorish Celts and centurions and pronounced emperor, plus medieval and Renaissance overlays, and is sauced and garnished with nineteenth-century eclectic revivalism. Using the Roman remnants for foundations, the abbots of Cluny, the Burgundian abbey where Roman winemaking was revived and perfected, built this to be their modest Paris town house and lived here from the 1300s until the end of the Ancien Régime.

Granted it's more colorful to imagine the Cluniac Order as a coven of incorrigible shellfish-worshippers, as the mansion's décor seems to suggest, but the truth is probably more prosaic. The abundant sculpted or ironwork scallop shells on the main carriage door, tower, and walls were added only in the 1840s during the medieval revival period to represent the cockleshell symbol of Saint James associated with Cluny. That's because in the late 800s AD the main north-south Roman road morphed into the main pilgrimage route from Paris to the shrine of Saint James at Compostella in Spain, near the scallop-scattered beaches of Finisterra.

Many of the route's way stations were created, owned, and operated by Cluny, like the fast-food franchises of today that blight the highways and byways of France. Pilgrims carried a scallop shell home to prove they'd made the months-long journey—until unscrupulous sellers got into the shell game. Presumably the scallops served along the Way of Saint James made for good eating, though salt pork, cabbage, and gruel were certainly more common fare. The wine flowed: The daily ration per monk or pilgrim was one Cluniac glass, corresponding to a modern liter meaning more than a quart. Cluny or not, to this day scallops are second only to oysters in the roster of Parisians' favorite shellfish. Is this due to pious Saint James or perhaps because in antiquity scallops and their briny ilk represented divine fertility—think of Venus flying lustily across foamy waves poised on the half shell. Maybe the reason is simpler: Scallops, especially those from the Atlantic shores of France are succulent, delicate, and addictive.

Beyond Cluny's scallops, the architectural hodgepodge as a whole seems magical to me, housing elements highlighting the Parisian—and my own—love affair with food. For instance there are several of the city's best-preserved late-medieval or Renaissance fireplaces, at least one of which, in the entrance to the museum, was used for cooking. The vestibule where you buy your tickets was the abbot's kitchen in the 1500s, at the time when the turkeys, chocolate, potatoes, peppers, beans, tomatoes, and other indispensable comestibles that revolutionized European menus first arrived in France from the New World. Did these new foods usher in a culinary Renaissance? Yes and no.

Ambiguity reigns the moment the words "medieval" and "Renaissance" are uttered, largely because individual countries, regions, or cities progressed at different paces. I have long wondered when the Middle Ages ended and the Renaissance began in Paris, for instance, and have yet to find the definitive answer. Florence, Pisa, Padua, and Rome were a century and a half ahead of everyone else, many historians agree, with a proto-Renaissance beginning in the thirteenth century.

In France a new dynamism in architecture could be said to start with Notre Dame and the other great Gothic cathedrals of the 1100s—the so-called native French style. Music, mathematics, and religious studies began to revive at the same time and in the 1200s, with the creation of Paris' Latin Quarter universities, the tempo quickened and the humanities were eventually folded in. The visual arts were slower to evolve in France, society was firmly stuck in feudalism, and cooking would have to wait several more centuries before it began to evolve. A convincing argument can be made that the rebirth of cuisine didn't begin in France until 1505 and the translation of Maestro Martino's recipes, or the seventeenth-century advent of François Pierre de La Varenne, author of *Le Cuisinier françois*. Profound changes in French cuisine—things that made it wholly different from other European court cuisines—only came during the Enlightenment.

TOOLING UP, DINING OUT

If you are as fascinated as I am by the mechanics and physics of cooking, you might be disappointed to learn there are no early kitchen tools and cooking devices on display at Cluny or anywhere else in Paris. That's not because they are esteemed unworthy of the nation's museum of medieval culture, but rather because such implements and proto-appliances are largely unfindable or impossible to move.

Having walked 750 miles across France on the Way of Saint James via Cluny, the town and abbey in Burgundy, and having driven probably 50,000 miles at 25 mph on the country's spiderweb of back roads as a reporter, I have been lucky enough to see a handful of historic kitchens. The most remarkable, intact, and justly famous is in Dijon at the Palace of the Dukes of Burgundy. Pierreclos, near Macôn, has another authentic small one with a fabulous rotisserie, and yet a third Burgundian château, Cormatin, preserves the hallowed site where La Varenne wrote his cookbook, though the kitchens were remodeled in the nineteenth century. The Loire Valley is littered with antique châteaux kitchens. Nearer Paris are Vaux-le-Vicomte and Chantilly where the celebrated François Vatel was maître d'.

The modern mind can't help being struck by the primitiveness of even the most magnificent, elaborately equipped antique kitchens. It seems miraculous anything edible other than roasted meat could come out of them—and the cost in human effort and health must have been enormous.

Filthy, broken, rotten, rusted, discarded—the rotisseries, ovens, cauldrons, and grills; the planks, tabletops, chopping blocks, and wooden buckets or barrels; the giant cooking forks and knives, hatchets, and saws of days gone by, are either deep underground or no longer, at least not in the City of Light. To be fair, how many microwave ovens and espresso machines and immersion mixers or sous-vide science sets will be preserved from our own era?

A curious fact I learned some years ago still gives me pause: There were refectories in monasteries, and mess halls in fortresses and palaces of course, but individual medieval or Renaissance dining rooms didn't exist, not in Paris.

Tables were set up on sawhorses or collapsible crutches wherever it was comfortable and convenient, meaning warm or cool, breezy or cozy, depending on the season. Proper purpose-built dining rooms only appeared in the seventeenth and eighteenth centuries.

More curious still: Most Paris homes and apartments had no cooking facilities until the late eighteenth or nineteenth century. When they weren't eating out, unless they were rich or had taken holy orders, city dwellers bought their food ready-made from those swarms of street hawkers, or from bakeries, butcher shops, and caterers. If a building did have a scullery, it was usually shared by various tenants and was of a most rudimentary kind: a place to butcher, chop, and peel; another place to spit-roast or boil—usually inside a broad chimney; a bucket for washing, a well for water, and access to an open sewer, back alley, or the river to dump waste. For practical reasons nearly all premodern kitchens were in basements, on ground floors or in outbuildings on courtyards—because of the fear of fire, the immense weight of stone fireplaces, the mess, stench, and noise. Isolation was imperative. In some areas in certain historical periods in Paris the municipal cleanup crews were staffed entirely by voracious pigs. Pigs will eat almost anything. There were no sewers and nothing was wasted. The rest of the equation is easy.

MY KINGDOM FOR A PIG!

Tout est bon dans le cochon goes the old French ditty meaning every morsel of the pig is good. Pork in all imaginable forms from trotters, bowels, and blood to rump, rib, and snout was the most abundant, beloved, and common source of fleshy protein—until, that is, the accidental death of young Prince Louis in 1131. It occurred when a panicked porker belonging to the Order of Saint Anthony headquartered east of what's now Place de la Bastille darted in front of the royal steed causing Louis to fall and suffer fatal

My kingdom for a pig! Prince Louis tripped by a porker in Paris, medieval woodcut, artist unknown

internal injuries. After this strange incident pigs were demonized by royal decree and many were put on trial, tortured, found guilty, and broken like heinous felons.

No such treatment was ever meted out to a unicorn, at least not in the vicinity of the Hôtel de Cluny. Of more esthetically pleasing interest therefore, than demonic pigs, a gastronomic quest to Cluny should include the museum's vast upstairs room displaying the celebrated *Lady and the Unicorn* tapestry series, a paean to the senses.

SENSE AND SENSIBILITY

Many stout men vie for the title but to my mind among the ultimate romantic sensualists, gourmands, epicures, and oenophiles of nineteenth-century Paris the most surprising of all may well have been a woman, George Sand, pseudonym of the cigar-smoking, cross-dressing, sexually omnivorous Amantine-Lucile-Aurore Dupin. When not penning racy novels or quaffing fine wines with her lovers, Sand was an avid cook and recipe writer and the first literary champion of *The Lady and the Unicorn* tapestries, which mark the transition from medieval to Renaissance art. In Sand's day they were moldering away in the gloomy château of Boussac, near Sand's own family property in the Creuze region west of Paris. Perhaps recognizing something of herself not in the slender, elegant lady, but in the subject of the tapestries—sensuality—Sand described them fleetingly in her first successful serialized novel *Jeanne* thereby bringing them to public attention. Ultimately they were bought, restored, preserved, and displayed at Cluny, where they remain to this day.

"Without question the most beautiful element of the décor in the salon of the château was the enigmatic tapestries," wrote Sand. Imagining them as having been made for a "famous faithless" lady to amuse her while in a gilded prison, Sand guessed correctly they had been designed and woven in the late 1400s, about the same time the abbots of Cluny remodeled and expanded their Paris pied-à-terre to its current configuration.

Each of the six masterpieces of wall hanging provides nourishment for modern sensualists, gourmets, gourmands, and epicures, not to mention horticulturists and enthusiasts of natural history. They exquisitely depict the lovemaking of mind and body, intellect, and appetite, underlying French and especially Parisian attitudes toward sex, the senses, and gastronomy, an utterly un-Puritanical openness at least five hundred years old and, given imperial Roman precedents, I would argue, much older still.

Enigmatic the tapestries may be but there's no question they are above all a celebration. In the tapestry dedicated to the sense of Taste an idealized, elongated, flaxen-haired beauty framed by a lion and unicorn is shown coyly plucking a candy from an elaborate dish held up for her by a handmaiden. The lady's attention is turned to the hovering varicolored parrot about to alight on her left hand, birds in medieval and Renaissance iconography being yet another reminder of sensuality or lasciviousness like the fertility-symbol rabbits nibbling around the periphery of the composition. The lecherous leering monkey at the lady's feet is devouring a bonbon or perhaps a ripe berry while looking at the lady's faithful dog—faithfulness being the operative concept.

The senses are also celebrated outside the museum. Wandering through the landscaped gardens of Cluny sandwiched between the abbots' mansion and the Boulevard Saint-Germain, you discover a potted re-creation of a medieval or Renaissance vegetable and herb garden reminiscent of the floral mille-fleur backgrounds in the tapestries. Researchers with magnifying lenses (and more patience than I possess) have identified thirteen species of tree and fifty-nine different plants in these backgrounds. Many of the species are now grown in the garden's carefully tended herb beds or vegetable plots. Several were key components in the kitchens and dispensaries of centuries past: cabbage, onion, cardoon, chive, parsnip, borage, plus sage, rosemary, hyssop, rue, mint, absinth, marigold, tansy, and lemon bath. Sound familiar? You might not want them in your food today but they are the herbal bridge from Apicius to La Varenne.

OF GEESE AND GASTRONOMIC THEME PARKS

When Emperor Julian scrubbed and bathed at Cluny, the imperial pleasure gardens swept all the way down to the banks of the Seine roughly following today's rue de la Harpe. Somewhere along this battered street a Roman butcher shop or slaughterhouse was unearthed last century. In the Middle Ages one of Paris' early Jewish districts grew here, and a well-known take-out "goose-roaster" spit-roasted geese and goslings to perfection.

The area is an atmospheric tangle of leaning landmark buildings but rue de la Harpe and the narrow alleys between it, the Seine, and the church of Saint-Séverin are now a low-level gastronomic theme park notorious for regulation tourist traps. Some feature self-styled *cuisine française* writ large on the marquee, others are faux Greek tavernas where patrons are encouraged to fling their empty plates to the ground as was the fashion in Paris in centuries past. There are North African couscous dens, kebab joints by the score, and a single, golden-arched fast-food outlet that perfumes the gardens of Cluny with the smell of burgers and fries.

Nostalgia is often bittersweet but can also be sickly sweet. A North African pastry shop, Pâtisserie Sud Tunisien on the corner of rue de la Harpe and rue Saint-Séverin has been broadcasting its patented honeyed, sticky scents for decades. Wild for the gooey, honey-soaked, layered lumps, probably not unlike the ones the lady and her unicorn enjoyed, I became a regular customer here in the 1970s, gobbling baklava, samsa, and yo-yo.

Back then Paris' ethnic eateries and specialty food shops seemed to me to vie for diversity and delightfulness with the lively ethnic offerings in America. Perhaps they still do, but, sadly, not in the high-rent core of Paris. In outlying arrondissements sizable Chinese, Vietnamese, Turkish, Maghrebi, and African communities thrive and the authentic eating reflects this. But Paris is no longer the great global city for non-French food. The ethnic food scenes in London, New York, Amsterdam, Berlin, Chicago, San Francisco, Toronto, and many other Western cities seem at least as rich and vibrant. That's got to be a good thing for the world.

Happily all is far from lost in the area beyond the Saint-Séverin theme park. On Boulevard Saint-Germain a couple of blocks west of the Cluny gardens you come upon the original luxury boutique of the garrulous philosopher-sculptor-chocolatier Patrick Roger, now a mini-chain operation. As a chocolate maker he is among the world's best: The quality and purity of his bars and filled chocolates can't be beat (I've held many blind tastings with chocolate lovers and professionals and Roger's creations nearly always come out number one or two). The less said about his philosophizing and sculptures the better. In the opposite direction down the same boulevard half a dozen blocks you reach Place Maubert, home to one of Paris' premier cheesemongers—Laurent Dubois—and the thrice-weekly outdoor Marché Maubert. Another five minutes east on foot along Boulevard Saint-Germain and you arrive at Chez René, the century-old Lyonnais-Burgundian bistro with penguin-suited waiters and premodern classics.

Jussieu, one of Paris' biggest university campuses since 1965, is a few more blocks east. Before the campus was built this is where the Left Bank's wholesale wine warehouses stood. Before the warehouses were built, up and down the gentle slopes of Jussieu spread the vineyards of the monks of Saint-

Germain-des-Prés and before them the vineyards and farms of the Romans of Lutetia. Two wonderful old-timer upscale bistros facing the campus are holdovers from the days of wine warehousing: Le Buisson Ardent, for updated, lightened traditional French fare and Moissonnier, for gutsy Lyonnais classics such as *tablier de sapeur*—tripe.

SERENELY SEEKING TAILLEVENT

In half an hour you can stroll from Jussieu or the chiaroscuro alleys of Saint-Séverin to Saint-Paul and the site of the former royal residence of Charles V in the Right Bank's chic Marais district, where medieval France's first stellar chef cooked and wrote.

When crossing the Seine on Pont de la Tournelle pause to crane your neck up at the glassy panoramic dining room of the ultra-classic La Tour d'Argent. I first lunched there decades ago when this weather vane of gastronomy had three stars in the Guide Michelin and could do no wrong. The second time I ate there it had two stars. The third time it had one.

Yet the perpetual house specialty, pressed duck, Torquemada style, was just as delicious as it had been, the tortuous preparation and service of it was a perfect performance of Escoffier-style showmanship, an absurd and gruesome entertainment, and the view of the Seine and flying buttresses of Notre Dame with its spires hadn't noticeably changed, either. Despite the slumping Michelin constellation the wine cellar was and is still one of the best anywhere. So what happened? Fashions change, even Michelin changes—the way glaciers melt, faster and faster. Novelty reigns supreme nowadays. Auguste Escoffier's spiritual grandchildren are demoted and *demodé* and perhaps that is as it should be: The style of food and service don't correspond to contemporary tastes. People ask: Is La Tour d'Argent exciting? Absolutely not—that's why I like it. Excitement isn't a state of being I enjoy while dining. I leave agitation to feverish foodistas.

Once you're on the sauce-boat shaped Île Saint-Louis, pause to lick a cone at Paris' only world-class ice creamery—Berthillon—or buy a steak at the outstanding butcher shop across the street from it, Gardil, home of the authentic Gallic ham and peerless dry hung beef. This pair of excellent establishments plus the unpretentious Boulangerie des Deux Ponts bakery down the cross street, give a gastronome hope.

When feeling generous about the exasperatingly slow service, I might toss in another restaurant on the island's main drag, a super chef's overpriced baby bistro serving solid traditional food with Alsatian touches to crowds of out-of-towners packed into a darkly upholstered interior: Mon Vieil Ami. Nearby is a comically pretentious hipster hangout with egregious attitude where beautiful people pick at the regulation artfully plated microscopic portions of verticality: Le Sergent Recruteur.

The island is also home to a must-see, one of the city's longest-running exemplars of what you might call gastro-kitsch, the theme restaurant Nos Ancêtres les Gaulois. That's Gaul as in gall.

What Vercingétorix, Emperor Julian, Charles V, or his chef Guillaume Tirel (aka Taillevent) would make of the restaurant, God only knows. Judging by the accounting and recipe books of the 1300s this wasn't the kind of fare King Charles or his trusted steward favored. Tirel appears to have earned his swashbuckling nickname "Taillevent" by the power and speed of his knife technique, the blade whizzing and whistling as it literally "cut the wind"—*taille-vent*. Carving before his master was an essential part of the dinner ceremonial. The pen being mightier and sharper than even Taillevent's knives, he is remembered

Taillevent's tombstone, 19th-century engraving

today for his literary output, meaning, of course, *Le Viandier*, which appeared in scroll or manuscript form circa 1390.

Unsurprisingly Tirel may not actually be the author of the book, or at least the whole book but no matter, he is a national hero; his tombstone is preserved in the antiquities museum of suburban Saint-Germain-en-Laye and his name on the marquee and menus of Paris' legendary, supremely luxurious, Michelin-starred temple of gastronomy, Le Taillevent.

Originality having no particular value in premodern times, Taillevent clearly didn't want to set a new trend by doing all the heavy lifting himself. As often happened in antiquity and the Middle Ages, recipes and manuscripts of unknowable provenance were gathered, reworked, unscrolled, stitched together, copied, and attributed to new compilers or writers, usually chefs or gastronomes, but also, in at least one celebrated instance, an exigent bourgeois husband eager to provide a housekeeping manual for his fifteen-year-old bride. This was the case of the fascinating, second-most-famous fourteenth-century French cookbook, *Le Mesnagier de Paris*, author anonymous but certainly not Guillaume Tirel, who would have been far too busy at court. Both authors were encouraged to shine light into the medieval cupboard by eager King Charles V the Wise and his successor Charles VI the Mad, respectively creator and perpetuator of France's first national library. By the stroke of these authors' magic quills suddenly all that was unwritten and therefore did not exist came into being, the Dark Ages of dining disappearing into brightness. Or so some historians would have you believe. In truth, there are other, earlier manuscripts and a good deal is known about the eating habits of medieval Parisians.

ANCESTRAL HUNGER

Somehow it's hard to believe everyone but the king and court was starving in Paris seven hundred years ago. Certainly, the Great Famine of the early 1300s lasted seven years and left psychological scars across Europe, reviving the age-old "ancestral hunger" that has haunted homo sapiens from the earliest days. But research hints that when things were good everyone but the poorest devoured unimaginable quantities of meat, most of it pork, all of it from heirloom breeds, free-range and organic, just think. It must have been delicious. By the late medieval period bourgeois households clearly had learned how to entertain. Pork wasn't often on the menu—it was bad form to have too much of it.

It's nothing compared with what Taillevent cooked, but here's an intimate dinner outlined in *Le Mesnagier de Paris*, a cinch for a young wife to whip up for a tableful of friends.

ASSIETTES (COURSES)

PREMIÈRE ASSIETTE: *Pastés de veel menu déhaché à gresse et mouelle de beuf, pastés de piopameaux, boudins, saucisses, pipefarce, et pastés norrois de quitus.*
(FIRST COURSE: Veal pasties finely chopped and cooked in beef fat and marrow, piopameaux pasties, blood sausages, sausages, stuffed pipefarces, and pasties from Norrois.)

SECONDE ASSIETTE: *Civé de lièvre et brouet d'anguille, fèves coulées, saleures, grosse char, beuf et mouton.*
(SECOND COURSE: Hare stew and eel soup, mashed fava beans, pickle, beef and mutton roasts.)

TIERS METS: *Rost chappons, copnips, veel et perdrix, poisson d'eaue doulce et de mer, aucun taillis avec doreures.*

(THIRD COURSE: Roasted capons, game birds, veal and partridge, seafood and freshwater fish, some gilded.)

QUART METS: *Mallars de rivière à la dodine, tanches aux soupes et bourrées à la sausse chaude, pastés de chappons de haulte gresse à la souppe de la gresse et du persil.*
(FOURTH COURSE: River mallards in sauce, tench doused with hot sauce and served with sops, fatty capon pasties with fatty soup with parsley.)

QUINT METS: *Un boulli lardé, ris engoulé, anguilles renversées, aucun rost de poisson de mer ou d'eaue doulce, roissolles, crespes et vidz sucre.*
(FIFTH COURSE: Boiled meats with lard or bacon, sticky rice, eels in an upside-down casserole, some roasted fish either saltwater or freshwater fish, meaty dumplings, crêpes, and sweetmeats.)

LA SIXIÈME ASSIETTE ET DERRENIÈRE POUR YSSUE: Flanciaux succrés et lait lardé, neffles, noix pellées, poires cijiites et la dragée. Ypocras et le mestier.
(SIXTH AND LAST COURSE: Sweet flan and larded milk, medlar fruits, peeled walnuts, stewed pears, and sugared almonds. Sweet Ypocras wine.)

Even if your medieval French is rusty you get the picture: twenty-four dishes all told brought out in six successive waves called *assiettes* and *mets*. There's plenty of meat, from the veal pasties to the roast beef and mutton, plus blood sausages and wieners—the only pork on offer. Hare stew is the standout wild game dish. Duck, capon cooked several ways, and partridge cover the poultry courses. Eel and fresh or saltwater fish swim in and out of the various *assiettes*. There are nice fatty soups full of soaked bread sops, and sweetmeats, fresh or cooked fruits, nuts, candies, and sweet Ypocras spice wine to wind things up and send things down. *Le Mesnagier de Paris* gives many such menus for "fat" and "lean" days, following the Catholic canonical calendar.

HEIRLOOM CHEF

Long-lived and irreplaceable Taillevent buried the wise father king Charles V and segued into the reign of his well-liked but mentally unstable son Charles VI. Both rulers were gourmands. Strangely it is said Charles VI was wild about the meat pies of a certain pastry chef on the Île de la Cité whose establishment was flanked by a barber's shop. Once the secret ingredient in the pies was discovered it was the outraged king who ordered the murderous anthropophagous pie maker and cutthroat barber be broken on the wheel then burned alive. Unwitting cannibalism is not why Charles VI was known as "the Mad," by the way, a tale too long to tell.

Gird your loins in the latest designer fashions, wander down the storied streets of the Marais between the seventeenth-century church of Saint-Paul and the Seine, and you'll note that the tang of Taillevent's acidulated, spicy cooking doesn't exactly hang in the air among the antiques shops, art galleries, and wine bars. Neither does the stench of open sewers and the great unwashed of 650 years ago. Hints of Taillevent and the two kings Charles do, however, linger in the topography and the evocative street names of this handsome neighborhood, much of it rebuilt in the 1500s atop the former grounds of the royal palace, the Hôtel Saint-Pol.

Here is proof that there is poetry in the humblest Paris street map: rue Charles V, rue de la Cerisaie, rue des Lions-Saint-Paul, rue Beautreillis. The first road is named for the king who built the Bastille and city walls of 1365–1380; moved the seat of government from the drafty, dangerous Île de la Cité to the Hôtel Saint-Pol; and most important of all, hired Guillaume Tirel to cook for him. The second street, rue de la Cerisaie, recalls the location of the king's cherry orchard, the third the site of the lion compound in the king's mini-menagerie, the last is a reminder of the king's vineyard—Beautreillis meaning "beautiful trellises."

Oh, wise, parsimonious monarch! Instead of wrapping his pleasure gardens around yet another vast purpose-built château—he already had half a dozen including the new Louvre and just as many hunting lodges—Charles

V wanted his flower beds, orchards, and vineyard to spill between four vintage mansions, all of them bought cheap, second-hand, remodeled, and expanded beyond recognition, the same modus operandi of contemporary American oligarchs in Santa Monica and elsewhere. The compound was known as the Hôtel Saint-Pol. The royal children lived in one mansion abutting a street now named rue du Petit-Musc and in another behind rue Saint-Antoine, the Ancient Roman road bisecting the Marais to this day. The queen's mansion stood behind rue Saint-Paul within sighing distance of the medieval church of Saint-Paul-des-Champs—"Saint Paul of the fields." It was linked by a portico to the king's palace, which filled the city block from rue des Lions-Saint-Paul to the Seine.

How many times have I wandered these streets, wondering if anything remains of the mansions and gardens and kitchens of the time of Charles V? That's hard to say. At least as many times as there were taverns in Paris in the 1300s—well over five hundred by one census. I live a few blocks away and can attest that the Marais certainly has many taverns today, several of them within the boundaries of the king's compound. Though they are but humble eateries unequipped with banqueting halls, Charles was a good fellow and might actually have enjoyed the straightforward, earthy fare and old-fashioned décor at Cave des Pyrénées and Le Temps des Cerises, both a century old, seen from our perspective, that is.

On second thought, Charles V might actually prefer the only regal restaurant in the Marais these days, L'Ambroisie, a perennial, unassailable Michelin three-star temple of gastronomy located on posh Place des Vosges. Presidents Jacques Chirac and Bill Clinton, followed by François Holland and Barack Obama, dug into the miniature, artistically displayed morsels at L'Ambroisie, the most expensive restaurant in Paris. The world-famous square edging the dining room would have faced the grounds of Charles V's Parisian hunting lodge, the Hôtel des Tournelles.

Though the king's neighborhood has been slightly reconfigured it hasn't changed much since the mid-1500s. The current mansions are five hundred years old. Some incorporate walls and cellars older still. Antique maps confirm that rue des Lions-Saint-Paul corresponds precisely to the queen's portico, widened and straightened. By sneaking into courtyards and surreptitiously stealing down steep stone staircases along this and other streets

I have discovered vaulted cellars, hidden gardens, miniature orchards, and other magical enclaves of the wealthy and retiring now viewable much to their chagrin using Google Earth. But I've never seen anything like a preserved medieval kitchen and, frankly, would not be able to accurately date the construction of a vault, well, or chimney if my life depended on it.

It's well-known where the king's kitchen gardens were: between rue Saint-Paul and rue des Jardins-Saint-Paul to the west of it. Closing for the kill, I've narrowed my search for Taillevent's main kitchens to the playground of a private school behind the notional remnants of the king's mansion. They could equally be beneath the property flanking it. As noted, cooking facilities were often in separate buildings. Pessimistic archaeologists and historians I've buttonholed over the years assure me little is left of the Hôtel Saint Pol and nothing of its kitchens. Why? Add to the reasons already enumerated at Cluny the reality that kitchens are the first things in a building new owners remodel then factor in the willful destruction of medieval Paris by a string of monarchs and modernizers and voilà. But hope is as eternal as springtime in Paris: The medieval cooking fireplaces and chimneys of the palace on the Île de la Cité and the kitchens of the Hôtel de Cluny still stand, massive and unmovable.

Equally massive and unmovable is the figure of Taillevent, the keystone in the foundation of the culinary identify of France. At last, a royal chef known by name! At long last, a French cookbook to rival Apicius!!

Though the recipes in Taillevent's *Le Viandier* are heavily indebted to the Ancients and the anonymous "others" of the Middle Ages they nonetheless represent something primordially Parisian linked to a specific time and place. "Here," you might say, "starts Parisian gastronomy, here begins the Parisian love affair with food."

Actually, I think it started when Paris was named Lutetia.

CRY FOWL

Who knows how many of Taillevent's dishes I'd enjoy making in my modest Marais kitchen? It only dates to the 1700s. That caveat applies equally to other centuries-old recipes, however: I have nothing against Taillevent. *Au contraire.* Modern tastes, the flavors of ingredients and produce, and today's cooking techniques, have evolved too far for literal re-creations from two thousand or six hundred years ago. But perhaps with a little tweaking a few things might do.

TAILLEVENT'S FAMOUS ROAST PEACOCK OR SWAN

Slaughter your bird as if it were a goose, keep the head and tail separate for later use, lard or bard it, roast it until golden, and season it with fine salt. A roast peacock or swan lasts a month or more once it is cooked. Should it become moldy on the surface remove the mold and beneath you will find it white, wholesome, and firm. (Author's note: Don't forget to pluck off the feathers before cooking. And before serving, use toothpicks to reattach the head and tail.)

Like his predecessors and many followers, Taillevent did not bother to list ingredients or weights, use standard measures, indicate cooking times, and give other tiresome details. His "recipes" like those of Apicius were intended first for himself, then for insiders and professionals. I know plenty of pros today who operate in the same mysterious way, especially when it comes to sharing recipes with journalists and cookbook authors.

In case you'd like a sauce or condiment to go with your roasted bird, or perhaps to slather on a boiled boar or side of beef, here is one popular suggestion I have rendered more or less comprehensible in modern American English.

TAILLEVENT'S FAMOUS GINGER-CINNAMON CAMELINE SAUCE

In a mortar, crush ginger, cinnamon, lots of cloves, grains of paradise, mastic, and, optionally, long pepper. Soak bread in vinegar, squeeze it out, force it through a sieve, add salt to taste, and thoroughly mix ingredients.

What is the most innovative thing about this recipe? Food historians have a quick answer: forcing ingredients through a sieve. Today we'd use a food mill, cheesecloth, blender, or processor.

In French, the word *saucier* sounds an awful lot like *sorcier*—sorcerer. Was Taillevent a saucy sorcerer? It seems so. Like an alchemist he took simple ingredients and turned them into something precious and complicated—the key to understanding French cuisine and its hocus-pocus magic. The first known great saucier of Paris, Taillevent called his three mother sauces *dodines*. One is whitish, the second is greenish, the third reddish. They are the indigestible springboard from which many later French sauces sprang.

TAILLEVENT'S GINGERY DODINE DE LAYT WHITE SAUCE

Use this on all kinds of waterfowl. As the fowl roasts catch the drippings in an iron pan and pour milk into the pan. Take half an ounce of ginger for two dishes' worth of sauce and force it through a sieve along with two or three egg yolks, boil this with the milk, add some sugar if you want, and when the fowl is cooked top it with this sauce.

Remember verjuice, that palate-bucking "juice" of unripe grapes or other sour, unripe fruit? Taillevent loved it. I have often used it in Burgundy, fresh off the vine, so to speak, when cooking fresh duck and other fatty fowl.

TAILLEVENT'S PIQUANT VERJUS-BASED SAUCE

This sauce is good on waterfowl, capons, and other roasted poultry. Pour verjuice on top of the roasting fowl and catch the drippings and verjuice in an iron pan. Take some hard-boiled egg yolks and half a dozen lightly roasted chicken livers and force them through a sieve with more pure verjuice. Add some ginger and de-stemmed parsley leaves and boil the sauce. Scatter some toasted bread crumbs on top of the roast and pour the sauce over it and catch it, add some more toasted bread crumbs.

CROWD PLEASER

The amazing thing about Taillevent is, he cooked and conceived menus for crowds—the entire famished thirsty royal court, as a matter of fact, plus visiting regents and aristos. In addition to the bread, fruit, vegetables, condiments, sauces, sweets, and suchlike, most of which had to be baked, picked, and prepared by the chef and his crew, on an average day in the 1380s the queen and royal children's mansions gobbled up 300 chickens, 36 suckling kids, 150 pairs of pigeons, 36 gosling geese, 11 sheep (then as now in France earthy mutton was preferred to delicate lamb), and 3 sides each of beef, veal, and pork.

In the king's mansion alone in a single day the valiant Taillevent and his crew butchered and prepared 50 suckling kids, 50 goslings, 400 pigeons, 600 chickens, 17 sheep, 5 sides of beef, 10 sides of calf, and 2 entire porkers, plus bacon and lard—the preferred cooking fat. Good thing the chef possessed great knife technique.

Now factor in the pageantry—most banquets included elaborate stage sets and machinery for wheeling in gilded chariots, sculptures, or siege towers out of which actors and musicians or live animals sprang into the dining hall. One popular, pungent banqueting trick was to cook a whole boar, mutton, or calf, then wrap it back up in its fur, pelt, hide, or feathers and set it on the table. Ditto the fowl and other beasts tame or wild. Ever smelled an untanned mutton pelt or boar hide? No wonder they burned incense and drank gallons of wine. How about making one animal taste or look like another: that was a favorite trick of Ancient Rome and medieval Europe. Talk about bread and circuses: The bread, as in the victuals, was the circus, as in the entertainment, the way nowadays the medium is the message.

At least Taillevent didn't have to worry about washing the guests' plates and tableware or laundering the napkins and tablecloths—there were none. Only the royal family was served food on plates of gold, silver, or pewter. Throughout the Middle Ages bread was baked into the shape of a cutting board—a *tranchoir*—the food was piled atop it and each diner (or pair of diners) got one.

When the meal was over, the greasy, gristle-flecked, wine-or-slop-soaked bread-boards were fed to the lowly servants or given to the poor—or flung to the dogs and pigs. No forks to wash, either! Forks for lifting dainty morsels off your plate into your mouth didn't exist, not in France. Charles V apparently had several tiny ornamental forks used for serving candied fruit. They were probably given to him as a gift by an ambassador from Venice or Genoa, places where forks of all kinds had been used since the eleventh century. French forks were huge and meant for cooking and serving, not eating.

Who gets to iron the napkins? No, *merci,* try your sleeve instead or the central fabric runner unrolled down the center of aristocratic tables, a napkin-cum-tablecloth. Bones, crusts, apple cores, rinds, and other items of detritus were flung gleefully to the floor—think Henry VIII, Falstaff, and Friar Tuck, or take a stroll on the Seine today on a weekend morning and see what young Parisian partiers do with their picnic supplies and bottles.

Judging by the size and excellence of his tombstone, Taillevent was a sturdy fellow, perhaps even larger than life and illustrative of that cliché. He certainly was an important figure at court, rich enough to lend money to Charles V and, later, was in command of seventy-three scullery workers under Charles VI. Ledgers prove it. That's an appropriate pedigree given the style of the contemporary grand restaurant named for Taillevent, just possibly the most palatial and among the most expensive in France.

Will I ever forget the time I ate at Le Taillevent? How could I? If nothing else, sticker shock remains, decades later.

Founded in 1946 and therefore older than I am and officially a near-antique, though in no way dusty or dowdy, Le Taillevent has always been and still is the place where monarchs, oligarchs, blue bloods, and the occasional red-blooded ordinary citizen dine when wishing to make sacrifice on the altar of classic haute cuisine. There's no molecular here: Le Taillevent's is a comfortable, delicious, and nonthreatening variety of haute that's as timeless as the décor and high-rent location in the 8th arrondissement. The aesthetics of plating match those of the surroundings. There are no triclinium couches, thrush-stuffed boars, or medieval bone throwing to distract diners. Recently redecorated in a twenty-first-century vein, everything is nonetheless as refined, understated, and difficult to date as always—a dash of *The Lady and the Unicorn* in the tapestries redolent of Saint James and scallops;

artful carved contemporary wooden geese to suggest foie gras perhaps or the gastronome Apicius sans vulgarity; wood paneling that merges *ancien*, imperial, and deco; well-spaced, capacious, handsomely napped tables for serious, discreet gastronomes large and small; and a soothing, exclusive, aristocratic, moneyed air blessedly disconnected from the vulgarities of the outside world most of us inhabit.

Appropriately enough, the restaurant is in the former mansion of the Duc de Morny, Napoléon III's imperial-bastard half brother, a renowned womanizer, cruel demagogue, and gastronome. The plummy service is more Second Empire than it is Charles V or Court of Versailles, with inspiration plucked perhaps from the memoirs of Escoffier, inventor of the palace hotel and palatial *grandes tables* of France's misty, golden-hued past. Yet the staff is neither obsequious nor condescending. The wine cellar's two thousand or so bottles are legendary. I can think of no better place to uncork a vintage Domaine de la Romanée-Conti, for instance, equal to the yearly wages of millions including me.

THE ROAR OF RABELAIS

Standing in the reconverted kitchen garden of Charles V where Taillevent got his green vegetables and herbs, now occupied by the quaint Village Saint-Paul antique dealers' quarter, pause to listen before straying into yet another boutique. Can you hear the hungry howling of the Rabelaisian giants Gargantua and Pantagruel gobbling and swilling everything and everyone in sight—bones, blood, and all? I can. In my mind's eye I see terrified patrons scattering from the cute little cafés and bohemian bourgeois bistros under the windows where the monsters' creator, bushy-bearded François Rabelais, the bawdy friar, doctor, and scholar, lives and writes in the first decades of the 1500s.

Gargantua, 19th-century poster by Gustave Doré

"Taking up the pilgrim, he ate him very well then drank a terrible draught of excellent white wine," gloats Rabelais wickedly. "The pilgrims thus devoured made shift to save themselves as well as they could by drawing their bodies out of the reach of the grinders of his teeth . . ."

Insatiable and sometimes cannibalistic, Gargantua and his son Pantagruel always had metaphorical and real bones to pick. It seems to me the gargantuan duo would especially love gnawing on the slender, fashionably dressed bobos and their chic nibbles at Pinot Grigio, a hipster restaurant on the village's northwest side. Would the brutes and Rabelais look out of place in the angular, chilly décor? Of course. Would they care? No, *au contraire.*

Earthy, irreligious, wantonly crude, rude, provoking, and uncontrollable, Rabelais' joyous heroes may have been intended as satires of the priests and noblemen of 1500s society yet, much more so than straitlaced Taillevent, they are models for the primal Frenchman today. Their gastronomic feats are still the measure of French manliness. They are the heroic eaters and drinkers who have nurtured contemporary myths like the French Paradox. Over the centuries the misinterpreted Gargantua and Pantagruel have spawned a host of imperious, macho, alpha, hard-drinking, tough-guy gourmands wantonly immune to Rabelais' deeper message. Which message? *Vivez joyeux,* the philosopher urges his readers on the first page of *Gargantua and Pantagruel,* live happily. What does he mean? Live thoughtfully with joie de vivre.

Gargantua is immortal but Rabelais, the author, died nearly five hundred years ago and was buried beneath the church of Saint-Paul-des-Champs once in Charles V's backyard. The church was destroyed, except for a single wall, during the French Revolution. Rabelais worshippers therefore have no shrine. Luckily a plaque marks the courtyard where Rabelais ate his last supper, somewhere in the confines of today's Village Saint-Paul. I like to think his was the slumping vintage building with Renaissance mullioned windows overlooking rue des Jardins-Saint-Paul and the city wall of Philip Augustus. That rampart was erected in the 1190s but had already started crumbling in Rabelais' day, ready to be blown down, as the author speculated, by "a cow's fart."

"Appetite comes while eating," Rabelais is credited with saying in one of his milder moments, "and thirst is slaked while drinking." The appetite and thirst for the rabble-rouser's words has yet to be satisfied or slaked. Some consider him the greatest French writer of all time. Why? Because the adventures of *Gargantua and Pantagruel* is stuffed with lewd descriptions of wild gorging and heavy drinking, and flecked with sexual innuendo unpublishable today. While talking about the doneness of meat, the color of shrimp and suchlike, and the pallor of a damsel's flesh Rabelais managed to coin a colloquial expression about the anatomy still in use today: "Where the sun never shines." The lists of dream-edibles the giants devour during the course of their travels read like surreal poetry and include the first-known literary reference to something called *poulle d'Inde*—"India hen" alias turkey, mistakenly thought to come from India. If your mouth waters while reading Rabelais, you're a Rabelaisian; if you feel queasy, you might be an effete modernist.

One thing is clear: By Rabelais' time Parisians were eating a huge variety of novel foods. Yet they clung to their Gallic traditions including the rotisserie. One episode in the Gargantua books stands out. When in sophisticated Renaissance Florence, Rabelais' rustic merry men find themselves in the company of a boorish monk from Amiens. He complains about the lack of pretty wenches—and rotisserie-style taverns with plump spitted fowl, mutton, and beef. "Who cares about this Florentine art and culture?" the monk exclaims, fed up with Brunelleschi's dome and baptistery.

JOIE DE MANGER

Given his cult status I'm surprised there's no decent restaurant in Paris named for Rabelais, unlike Apicius or Taillevent, who get pricey establishments with high-profile chefs. But Rabelais does have a university, publishing house, and asteroid named for him, plus a grand confraternity of gourmands, l'Académie Rabelais, founded in 1948. How its members stay sober enough to judge I do not know, but they award an annual prize to the best wine bar-bistro in Paris and the best book with Rabelaisian gourmandizing or tippling as a theme. Some of the Académie Rabelais' favorite wine-soaked spots are also my own.

I have observed members in action at the *comptoir*—the zinc bar that is obligatory to their definition of *bistrot à vin*. But I am no longer in the Gargantuan-class of drinkers so do not seek the brethren's company, preferring to remain a voyeur.

Historians and academics assure the unregenerate reader that Rabelais' roistering style marks the end of the Middle Ages and the birth of the Renaissance in French letters. He certainly had impressive credentials, traveled and feasted widely, particularly in Italy, and had some powerful patrons who changed the course of their times. Rabelais' royal protectors were no other than King François I and his older sister Margaret, Queen of Navarre who, incidentally, was the first to use the term "restaurant" in reference to a restorative food. Though these siblings were both hearty medieval eaters, each was capable of displaying refined Renaissance taste, the king adoring his tongue of carp and liver of monkfish stewed in Spanish wine, and Margaret favoring delicate almond-chicken soup, delicious then and delicious today.

Ironically given his ecclesiastical profession, it was the bon vivant Bishop of Paris, Jean de Bellay, who whisked Rabelais to debauched Rome and played the greatest role in Rabelais' training as an anticlerical, intellectual, "priest-eating" gourmand—the real reason he's so important to your average atheistic food-loving Frenchman.

A dangerous subversive, Rabelais' satires bent many in the church hierarchy out of shape. His writings were condemned as sacrilegious and heretical at a time when Protestantism was on the rise, the Wars of Religion were set to erupt, and the Holy Roman Emperor Charles V of Spain was subduing and uniting Europe for the greater glory of God—and himself.

Meanwhile the great French humanist François I was fighting the emperor while simultaneously modernizing and centralizing France, wiping out feudalism and making himself the only king of the French castle. François was a large, energetic fellow whose Rabelaisian nicknames coincidentally allude to the exaggerated proportions of certain parts of his anatomy. With one large hand tied behind his broad back, François ushered in a renaissance of arts, letters, etiquette, and, perhaps cooking, and started the rebuilding of Paris as the "New Rome."

NEW ROME OR NEW FLORENCE?

Up from the Italian Peninsula came not a Caesar but rather little old Leonardo da Vinci, escaping accusations of sodomy. Following him were the Mannerist capo Giulio Romano, Francesco Primaticcio, Rosso Fiorentino, and Benvenuto Cellini, with their paint pots, calipers, and silversmith tools in tow.

Blame it on Leonardo and the *Mona Lisa,* or maybe the pesto and other great Ligurian food at the charterhouse of La Cervara, near Portofino. That's one of the places François I was held prisoner after being defeated by Charles V in yet another Italian Campaign at the Battle of Pavia, in 1525.

Actually the first conqueror of Paris kitchens probably wasn't Italian Renaissance court cuisine, but rather the rustic *zuppa pavese* whipped up for François on the spur of the moment. Made with free-range organic eggs poached in meat broth with fried slices of bread and grated Parmigiano, it was prepared for the king by the trembling hands of a peasant woman whose services were requisitioned to sooth the royal ego after the debacle at Pavia, where the king was made prisoner and put up for ransom. Already conquered by Italian culture and food, the regal Frenchman imported both in abundance to his riverine capital. *Zuppa pavese* reportedly remained on the royal menu for many a year, perhaps, who knows, nourishing François' son and successor Henri II and, having shaped his taste buds, inducing him to marry the indomitable Caterina de' Medici. Known in France as Catherine de Médicis she was the mother of a series of suspiciously dainty Florentine-French kings and proved herself capable of cooking up murders, massacres, and conspiracies galore.

The Pavia soup story may be apocryphal and the supposition absurd, but maybe not, stranger things have happened. What's sure is the French term *soupe* became common at this time and *la soupe* always meant potage with bread in it. Etymologists might be spoilers by pointing out that both *soupe* and *zuppa* are dauntingly ancient, deriving from early Gothic and perhaps even more remotely from Indo-European roots. We're all an alphabet soup of genetics and cuisines.

Those dusty history books I read suggest something even more curious: that the renascence not the Renaissance in French cooking began about twenty years before the Battle of Pavia, when François was a mere whippersnapper. Why then?

Hello, Columbus!

In from the New World flooded foods from the Spanish Main. While the beans and turkeys and tomatoes were being unloaded and cooks across Europe were trying to figure out what to do with them, an Italian culinary army of conquest was traversing the Alps and would soon subdue Parisian palates. At least that's how the story goes.

As of 1505 aristocratic kitchens throughout the realm of France began to be infiltrated by the recipes of one Maestro Martino, a Lombard (or Italian-Swiss) whose fifteenth-century collection of culinary secrets was published in Latin, with comments by the Renaissance scholar Bartolomeo Sacchi aka Platina. This is astonishing stuff. Kitchen clocks were unknown. But for the first time ever cooking times are given—in paternosters, Ave Marias, and the time it takes to say other prayers. Timing was no longer done with a wing and a prayer, but with a prayer and a stir. Martino supplies a banquet menu with 180 different dishes. Impossible, you say? Not with enough paternosters.

Thanks to Martino's recipes and Platina's impressive tome on health, morals, and domestic happiness, a bestseller with the gripping title *De Honesta Voluptate*—of "honest" or wholesome voluptuousness—Maestro Martino was soon recognized as the great chef and recipe writer of the Renaissance—except, perhaps, retrospectively, by modern Frenchmen.

François did not have modern French prejudices, however, and gaily trotted back from one of his many Italian Campaigns bearing newfangled contraptions, i.e., a set of fancy ceramic plates the likes of which had not been seen in Paris since the days of Emperor Julian. In 1538 the Italian cloche arrived just in time to cover the dishes and keep the food warm. It felt like the beginning of the end of Gallic tabletop boorishness and the birth of the modern French notion of art de la table.

Following Maestro Martino the march of other Peninsular Italian cookbooks, chefs, and paradigm-changing items of tableware into France could not be stopped, continuing throughout the 1500s and into the 1600s.

As ever with these cousin countries, the exchange went both ways, the imported Italians often pleasantly surprised by the excellence of French cuisine and ingredients. It was a marriage made not in ecclesiastical heaven but in François' lusty, possibly anticlerical Renaissance Franco-Italian kitchen where the gluttonous love of food and drink, as refined by Platina and expounded voraciously by Rabelais, if not a virtue, was at least not a mortal sin. The benefits of this unholy culinary union are still felt today. If you doubt my word, you may inquire at Chez Panisse for elucidation.

GULLET SCIENCE

A place of honor among passionate food- and wine-loving Parisians goes to the essayist and indefatigable traveler Michel de Montaigne, a contemporary of Rabelais. Another heroic eater and drinker Montaigne is credited with a great knowledge of the "science of the gullet" or of the palate, if you prefer delicacy over accuracy. He certainly loved wining and dining, delighting in meat, fish, sauces of all kinds, and fruit, especially melons. Montaigne was mad about melons. A wise and reasonably modest man he never considered himself a "scientific gourmet." The real connoisseur of Montaigne's essays was a servant Montaigne met and employed. This anonymous gentleman may have been the first fully fledged modern gastronome, a proto-foodie, the heir of Apicius, Terence, and other Ancients, and the forebear of Grimod de la Reynière and Brillat-Savarin, whose early nineteenth-century books echo so many of the servant's reported words.

"An Italian I lately received into my service was maître d' of the kitchen to the late Cardinal Caraffa until his death," noted Montaigne affably. "I asked him for a description of what his duties had been. He began discoursing on the 'science of the gullet' with so calm an expression and such magisterial gravity as if he had been handling some profound point of divinity," Montaigne continued with only a hint of irony. "He made a learned distinction of the several kinds of appetite: the appetite a man has before he begins to eat, and those he feels after the second and third service. He spoke of the means simply to satisfy the first and to stimulate and activate the other two. He discussed the ordering of the sauces, first in general, and then he proceeded to the qualities of the ingredients and their effects on the diner. The differences of salads according to their seasons, those better served hot and those cold; how to dress and decorate them to make them appealing to the eye. After this he talked about the order of the whole service, full of weighty and important considerations."

At this point in the narrative the erudite maître d' quotes Juvenal to Montaigne on knife technique and good taste: "Nor with less discrimination does he observe how we should carve a hare, and how a hen."

Montaigne closes by giving this unknown Italian the highest accolade of all from his perspective: "He spoke using lofty and magnificent words, the very same we make use of when we discourse on the government of an empire." Sound familiar? Keep reading.

Nowadays an effigy of Montaigne lounges in bronze on a monument in the Latin Quarter bordering a corner park fronting the medieval museum at Cluny. On the statue's limestone plinth are Montaigne's celebrated words:

"My heart has belonged to Paris since childhood. I am French only by association with this great city, the glory of France and one of the world's noblest ornaments." I second the emotion.

PARACHUTE KERFUFFLE

The ornamental quality of Paris is undeniable. Baubles abound. Sitting on the narrow terrace of Brasserie Balzar kitty-corner to the Montaigne monument, I always try to forget the silly controversy that raged here over the 1998 takeover and subsequent remake of this nineteenth-century landmark.

The French corporate restaurant group Flo bought Balzar, cleaned it up, redid the Art Déco elements, rejigged operations, and then things went back more or less to normal. It was a new, self-conscious, ill-at-ease normal. Groupe Flo also run Brasserie Bofinger and over a dozen other landmarks in Paris. The décor and theme change, but the food is unsurprisingly similar and surprisingly edible though it will never win stars or plaudits.

It might have been worse: A phony bobo bistro or fast-food franchise, for instance, could have taken over. Strange no one wept or spilled ink when Groupe Flo took over the other dozen Parisian monuments to the science of brasserie-style gullet. Maybe a new role for corporations and star chefs is the quasi-preservation of historic eateries. Chain restaurants were born in Paris after all—in the nineteenth century. Before gaining independence for a spell, Balzar had already belonged to the owners of another place with so-so food but a great rep and superior attitude, made famous by that peerless epicure Hemingway. I'm speaking of course of the eternal Brasserie Lipp in Saint-Germain-des-Près.

Another contemporary of Montaigne, Rabelais, and Catherine de Médicis was a scholar and humanist named Jean Nicot. Who he? In warm weather when the folding glass panels are open on every terrace in town you can smell Nicot's lingering Renaissance legacy. He was King Henri II's ambassador to Lisbon. Thinking he was doing humanity a favor he brought New World tobacco plants to Paris hence "nicotine" and the lovely flowering garden plant "nicotiana." Nicot earned kudos by giving Queen Catherine a bundle of tobacco leaves to chew, to fight off her headaches, thereby turning her into an early nicotine addict and French role model. She is the forebear and patron saint of countless millions of proud Frenchmen and especially Frenchwomen.

Nicot has no monument but there is a street named for him. He is worshipped by the tens of thousands of tobacconists scattered across the land, and millions of French teenagers and adults. Daily they engage in the ritual burning of billions of cigarettes at his altar. Every garbage truck in Paris is emblazoned with an uplifting Nicot statistic: 350 million tons of butts are swept up each year in the City of Light alone. Perhaps it should be renamed the City of Lighters and strike-all matches? On average, a mere one-in-three French are tobacco addicts, but in the food industry the ratio must be close to one-in-one.

Why butchers, bakers, pastry makers, and restaurant workers from dishwashers to star chefs are such passionate smokers is a question worth asking. Are they weaned on butts and the words of Molière? "He who lives without tobacco is unworthy of living," said the French Shakespeare. Why *Kitchen Confidential*–style machismo rules in the food industry is another good question. Might the two be related?

THE MEDICI "MYTH"

The French spend their money on nothing as freely as they do on things to eat and what they call *faire bonne chère*," wrote the Venetian ambassador to Paris, Girolamo Lippomano, in 1577. "That's why their butchers and meat merchants, roasters and retailers, their makers of pastries, cabaret and tavern owners are found in Paris in such huge numbers that it's downright confusing."

Lippomano prefaces and follows this flattering remark with a long description of the foods and eating habits of the Parisians. Vast quantities of meat, meat pies, pastries, and certain vegetables—peas for instance—are devoured. There are fish sold fresh or preserved, mountains of butter and pools of milk, the proverbial land of plenty. "The population is countless in number yet nothing is lacking: everything seems to fall from the sky," Lippomano gushes. Then as now delicacies are shipped up the Seine from Picardie, Normandy, and the Atlantic, or arrive from Auvergne, Burgundy, and Champagne, he remarks approvingly. It seems cheaper to eat out, or buy your cooked food from rotisseries, bakeries, and caterers, than to buy it at the market and make it at home, the ambassador exclaims, thrilled by the cornucopian *bonne chère*.

What, you might ask, does he mean by *faire bonne chère*? Essentially the expression signifies "eating well," "entertaining," "dining out," and "having a cheery time at table," all wrapped in one. If you know French or think you do, you might also wonder why it isn't spelled *bonne chair*, as in good flesh or good meat. Why? Because, linguists say, *chère*, as in *ma chère* or *ma chèrie*, refers to a dear woman's face and therefore *bonne chère* means the lady of the house is putting on a good face, in other words she is welcoming guests. From this simple French fact *chère* has come to mean anything having to do with the quantity, excellence, and so forth of food and cheerful consumption. "Cheer" is a perverse derivative of *chère*, by the way. Go figure. Instead of correcting a medieval spelling error the linguists of the Académie Française got ahold of *ma chèrie* and by pinching a syllable performed a Jesuitical retrofit of her fleshy cheerful cheek.

Who can be surprised by either the expression or the verbal contortionism? Already in the time of Emperor Julian partying was the favorite pastime in Lutetia.

Little did François I realize what he was getting into when he arranged his second son's marriage to the Medici heiress Caterina, a feisty young thing with fish lips and bovine eyes, but shapely pretty hands sparkling with gold. Caterina's mother was a spirited Frenchwoman, her father Lorenzo II, rich, influential, and magnificent, though nowhere near as magnificent as her grandfather Lorenzo il Magnifico. From a family of ennobled bourgeois doctors, she was not of a royal bloodline, but she compensated with a papal dowry and some pretty promising political and spiritual connections. Caterina was bundled off at the tender age of fourteen in 1536 to marry Henri II of France, who not being the eldest son had little prospect of ruling. When Henri's older brother caught cold and died after playing racketball and, later, when François I also departed for the banqueting hall in the sky, Henri II inherited the throne.

Becoming queen in 1547, Caterina was given a bang-up coronation banquet in Paris two years later—and by some strange twist of archival fate the expense account has survived.

A ROYAL BANQUET FOR QUEEN CATHERINE, JUNE 19, 1549

There shall be thirty courses served to seated guests and eight courses to the commoners.

For one and all: 2,995 bottles of claret and white wine

For the seated guests:

Roasted, boiled and otherwise cooked to perfection: thirty peacocks, thirty-three pheasants, twenty-one swans, nine cranes, thirty-three spoonbills, thirty-three large herons, thirty-three egrets, thirty-three young herons, thirty fattened kids, thirty-six turkey-hens, thirty capons, six pigs, sixty-six chickens, sixty-six grouses, ninety-nine rennerons deer, ninety-nine each of squabs, doves, and chickens, the latter cooked with vinegar, thirty-three young hares, seven turkey cocks, sixty-six young bunnies, thirty-three goslings, thirteen young partridges, three young bustards, eighteen cockerels, ninety-nine quail for roasting and ninety-nine more for making quail-meat pies, twenty capons also for meat pies.

For the Queen's pleasure: twelve dozen artichokes.

Desserts &tc: forty each of marzipans, croissant-shaped gateaux, bracelet-shaped Royal pastries, cheineaulx curved wafers, lésardeaux zigzag-shaped cookies, &tc, &tc, &tc . . .

Also on the accounting books were twenty-dozen violets to decorate the tables, plus linens, cheeses, a host of savory pastries including verjuice-flavored tarts, and huge quantities of spices and herbs many of them familiar to Taillevent—in other words, the banquet chef favored the usual medieval cupboard.

Remarkably absent from the *festin* was fish. Perhaps the queen or the king weren't big on it, especially in summer, or June 19 wasn't a "lean" day in the canonical calendar.

Remarkably present were the marzipans, sweet pastries, and cookies—totally Renaissance Italian—and especially the artichokes. Since antiquity, artichokes have been an Italian obsession. Caterina was wild about them, ingesting immodest and dangerous quantities—dangerous because they clearly worked magic, leading to her many life-threatening pregnancies. Everyone knows that artichokes were and still are classed among the most genial of aphrodisiacs, at least in Italy. Caterina might well have needed them to please the king, who during her infertile years threatened to have the marriage annulled. She may also quite simply have adored their subtle, slightly bitter flavor, as I do.

Of special note were the crescent-shaped gateaux. Might they be the ancestors of today's croissants? Probably not, but then again the true origins of croissants are still unconfirmed. What's guaranteed is Caterina would not have ordered them and must have been furious to see them on the menu: The crescent moon is a symbol of Diana, the Huntress, and the king's favorite mistress was none other than Diane de Poitiers, a relentless cougar old enough to be his mother.

How many sit-down guests were at the banquet? The archives don't tell. Judging by the numbers of servings, there were probably enough diners to fill twenty or forty tables or to be easily divided by twenty or forty. But there may have been many more. What's really curious are all the thirty-threes, sixty-sixes, and ninety-nines. Students of arcana argue the numbers were of vital interest to Caterina. She believed in numerology. In Italian culture then and now, threes, sixes, and nines are good luck: three for the Trinity, six for twice the Trinity, nine for three times the Trinity, thirty-three for the age Christ was crucified, ninety-nine for the Trinity times Christ's age when crucified, and so forth.

The victuals were brought out in massive, successive waves of multiple dishes, with many small portions of each placed strategically on a table smorgasbord-style so that guests could serve themselves from platters within easy reach. This style of entertaining is known in France as *service à la francaise* but there is nothing particularly French about it. At the Louvre, take a look at Paolo Veronese's *The Wedding at Cana* painted in 1563—it's the biggest canvas in the museum. Most banquets in Europe were organized this way from antiquity forward and some still are. The expression *service à la francaise* was adopted by the French after the modern, course-by-course or dish-by-dish so-called *service à la russe* was introduced into the country from Russia in the early nineteenth century. Given the culinary hegemony of France and the propensity to gerrymander history, *service à la russe* has of course long been considered typically French.

THE PARTY'S OVER

Hangovers come in many shapes and sizes. After the banquet, Caterina's philandering royal spouse went back to shunning her and leaped into a familiar saddle. As noted, the king's longtime mistress and de facto co-regent was Diane de Poitiers, still comely though long in the tooth. What would a Freudian say? Maybe mother-love is why Henri was seen to practically breast feed on Diane de Poitiers' lovely bosom in view of the court. Diane was Caterina's greatest enemy and ally. They had a symbiotic relationship. The huntress wasn't interested in claiming the throne with her uterus. She ordered the king to do his duty as husband with Caterina. By dint of eating artichokes somehow Caterina managed to spend enough quality time in bed with Henri to bear ten heirs—her assigned function. She nearly died in the process, giving birth to a pair of ill-fated twins. One died in childbirth, the other shortly afterward.

Eventually Caterina got her revenge. Cocky Henri II was skewered through the eyeball in a jousting match on rue Saint-Antoine on the tenth day of July in the year of our Lord 1559, in other words precisely a decade and twenty-one days after the royal banquet. Twenty-one is three times seven and seven is very unlucky. There were twenty-one cranes served at the banquet to boot. It's all a question of numbers. And then there were those crescent-shaped gateaux . . .

From a purely contemporary gastronomic standpoint the fatal accident happened at the corner of Impasse Guémenée near the neighborhood's best little family-run bistro, Le Gorille Blanc, halfway between the vinous old Cave des Pyrénées and Bofinger, the brassy brasserie that still serves the city's best *choucroute,* if you ask me, and no, it is not exactly the same as sauerkraut. Two outstanding cheesemongers, a great butcher with some of the city's best rotisserie chickens, and Benoit, an excellent artisan chocolatier, operate within minutes of the site of the royal accident, not to mention several wonderful wine shops and a great old-fashioned family-owned catering establishment with the Rabelaisian name Au Sanglier—The Wild Boar. A Renaissance king or Venetian ambassador would be pleased with the comestibles and potables on rue Saint-Antoine.

Back to Henri who spent five agonizing days dying: Whose colors was he wearing on his fluttering ribbons during the joust? Not the queen's but rather Diane de Poitiers'. The adulteress sorceress was therefore clearly to blame and was ousted, spending most of the rest of her long and adventurous life at the exquisite Château d'Anet.

Understandably somewhat embittered by her early experiences and left with eight surviving children—a disappointing number—Caterina henceforth ruled France, with occasional help from the reactionary Catholic Guise clan. A skilled backseat-driver, she drove through the reigns of her three ineffectual sons until she died in 1589 still full of Florentine pizzazz.

So when is a myth not a myth? Answer: When it's true. French culinary chauvinists can't seem to stand the notion that their country lived in the shadows of Italy those many centuries ago. Certainly the process of Italianization of French court cuisine and what you could call "good manners" and art de vivre had already started thirty years before Caterina's baggage train parked in Paris. Strictly speaking it wasn't initiated by the Medici gang. But it continued throughout her lifetime and picked up pace, and then returned in the 1600s with a Medici cousin. Who knows, without the Medici influence the Parisian royal dining scene might have reverted to bone-throwing, dirty sleeves, and dogs or pigs under the tables.

As the inventor of food writing, Grimod de la Reynière noted in 1803, gourmet eating "had long flourished in Italy, where the Medici awoke arts that had slept for fourteen centuries."

The Medici ruled long, perhaps too long, arriving in distinct waves like a banquet with *service à la française*. Caterina's first son François II was a teenage weakling who lasted seventeen months on the throne. Charles IX held on for fourteen years, his mother peering over his shoulders as he toyed with mistresses and failed to produce a legitimate male heir. Becoming unhinged and increasingly uppity toward the queen mother, some authors including the imaginative Alexandre Dumas claim mamma Caterina poisoned Charles to get him out of the way.

Remember the Venetian ambassador's glowing words? In the 1570s while the Florentine-Frenchman Charles IX putatively ruled, the *bonne chère* got seriously great. Not just visiting Venetians, but also the gourmets of the subsequent Ancien Régime and early modern France confirm it. This wasn't the king's doing—he was ten when he took over and his main interest as hormonal teenager was blood sports and skirt-chasing. The food got better because his mamma ran the show as in all good Italian households.

The biggest banquet Charles IX and Caterina planned turned out to be the Saint Bartholomew's Day Massacre. It wasn't hugely appetizing. The guests of honor were Charles' nymphomaniac sister Marguerite de Valois aka Queen Margot, a staunch Catholic, and her husband-to-be Henri II of Navarre, a hereditary Huguenot, the future Henri IV of France, the guy who force-fed his confessor partridges and famously quipped "Paris is worth a mass" when he converted to the Roman faith in order to enter the besieged capital.

Charles' and Caterina's nefarious plan was to lure the leading Protestants into Paris to the marriage and wipe them out—a different kind of banquet pageantry. The plot worked pretty well. Over three thousand Protestants were dispatched in the space of three days. The Marais in particular was awash in blood. Butchery marked the reign of Charles IX who, if he wasn't already deranged, went seriously mad after Saint Bartholomew's Day. His ambiguous successor Henri III increased the bloodletting as the Wars of Religion played on.

FILET MIGNON

Oddly Paris was Europe's great food city, a cornucopia afloat in blood and guts and not only in the form of blood sausages and offal. Refinement of manners reached a peak. By all reports the *bonne chère* wasn't substantially different from what it had been for centuries, both at the top and bottom of the scullery ladder. The biggest change was the increasing shift from caustic, acidic verjuice to an Italianate preference for sweet and sour. Even more important was the change in the way meals were prepared, served, and consumed.

Despite French attempts at revising history it's a proven fact that thanks to Henri III the table fork—as opposed to the serving or cooking fork—at last graced the better tables of the realm, starting in Paris. There was no guarantee, however, that anyone but this peculiar king and his entourage would actually use his forks. They were deemed effeminate and overdelicate—*très mignonne*. Whether the young king was gay or bisexual, as many have alleged, and whether he disliked violence, war, and manly activities including hunting, making him the opposite of his grandfather, François I, and therefore perverted by Florentine ways, seems unlikely but not impossible. It may not seem like an issue to progressives nowadays, but in the 1500s it was a big issue. The spinmeisters and revisionists were active then and are active now on both sides of the equation.

Strangely, given his supposed love of luxury and peace, the record suggests it was Henri III and his iron-sided mother, Caterina, who masterminded the massacre of the Protestants—not Charles IX. There's no question Henri's hitmen murdered his rivals from the House of Guise in his presence. What's also pretty sure is Henri was a sensitive guy who liked finery, art, and architecture, and had what a modern physician might call a phobia for sticky things and dirty fingers. He and his dandy mignon-minions loathed coarse French fashions and table manners, and lived in terror of staining their ruffled collars. Despite efforts to induce change, even the top-drawer Parisians including Montaigne still ate messily with their knives and fingers—no napkins, no forks, not even spoons, unless served soup.

Henri and his long-haired, divinely scented mignons would have none of this—and neither would mamma Caterina. Forks and silver spoons in fancy personalized cases flooded France, and so did napkins. If forks were good enough for Caesar and Julian, they were good enough for Caterina and Henri. The fact that no one in France opened their fancy fork-and-napkin cases except in the presence of the king or queen is another matter.

The reign of Henri III, the last of the Valois kings, was astonishingly violent. Even his supposedly delicate, effeminate favorites became dueling dandies and a number of them died senselessly defending their honor. After ordering the murder of many, Henri III was in turn murdered in 1590, leaving the throne to his coarse Bourbon cousin Henri II of Navarre. Crowned as Henri IV of France, the new king swiftly annulled his barren union with Margaret of Valois and was ready to go. He got off to a great start by besieging Paris for long enough to starve 50,000 or so Parisians, about a quarter of the population. The siege failed, inducing Henri to famously embrace the Roman faith. No wonder he had himself dubbed "le bon Henri"—good Henri—and went out of his way to promise stewing chickens for peasants' pots, still on menus today as *poule au pot,* plus lots of partridges and other volatile game for the upper crust, and lethal quantities of raw garlic and chilled Jurançon or other wine for one and all. Like many heroic French kings Henri's passions were hunting, skirt-chasing, and making war—fine food was the proverbial icing on the regal cake of life. It's ironic he wound up remarrying a remarkable glutton.

This messy royal transition is proof if ever it was needed that there's no such thing as linear progress in cooking, table manners, or politics.

French-eating habits were set to slide under the rule of the garlic-scented bon Henri until another Medici lady was hustled up to Paris in 1600 to provide proper Catholic heirs and restore order in the kitchens and banqueting halls. Enter Maria de' Medici, Caterina's equally fertile and forceful cousin, another adept of forks, spoons, napkins, and *bonne chère* with a Florentine accent. Lots and lots of *bonne chère*.

PART FOUR

Entrées, Second Service:

Medici *à la Parisienne,* Early 1600s

BOURBON STREET

When married off by proxy at a tender age, Maria de' Medici was slim and attractive, her face an elongated, delectable almond—that's what the portraits purport to show. After a few too many banquets, six pregnancies, and, I suspect, the binge-eating stress induced by her husband Henri IV's assassination in 1610, Maria ballooned into a voracious gargantuan queen mother. Her magnificent girth was captured by Peter Paul Rubens on enough canvas to sail fleets of galleons.

Rubens' celebrated cycle of monumental paintings now hangs in the Louvre—room is needed. They were conceived for Maria's cozy new Florentine-Parisian mansion, the Luxembourg Palace, crown jewel of Paris' prettiest park, the Luxembourg Garden, home to the French Senate. If the Luxembourg reminds you vaguely of Florence's Palazzo Pitti, there is a reason: That's where Maria grew up and what she tried to re-create.

Rubens' extravaganzas of the baroque are bizarrely beautiful. Glorifying and deifying Maria, her arrival and life in France, they include the episode of the blessed birth of an heir, the Dauphin Louis, dubbed upon his coronation Louis XIII. Cornucopias, puffy clouds, a storm-wracked ship—Rubens knew how to flatter by using themes and backdrops from classical mythology. The paintings also cleverly suggest other providential Christian lives—the Virgin Mary and Mary Magdalene's, for instance. Standing before these sumptuous smorgasbords of color with mouth agape you can't help wondering whether Maria was not just gluttonous but also the prototypical narcissist. As God's gift to France she ensured the continuation of the newborn Bourbon line sired by Henri IV.

In the déjà vu department, Maria played Caterina de' Medici to her son Louis XIII, ruling in his stead when he was underage, then driving the royal coach from the backseat until the rebellious teenager wisely ran her out of Paris and took the reins. He made the strategic error of allowing her back in. No slacker when it came to vanity or ferocity, Louis inherited his father's passion for hunting and butchery, and a singular indifference to refined food or table manners. His greatest culinary distinction—a big black mark in his book if you ask me—was to reject the potato, recently imported into France and presented to him at the royal dining table.

He also shared his predecessor Henri III's love of male company. No dainty mignons for macho, mustachioed Louis—he liked his favorites full grown. Left to his own devices Louis would have happily rolled the royal menus back to the gamy days of the Middle Ages except that he hated medieval feudalism and was bent on stamping out its last writhing vestiges, hence the need for national institutions emanating not from clannish, rebellious aristos but from the Crown of France. Besides, mamma Maria was there to gobble her marzipans, wave Florentine forks, and spread finery. She imported an army of Italians, including many scoundrels, to cook, entertain, rule, pilfer, and terrorize the populace and recalcitrant aristocrats desirous of feudal privilege. Only the church escaped her wrath. Actually the church in the form of pope, prelates, bishops, and cardinals encouraged her righteous wrath against others.

Louis took credit for many projects begun by his father, starting with the so-called Louis XIII style, pioneered by Henri III and continued by Henri IV. The handsome brick-and-stone pavilions of Place des Vosges were his papa's pet project. Given the young king's lack of taste and his disdain for delicacy, a cynic might say it's fitting that the Square Louis XIII, the fountain-dotted green centerpiece of the Place des Vosges, is framed by a culinary desert, a certified gastronomic disaster zone stuffed cheek by jowl with fashion boutiques, third-rate eateries and ice creameries, glitzy pastry shops, and self-styled art galleries.

But wait, the great unassailable Michelin three-star temple of miniaturized perfection L'Ambroisie is on Place des Vosges. One day perhaps we'll know whether Barack Obama actually enjoyed his meal there. Obama reportedly pleaded for authentic bistro fare—he loved La Fontaine de Mars near the Eiffel Tower—but was overruled by plump, luxury-loving, protocol-sensitive President François Holland who wasn't likely to pass up an all-expenses-paid three-star experience.

DESERTS AND DESSERTS

A desert did you say, or a dessert? If you stick to the housemade pastries and avoid the luncheon or dinner fare, Carette under the square's north portico certainly has a nice view. Ditto Ma Bourgogne on the west side, the perfect breakfasting or aperitif spot, as long as the excellence of the coffee or wine or anything else but the panorama and atmosphere isn't an issue.

I wonder if the unholy trinity of pretentiousness, mass tourism, and historic site always breed mediocrity. Rome is cursed by a similar glut of wonders and wanderers. But stop again. Flare your nostrils. Some of the world's best tea comes from the Dammann Frères boutique sandwiched between L'Ambroisie and Ma Bourgogne. There's a perfectly good "artistic" chocolate shop, Joséphine Vannier, a hundred yards east of the Place des Vosges, on rue du Pas de la Mule. And how could I forget, among the greatest chocolatiers of all, Jacques Genin has set up his jewel-like shop a quarter-mile north on rue de Turenne. This is fitting: Chocolate first came to France from Spain with Louis XIII's wife Anne of Austria—her great, failed contribution to gastronomy. It failed the first time around because Louis XIII and the French court didn't care for it, only embracing *chocolat* decades later, thanks to Maria Theresa, Louis XIV's chocolate-addicted Spanish queen.

Did someone really say culinary desert? Several blocks east of the Place des Vosges is the twice-weekly Boulevard Richard-Lenoir market and its outstanding purveyors of farmyard chickens, fresh wild fish, organic vegetables, cheese, and Lebanese street food. For the *choucroute* and shellfish, the perennial Bofinger is five minutes away, ditto Le Gorille Blanc, my favorite Marais bistro. On a few of the more remote back streets of the Marais, great pastries, outstanding coffee, peerless smoked salmon, world-class falafel, and good or even great restaurant eating and drinking can still be found—if you bother to look for yourself and skip the *vox populi* websites where the difference between shoe leather and sirloin is unclear.

Chez Nenesse, a throwback bistro with great grub from circa 1970, is still in business near the Temple neighborhood. For those who can afford to splash out, one of the city's best and longest-established terroir restaurants L'Ambassade d'Auvergne and the paragon of overpriced, exquisite, changelessness L'Ami Louis are nearby on the northwestern edge of the Marais. Bobo paradise isn't the gastronome's hell after all. As ever, amid the blight are blossoms, some of them fragrant.

RELAIS RACE

Ironically no matter how you spin it, one of the city's most reliably good, traditional Michelin one-star restaurants is named for this unloved, rather villainous king: Le Relais Louis XIII. It may well be the finest, traditional *grande table* left in that other quintessentially charming, chic, and therefore gastronomically challenged Parisian neighborhood on the Left Bank bridging the Latin Quarter and Saint-Germain. The meals I've shared with friends at Le Relais Louis XIII have been superlative in the seventeenth- or perhaps the nineteenth-century vein, and deeply reminiscent of the old Tour d'Argent. That's because the longtime chef Manuel Martinez was in charge of the Tour d'Argent's kitchens for nearly a decade. His menu is seasonal, but the house specialties are perennials, like the atmosphere and décor.

Portraits of Louis XIII and Anne of Austria watch over you in the dining room. The exposed timbers and rough stone walls exude woodworms and authenticity: The building was part of the medieval Grands-Augustins convent. The place is an antidote to the ephemeral trendy Paris restaurants that spring up and blow away like the crocuses in the Medicis' gorgeous Luxembourg Garden.

History tastes good, too—as long as novelty and "excitement" isn't what you're after. Dainty Henri III reportedly dropped by here in 1579 to found a club of broadminded progressives, the Order of the Knights of the Holy Spirit. Whether he brought his forks and napkin with him wasn't recorded. The decisive moment in the site's pedigree came on May 14, 1610, when the bon Henri IV, on the way to the Arsenal and Place des Vosges, was stabbed to death by a Catholic fanatic brimming with Christian charity. The nine-year-old heir Louis was snatched from the Louvre, bundled across the Pont Neuf, and crowned in the safety of the convent.

The ceremony may well have happened right where you're sitting, supping, if I were you, on duck pressed à la Tour d'Argent. You can also have your waterfowl roasted and spiced in the style of the Renaissance, or opt for succulent braised veal sweetbreads with mushrooms, peppery wild hare *à la royale,* and the perfect, classic Bourbon vanilla *mille-feuille.*

Even if the coronation of Louis XIII took place upstairs, as some think, who cares? A fascinating yet distinctly unappetizing oddity of the décor is the rusted chastity belt displayed on the staircase to the medieval cellar. It's a reminder of the joys of the convent, certainly not of the bonhomie of the premises' former tenants, a boisterous working-class café that was Picasso's coal depot and hangout when he lived across the street from the late 1930s into the 1950s.

Other clickable gastronomic and topographical links to Maria de' Medici, Louis XIII, and the Bourbon dynasty connect this restaurant to the Louvre, Palais-Royal, and Versailles; the Mazarin Library and the Luxembourg Palace. Since it's about time for another meal let us reconvene there, half a block from Maria de' Medici's manse.

BLUNT IS BETTER

It's tough to imagine the red-robed Cardinal Richelieu—think the evil mastermind of *The Three Musketeers*—as the widowed queen Maria's lover. Can you see him sneaking down secret passageways and staircases from his Petit Luxembourg Palace to the queen's massive, sprawling mansion next door?

Heftiness and triple chins aren't necessarily unattractive, and goodness knows the aesthetics of the baroque were different from our own. Maria was clearly appetizing enough to her husband and subsequent comers, including the Florentine adventurer and mercenary Concino Concini alias Le Maréchal d'Ancre. Concino was married to the queen's lady-in-waiting. Like Maria, both were colorful imported Italians who wreaked havoc on Paris. Concino had a private army of seven thousand men and alongside Maria virtually ran the country into the ground.

It was as an assistant to Concini that the youthful Richelieu became the queen's closest advisor, some say more than that. In his youth, Richelieu was a well-fed morsel of manhood. If ordered to do service, would he have refused to climb the social ladder into the royal bedchamber? Does it matter? Of course it matters! Dalliance was de rigueur then as it is today among a certain kind of Parisian. Philandering and sex in general are firmly believed to stimulate the appetite. They are forms of gastronomic foreplay. Aphrodisiacs abounded then and still do. If not garlic or artichokes, it's oysters or caviar and rivers of Champagne.

What makes the liaison hard to credit is Richelieu's mature physique and reputation as the chilly "Red Eminence." He shriveled from his rotund prime into a slight, sickly, dry statesman whose only appetites were for power and politics, certainly not feasting and debauchery. But he did share the Medici delight in plots, assassinations, and intrigue, and the horror of bad table manners. As a diplomat he spent a great deal of time at table dickering with rival factions for the queen's benefit and, later, for her son's. He ran Louis XIII's kingdom with authoritarian panache, living just long enough to witness and perhaps cause the miraculous birth of Louis XIV, heir to the Red Eminence's ingeniously engineered theocratic Divine Right absolutism.

Richelieu was neither a gourmet nor a gourmand. The many classic dishes à la Richelieu—including *pâté en croûte Richelieu* (veal and pork in a buttery crust), *filet de boeuf Richelieu* (carrots, onions, butter, Madera sauce), *sauce Richelieu* (mushrooms, truffles, butter)—are named for the libertine gastronome Maréchal Duc de Richelieu, the cardinal's eighteenth-century descendant.

But it's thanks to the cardinal the world has round-tipped, blunt-ended table knives—the ancestors of today's butter knives. Why?

Here's a hint. At my favorite old-fashioned bistro near the Luxembourg Palace, Café Tournon, I once watched with fascination as a suited diner attacked his steak with a lethal Laguiole pocketknife then prepared to discreetly pick his teeth with the pointy blade. He hesitated, knife in midair, knowing he'd been spotted. The providential arrival of toothpicks spared an embarrassing spectacle.

In Richelieu's day it was common for everyone, especially the quarrelsome menfolk, not merely to disdain the forks and napkins bequeathed by Henri III, but to pick their teeth at table with their knives—or stab tablemates. Richelieu abhorred coarseness and petty violence, especially if it stained his table linens. So he had his maître d' commission an artisan to produce the world's first known innocuous and, it must be said, often useless knives. Problem resolved—at Richelieu's table. Elsewhere, the sharp, pointed, flicking blades and greasy fingers prevailed for a century or more, despite Louis XIV's banning them in public and at court in 1669. The unspeakable truth is the Sun King preferred eating with his fingers—like a Roman emperor. Knife control proved to be about as effective as gun control today.

ROYAL JACKRABBITS

Close your eyes and imagine a cross between the pleasantly frayed Brasserie Balzar of decades past and your dream Parisian café circa 1958. Lift your eyelids and gaze upon Café Tournon, a roistering place with moleskin banquets, wooden bistro chairs that make the backside ache, multicolored broken-tile floors, a zinc-topped bar, mirrors and murals on the walls, spunky waitresses, an ambitious yet unpretentious chef, and a real husband-and-wife team of owner-managers referred to by the Rabelaisian regulars as *le patron* and *la patronne.* The murals are a touchstone for aging boomers. They were painted in the late 1950s in the naïf Douanier Rousseau style and show sunny scenes of smooching and playing in the Luxembourg Garden.

The hard-drinking Austrian novelist Joseph Roth lived above Le Tournon. You can hear echoes of the café in his haunting books. After World War II this was where James Baldwin hung with Chester Himes and Richard Wright. Duke Ellington reportedly did his Paris debut here before setting the jazz scene on fire in neighboring Saint-Germain-des-Prés. The Tournon has long been one of my preferred watering holes in an area where the restaurant food, wine, pastries, and chocolates are often fabulous. Three of the city's top pâtissiers and chocolatiers Gérard Mulot, Patrick Roger, and Pierre Hermé are within a five-minute radius. The Académie Rabelais honored Café Tournon some years ago as the best wine bar-bistro in Paris and the city's top French food critic François Simon gave it a rave. Luckily the publicity eventually died down, the vogue passed, and the regulars have returned to their usual roosts.

Besides serving a roster of nineteenth- and twentieth-century classics, including celery root salad and divinely simple boiled eggs with real house-made fresh mayo, the Café Tournon's fall feature is the inimitable ancient-medieval-Renaissance-modern specialty of kings, *lièvre à la royale.* This is the same long-cooked, peppery, pudding-like wild hare concoction you might already have tasted in an excellent rendition at Le Relais Louis XIII. Apicius ate his hare in a somewhat similar fashion, with pounds of black pepper, and *Le Mesnagier de Paris* recommends something like it in the form of a *civé* or stew. *Lièvre à la royale* is known as the cult dish not of Louis XIII but of his son, the Sun King, born in 1638 and already an adolescent big eater. Naturally enough the *à la royale* handle wasn't added until long after both monarchs died.

Whenever senate sessions at the Luxembourg Palace are suspended Café Tournon is pretty quiet. But when the politicos and their advisors, the lobbyists, journalists, and other famished hangers-on show up, the smoke on Café Tournon's terrace thickens and the pace picks up. When the editors and authors from nearby publishing houses show up, the stage show can at times be as good as it gets in Paris.

Given that the Luxembourg Palace provides the café with its hungriest and most free-spending, state-subsidized clients, it's only right chef Patrick Canal uses the "classic" nineteenth-century recipe for hare supplied by Senator Aristide Couteaux. Couteaux's recipe runs to five pages, transforms the hare into a spoonable pudding, and requires poor Patrick Canal and anyone else rash enough to follow the instructions to spend several days in preparing royal hares.

Couteaux, a possible model for Elmer Fudd, was not only a gastronome: He was rarely seen outside Paris without his trusty shotgun. "A jack-hare is what is needed, the kind with red fur, shot preferably in the mountains and of solid French pedigree (distinguished by the slight nervy elegance of the head and limbs)," Couteaux begins. "It should weigh five to six pounds, meaning older than a leveret but still adolescent." The senator pauses before moving from the essential to the quintessential. "The most important thing is to shoot the hare cleanly so it doesn't lose a drop of blood."

Blood! The secret ingredients in *lièvre à la royale* aren't only the poor jackrabbit's blood, and its lungs and entrails, as you might imagine, or the streaky bacon and goose fat. It's not the vinegar, mounds of garlic, and heaps of shallots, or the optional black truffles, the inky wine at least two years old, and preferably from Burgundy or Bordeaux. The secret isn't secret at all—everyone knows it is foie gras.

A PROFESSION OF FOIE

What I do not know and want to know is how Steinway-sized Maria de' Medici and her gargantuan grandson Louis XIV—when full grown he consumed seven thousand calories per day—how, I ask, did these two avoid becoming specimens of walking, talking foie gras? Did they feel cannibalistic when they ate it? Maybe this is how the French homophones *foi*, *foie*, and *fois* got jumbled up—"faith," "liver," and "time" sounding identical to the ear. Was foie gras a common feature on the royal or bourgeois menus of the 1500s and 1600s? Did the Florentine invasion of France include fattened geese, or did the Jewish community in Paris already have them during the Medici queen's reign? The jury is still out.

Anyone who uses Wikipedia or has read this book attentively knows by now that foie gras has been around since the Egyptians first embalmed it. To recap, it's assumed, without documentation, that the delicacy clandestinely entered France many centuries ago. The French national propaganda department funded by various government ministries posits that the explosion of foie gras production in France can be explained by the planting of corn from the New World in the foie gras heartland of the Southwest in the 1500s. Suddenly it was a cinch for proud Gallic peasants to fatten geese and ducks. The livers, other organs, and fatty padding of these fowls are made for stuffing and swelling—a proven scientific fact, ask any Canada goose overnighting on the Seine. The fat stocked up in their bodies is the energy reserve that allows them to fly on intercontinental routes.

Sound plausible? What a funny coincidence that the New World corn and Old World diaspora of Jews appeared in France—and Italy, Germany, and elsewhere—at about the same time, at the end of the 1400s. Might the Spanish Inquisition and Alhambra Decree forcing religious conversion be responsible for the spread of *foie gras*? "The liver of domestic geese raised by the Jews is extremely large," observed Bartolomeo Scappi in his 1570 *Opera*. "It weighs two or three pounds."

Parbleu! The hallowed tradition protected by the French government and

United Nations culinary defense troops, the "noble product" touted as quintessentially French, is really an Egyptian-Mediterranean-Jewish specialty of relatively recent Gallic adoption? Scandalous! So let's get skeptical. What's "recent"? That depends on your frame of reference. I've found no mention of foie gras or fattened waterfowl livers of any kind in French medieval or Renaissance literature, cookbooks, and household manuals. But *foye gras* with a "y" does show up in a number of solid recipes in François Pierre de La Varenne's celebrated *Le Cuisinier françois,* first published in 1651, i.e., during the reign of the jackrabbit-loving, Rabelaisian Sun King.

This makes perfect sense. So let us conjecture. Things moved slowly in those days. Figure that, following the Jewish diaspora of the 1490s *foie gras* and corn probably took a century or so to gain popularity in France, and another half century to be so common that *foie gras* is included in a French cookbook with no explanation of what it is or how to find or produce it. You're easily into the first decades or middle of the seventeenth century say, around 1635, when the French Academy was founded by Cardinal Richelieu. The Academy put the language and culture in aspic and hasn't updated its statutes yet. Why update myths about *foie gras*?

LA VARENNE, *LE CUISINIER FRANÇOIS*: "*FOYE GRAS* CUIT DANS LE CENDRE"

Il faut le barder &: le bien assaisonner de sel, poivre, clou battu & un bouquet fort petit, puis l'envelopper avec quatre ou cinq fueilles de papier & le mettre cuire dans les cendres comme un coing. Estant cuit, prenez garde de perdre la sauce en le remuant; ostez les fueilles de dessus, & le servez avec celles de dessous si vous voulez, ou sur une assiette.

Here's my decryption of the chef's un-Kosher "Foie Gras Cooked in Ashes." Nothing could be simpler for a regal chef with a fireplace designed for cooking quinces. La Varenne instructs his readers to bard the uncooked foie gras, presumably with bacon or lard, season it with salt, pepper, powdered cloves, and the tiniest *bouquet garni*—a pinch of minced or crushed bay leaf, thyme, sage, or tarragon will do. Then wrap it in four or five sheets of cooking paper and set it to bake slowly among the hot ashes like a quince—or a foil-wrapped potato in a BBQ unit, if that's easier to envision. When it's cooked—the timing and degree of doneness is up to you, the French like it *mi-cuit* meaning half-cooked—be careful not to let the juices run off as you remove the foie gras from the ashes and unwrap the top sheets of paper. Serve it still enveloped in the bottom sheets, or unwrapped and on a plate if you prefer. Voilà, le famous barbecued fattened goose liver.

It's odd, don't you think, that La Varenne is so closely associated with the Sun King and Versailles' court cooking when in reality his career began during the reign of Louis XIII and he was born, worked, and died in Burgundy? The reason lies in the title: the *French* cook. It was followed by *The French Pastry Chef* and other books proclaiming French citizenship. With La Varenne, culinary nationalism begins. Throughout the reign of Louis XIV everything from cooking to art, crafts, table manners, and morals was rebaptized as "French."

Why? First to secure the Sun King's position as Divine Right monarch not only of the Île-de-France, but of *all* of France—including many recalcitrant former provinces, kingdoms, and duchies such as Normandy, Burgundy, and Provence—and, second, France's natural, God-given superiority over its rival European neighbors.

Still, all those *à la Duxelles* dishes with buttery mushroom-and-onion sauce you see on French menus today were excogitated when La Varenne was chef to the plutocratic Nicolas Chalon du Blé, Marquis d'Uxelles, lord of the riverside city of Chalon sur Saône far from Paris and Versailles in southern Burgundy. La Varenne cooked and wrote in the cozy little kitchen of a handsome small, moat-ringed château floating on the edge of the storybook village of Cormatin. As the Guide Michelin says of three-star restaurants and remarkable sites, Cormatin is worth a trip.

Reasonably enough La Varenne's kitchen was remodeled in the 1800s but some features are original. Under twenty five-foot ceilings with giant exposed timbers stands a gargantuan cast-iron stove. In the yawning fireplace the wind-up rotisserie kept spitted beasts turning slowly until roasted to perfection. A cast-iron cauldron dangles inside the chimney, suspended from a toothed pothook. There are copper pots everywhere—a whole battery of them on one wall—and terra-cotta cooking vessels, too. The double-wide, tile-topped, coal-or-wood-fired *potager* cooking unit is among the only *potagers* preserved in France and faces a big bright window giving onto the garden.

Here the happy chef could shine. At Versailles he would have been scorched by the brilliance of the Sun King like Louis' other chefs, valets, and maître d's. Few today would know his name.

LA VARENNE'S RUDIMENTARY HARE RECIPE

Saddle of Hare: Once you have skinned and gutted the hare, cut it into a saddle, that is to say, cut it below the shoulders, afterward remove the overlapping layers of inner skin atop the saddle, then stuff the hare (with its liver and offal) from the rear, spike it (with bacon and herbs), roast it, and serve it with pepper sauce. To make Pepper Sauce: vinegar, salt, onion or shallots, orange or lemon peel, and (ground) pepper. Cook these ingredients and serve the sauce on your meat.

Sound fairly basic? La Varenne's book was seminal largely because nothing French of note had been published since Taillevent. It still features *verjus* and lots of spices. The novel foie gras has been married with capon but not hare, not yet. Still, *Le Cuisinier françois* went through thirty French editions and twenty foreign editions in a century or so and established the reputation—some might say the myth—of the supremacy of French chefs and French cuisine. It appeared when Louis XIV was only thirteen, living not at his father's rustic hunting lodge at Versailles but alternately in the Tuileries Palace at the Louvre or with his mother Maria and Cardinal Mazarin in Richelieu's Palais-Cardinal, later dubbed Palais-Royal to recognize the crown's ownership of the property after Richelieu's death.

The year 1651 was memorable not only for the publication of La Varenne's book. It was the year when young Louis was rousted out of his royal bedchamber by rioting aristocrats, members of the Fronde Conspiracy, an experience that led him, decades later, to move the court from dangerous Paris to sleepy Versailles. Coincidentally that incident may also have led to the birth of French cuisine as an institutionalized soft-power weapon, a Parisian then Versailles-based *French* national identity card.

By the time the Fronde got going, civil war–torn France was run by another lay cardinal, Jules Mazarin, long thought to have been the other leading candidate for the Sun King's biological father.

PARDON MY FRENCH: DID YOU SAY MAZZARINO?

Hovering six scenic blocks downstream from Le Relais Louis XIII is a scaly slate-covered dome. I think of it as Mazarin's Cloche and see the kind of bell used in fancy restaurants to cover a plate to keep the food warm. Under the bell is the country's cultural sancta sanctorum: the French Academy, French Institute, and Mazarin Library, a holy trinity housed in the same harmonious, horseshoe-shaped complex fronting the Pont des Arts directly across the Seine from the Cour Carrée of the Louvre.

As mentioned, I am a regular at the Mazarin Library in part because it's a repository for rare cookbooks, including a priceless fifteenth-century manuscript copy of Taillevent's *Le Viandier* kept in the reserve-of-reserves. In the vast, high-ceilinged reading rooms the tidal swoosh of traffic along the quays is barely audible. Stony busts stare watchfully, grandfather clocks tick and tinkle, pencils scratch, fingertips hunt and peck. Silently researchers and white-gloved librarians delicately turn pages. Silently, reverently I pore over the thick pages swarming with the tobacco-hued script of *Le Viandier,* or a curious Italian translation of La Varenne, or the revolutionary eighteenth-century *Le nouveau cuisinier royal et bourgeois,* a 1714 edition, by François Massialot, and the proto-molecular *Les Dons de Comus, ou les Délices de la table,* from 1739, by François Marin, maître d'hôtel du maréchal de Soubise. Note the "nouveau" and "bourgeois" in the title of Massialot and get ready for real change in a few chapters.

Certainly it's more practical to consult these fragile works online and I do. But seeing the slanting, swirling script and thick red capitals for each first letter of each recipe in Taillevent, feeling the wear marks made by long-dead fingers, smelling the distant smells of the original books so preciously preserved, turning the curled, yellowed, stained, and pocked pages, is another thing altogether.

Reading brittle descriptions of luscious delicacies, of stuffed roasted geese, plump crispy-skinned capons and spicy royal hares, of partridges and cranes spitted, and stewed suckling veal, of wild mushroom ragout, truffles, pâtés, sturgeons and turbots, of soups and savory tarts and sweet creams, cheeses and sauces, the bounty of cupboard, larder, kitchen, and scullery from egg to apple and nuts, all swimming with the dust motes before me, makes a body hungry, makes my mouth water, nose twitch, and eyes sting. I close these sacred books, nod thankfully at their keepers, and pity those who come to Paris yet fail to find the good and great remaining in the city's cavernous maw.

Within a snail's crawling distance are bistros, cafés, and high-end restaurants, some worthy of Mazarin, Louis XIV, and his heirs, favorites of today's lusty French academicians. Wait for the lunch bell to tinkle under Marazin's Cloche then follow the togas to ancient Lapérouse, spanking new Guy Savoy appropriately located inside the former mint, Le Voltaire, La Frégate, and Le Relais Louis XIII, or, for fine spitted fowl, La Rotisserie d'en Face. Have plenty to drink at the first three of these. You'll need courage when the check comes and your plastic melts. If you prefer attitude, youth, beauty, confusion, and trendy fusion cuisine, you can always head instead to Ze Kitchen Galerie—it's exciting and recommended by certified foodistas.

On your way out of the Mazarin Library, take a moment and detour to the middle of the Seine on the Pont des Arts. Turn around to admire the cardinal's cloche as it was meant to be seen: from the Louvre, the resplendent residence of the Sun King and other kings. Mazarin and Louis were eager to be within skipping distance of each other. You may be forgiven for wondering if you're not in Paris but in the Eternal City admiring a late-baroque merger of Bramante and Bernini. That's because Mazarin's library was modeled on the Barbarini Library in Rome. The aesthetics may also have something to do with the fact that Jules Mazarin was none other than Giulio Mazzarino, another pesky Italian come to make his fortune at the court of France. Was he really Louis XIV's father?

THICKER THAN WATER

As any cook will tell you, blood is not just thicker than water it takes longer to come to a boil or reduce in a recipe for slow-simmered pressed duck or, better, *lièvre à la royale*. The creature's vital juices are an essential part of the regal hare recipe, and blood is equally essential in the tale of Mazzarino and Louis XIV.

For centuries a controversy has boiled and bubbled about Louis XIII's presumed inability to sire an heir, and the "miraculous" birth of the little Sun King after decades of barren wedlock to Anne of Austria. Both putative parents were thirty-seven years old, he a geezer with "the libido of a goldfish" as one pundit has put it and she an old maid by the standards of the day. Royalists and other apologists explain the miracle with meteorology, calendars, and dynastic pressures, which presumably spurred performance. Conspiracy theorists, most of them left-wing "republicans," ferret out "real" biological parents and have turned up many, especially on the woman-shy father's side.

Among the candidates for biological father is the sly, red-robed Cardinal Richelieu, though he was an antique by 1637 when conception occurred. Alternates are a collection of noblemen including a naturalized German, and that other wily lay cardinal, Jules Mazarin.

As the godlike Divine Right arm of church and state, the Sun King was not just any old French monarch. It is bad enough Louis' putative mother Anne was a Habsburg therefore a blend of Austro-Hungarian-Spanish. Imagine him a bastard with a German or, God forbid, a low-born Italian father—and no French blood *à la royale*. Maria's grandson, Luigi, not *français, impossible*!

Mazzarino wasn't just Louis XIV's closest advisor and minister, the anointed heir of Richelieu. He was said to treat the king as if he were his son. It's clear from the secret correspondence of Mazarin and Anne of Austria that they were in love. Louis responded to Giulio with filial adoration. Not even the most flagrant nationalist hagiographer can deny Mazarin molded Louis' taste in everything—especially art and culture—and they even looked like father and son.

Blood to the rescue again! After centuries of quarreling, a Franco-Spanish crack team of historians, forensic scientists, DNA experts, and others in the medical community joined the fray a few years back. Exhibits were produced. One was the presumed mummified head of Henri IV, fountainhead of the Bourbon bloodline, another an heirloom handkerchief soaked with the presumed blood of Louis XVI, blood mopped up by an admirer when the king was guillotined in 1793 and jealously preserved since then by an aristocratic Italian clan.

What were the conclusions? Initial reports claimed the two samples had an identical genetic profile determined by male descent. What did that mean? It meant Louis XIII was perforce Louis XIV's father and therefore the genetic, biological forebear of the rest of the Bourbon kings. Joy! The honor of the nation saved!

Like rival chefs cooking up the same royal jackrabbit, however, hairsplitters soon spoiled the dish. The controversy continues to simmer. Richelieu and Mazzarino are still in the running much to the chagrin of royalists, of which there are distressingly many in France. Why Richelieu isn't exhumed from the crypt of the Sorbonne and why Mazzarino's many relatives' genetic material is not tested is an open question. Maybe no one has thought of that or maybe the investigators fear the results?

The upshot is there's no guaranteed genetic explanation for why the Bourbon dynasty boasted so many Maria de' Medici spin-offs: large, ravenous specimens of humanity; robust eaters, lovers of strong meat and flowing wine; kings, queens, princes, and princesses whose tumultuous Old-Régime love affair with food has inspired generations of Frenchmen and -women who emulate their example today and devour *lièvre* whenever possible.

Peppery, winey, long-cooked jackrabbit in roulade or pudding form, with or without foie gras has become a cult revival dish served by better bistros like Café Tournon and multiple-starred temples alike. The televangelists of revamped nouvelle and the high priests of haute have conveniently rediscovered not just terroir but also their royal roots. Alain Ducasse, Pierre Gagnaire, Eric Fréchon, Paul Bocuse, and who knows how many other stellar performers feature the dish on their menus at premium prices. Some insist on Chambertin for the marinade and sauce—that's $50 a bottle and up, up, up for a single ingredient. The foie gras comes gilded.

Perhaps part of the attraction of this longest, most complicated and challenging of classic recipes of early haute cuisine derives from the prophetic words of Senator Couteaux: "The garlic and shallots must be minced so fine that each attains a near-molecular state." *Molecular,* did he say? There really is nothing nouveau under the Parisian sun.

Paroxysms of contemporary jackrabbit fever have even engendered an annual competition in the town of Romorantin in the hare heartland of the Sologne region south of Paris. Battle lines are drawn, there's no running with the hares and hunting with the hounds, you belong to one side or another. Historians writing in learned journals wrangle with populists and their tabloids. Chefs fling spoons, roulades, and molecules; gourmands and gourmets come to blows over which recipe is the most "authentic," "oldest," or "the best." No one is really sure when the concoction was invented or named and by which chef, probably because there are so many variations on the theme spanning centuries. The deboned "pudding" recipe was supposedly perfected for the elderly, toothless Louis XIV who died in 1715, but the closest thing to it I've found only dates to 1755 so this may be yet another apocryphal tale.

As Anglo-Saxon partisans of simplicity have observed, it's instructive to recall what the original gastronome Archestratos urged four centuries before the Christian era. "Many are the ways and many the recipes for dressing hares," the wise man wrote. "But this is the best recipe of all. Place before hungry guests a slice of roasted meat fresh from the spit, hot, seasoned only with plain simple salt, not overdone. Do not be put off by blood trickling from the meat. Eat eagerly. All other ways are superfluous, especially the cooks' pouring of sticky gooey sauce upon it, shavings of cheese, and lees, and dregs of oil, as if they were preparing a dog's breakfast."

A select reading of Archestratos by French chefs focuses on the appetizing "blood trickling from the meat," not for this recipe, perhaps, which requires long simmering, but for so many others.

Conventional wisdom has it that to understand the modern French, questers must unravel the mysteries of the Sun King's court. Louis XIV is a French god even to republican atheists. This adage is assumed to apply not just to politics, culture, and behavior in general, but also to cuisine, manners, and art de la table. Conventional wisdom is not always wrong.

Now that you know the Sun King's hare was around in one form or another and perhaps under a pseudonym before he was born, and the French Academy was also already in session, and that nothing comes from nowhere, including forks and foie gras, you can safely board an RER commuter train a few blocks upstream or downstream from the Mazarin Library and ride out to Versailles for a look-see.

PART FIVE

Entrées, *Troisième* Service: Versailles *à la Royale*, 1638–1715

The Royal Treatment: Louis XIV dining at court with Molière, from painting by L. Gérôme, 1893

VERSAILLES DETOUR

Ask Henri IV: Paris is worth a mass. To some it's worth a transatlantic voyage. Versailles is certainly worth a forty-five-minute detour.

As your train rolls west those twelve strategic miles from Paris to Versailles, gaze out through streaky windows upon the proverbial land of milk and honey, butter and cream, good and plenty—plenty of flour among other good things. The seventeenth century was the century of butter, cream, and flour in everything—especially in the rich sauces and pastries beloved of the royal court. Once the old milk cow had been milked to death she went into a pot and became a bouillon—Louis XIV's breakfast and ironically the last meal of the condemned, the ubiquitous base ingredient for sauces and stews, the basso continuo note in classic French cooking until the advent of the nouvelle cuisine of the 1970s. No worries, you'll hear plenty more in these pages about bouillon, *ancienne* nouvelle, and *nouvelle* nouvelle.

The outskirts of Paris today may be an asphalt jungle crossed by battered greenbelts but in the bad old days of the Ancien Régime, the vineyards, orchards, fields, and cow-dotted pastures began right outside the city gates. Local meant local. The entire Île-de-France was extraordinarily bounteous and coveted. Beyond it stretched the Beauce, the breadbasket and flour mill of the realm.

Watery, far-flung Versailles had the unlikely advantage of thick forests and marshlands—drained not to destroy the mosquitoes but to build the king's gardens, fountains, and magnificent monumental pools and lakes. Waterfowl, venison, and hare flapped, leaped, and scampered here, there, and everywhere. That's why before Louis XIV was born, his father Louis XIII, the

Great White Hunter, had a nifty little gilded hunting lodge slapped together and poised on the heights overlooking endless woodlands. To this day the lodge is the core of the Château de Versailles.

Louis XIV was also an indefatigable hunter but as regards Versailles it wasn't the wild game that interested the Sun King. It was the breathing distance from Paris and the beneficial isolation. Twelve miles seemed enough to keep the ravenous rabble and disgruntled aristocrats at bay, giving the army time to muster, mount, and aim cannons.

Who can be surprised Versailles grew into a gilded loony bin for bored nobles overseen by royal bewigged pooh-bahs? The place was devised to thwart, baffle, and occupy potentially troublesome courtiers. It was a make-work, make-fun, gated community of from 4,000 to 6,000 residents and their retainers, among them 500 cooks, valets, and waiters; 324 of them assigned to the so-called Bouche du Roi team reserved for making the king's meals.

Versailles' etiquette alone would drive any sane person mad—the constant dressing for ceremonies and the hour-by-hour activities were strangely reminiscent of an interminable Catholic mass. Maybe it was not so strange: Louis' humorless, ruthless bishop Jacques-Bénigne Bossuet had codified a nouvelle form of Divine Right theocracy. "I *am* the State," the delusional king repeated like a deranged parrot. His subjects owed him obedience as to God himself, Bossuet proclaimed. There was no appeal against Louis or his decisions except through prayer.

Hallelujah! In his bleak, nasty memoirs the deliciously acerbic Duc de Saint-Simon tells how time and timing were everything at Versailles. "With an Almanac and a watch," he noted, "one might say exactly what the king was doing at a distance of three hundred leagues." Courtiers cooled their gilded heels six to eight hours each day to see Louis, be seen by Louis, and attend with slavish sycophancy on Louis. Remember, in French "attend" merges "wait" and "serve."

What did these charming "noble" gentlemen and ladies do? There was the delousing and powdering of the king's wigs, which he changed seven times daily, the lighting of the king's candles, the viewing of the king's 7:30 A.M. ritual rising and gulping of beef bouillon for his first breakfast, and his 11:30 P.M. bedtime. The terms "rising" and "setting" were used to designate the sun—as in the celestial orb—and Louis.

The king was lathered and shaved every second day surrounded by his favorites. There were the king's twice-daily promenades, the inspection of the king's feces, the spectacularly earthy bimonthly bowel purge, and other entertainments—card games, billiards, ballets, ballroom dancing, theater, opera, and *la chasse,* i.e., hunting. Attendance at all was de rigueur. Everyone knew the time to negotiate contracts, ask for favors, and present a petition was immediately after a purge.

Above all there was fashion and feeding—endless discussion of clothes, food, and drink; who got drunk; who pigged out or ate like a wolf; what was good, bad, and middling. You'd think the most popular dish was carp—that's what the courtiers did best, carp and gossip. The institution of the food and wine bore, the fashionista and foodista, was born in Versailles. Did the menus mirror society or was it the other way around—or both? Versailles became a Hall of Mirrors of narcissistic vanity and gluttony, the king's reflection an infinite regress.

Between his rising and bedtime Louis' main meals included a second, 10 A.M. breakfast, lunch at 1:00 P.M., and the public 10:00 P.M. *souper* du Grand Couvert taken in the king's antechamber and lasting precisely forty-five minutes.

Unsurprisingly inebriation was commonplace. "Drink up!" was not a friendly toast but a command. Court ritual forbade putting anything but empty glasses back on servants' trays. No wonder the minute they could the courtiers ran wild outside the gated community. Once Louis was safely in bed the aristos would gallop off and party at nearby châteaux or head into Paris for serious debauchery, setting the style that was later openly followed at the Palais-Royal during the Regency of Louis XV—and continues in contemporary iterations to this day.

The Duc de Saint-Simon reports that the Duchesse de Bourgogne threw a bash at her château with the notoriously debauched Duchesse de Barry, for instance. De Barry (not to be confused with the lusty Jeanne Bécu, aka Madame du Barry, who came later) and the rowdy Duc d'Orléans, the future Regent, got falling-down drunk and the duchess was still blitzed when her lackeys wheeled her back to Versailles. That kept tongues wagging.

Many naughty nobles got up to hijinks on site, just like today's adolescent reprobates. Two high-placed duchesses, one of them the Rabelaisian gourmand Princess Palatine, Louis' sister-in-law, secretly smoked tobacco, a male preserve. The king's brother, Monseigneur, forbade it, but the ladies continued and were eventually scolded in the presence of the court. The petulant childishness of spoiled children grown into vicious adults became the norm. Versailles degenerated into a hatchery of narcissists later transferred to Paris where self-adoration still thrives.

Were court meals as delicious as nostalgic royalists claim? Sometimes, possibly, but mostly they weren't. The king's self-aggrandizing, enormous suppers at which courtiers and commoners looked on were "drowned in apathy and grease" as Saint Simon puts it poetically. Louis famously "swallowed his food like a wolf but supped like a monarch," wrote nineteenth-century critic and historian Hippolyte Taine, whatever that means. To me it indicates bad teeth that made chewing painful. "His table was noble," Taine hastens to add, "with none of the buffooneries of a medieval court."

No buffoonery perhaps. Try sadism instead. Cruelty was the most common strategy for getting through the tedium of meals. Madame Panache, a celebrated elderly half-wit, crashed the king's suppers and his brother's dinner parties. Instead of escorting her out, the noble guests insulted, poked, and provoked her, chortling at her angry outbursts and filling her pockets with oily cooked meats and sloppy stews. The juices and sauces ran down her fancy dresses to the amusement and delight of all.

What and how did Louis eat? His plate, knives, forks, and spoons were solid gold. But he wouldn't use them, eating with his Augustan fingers instead. Louis' best-known valet de chambre, Nicolas de Bonnefons, indiscreetly remarked in his works that his Lordship was too fat to reach dishes placed in the middle of his dining table. Placement of people and delicacies was therefore as essential as it had been in the Middle Ages and Renaissance: Your importance and the excellence of the *bonne chère* were measured by how close you and it were to the king.

As to his favorite foods and habits, three years after Louis died, in 1718, the plump Princess Palatine recalled wistfully that "He could eat four servings of soup, an entire pheasant, a partridge, a big serving of salad, two slices of ham, garlicky mutton au jus, a dish of pastries, then follow with fruit and hard-boiled eggs."

Princess Palatine was no slouch herself. A Maria de' Medici look-alike with a refreshing sense of humor, she boasted that if anyone were to sup on her flesh, she would be as tasty as a roasted suckling pig.

At Louis' table, eggs came after the proverbial nuts. Eggs became the rage, with one seventeenth-century cookbook giving 56 recipes for them. Egg mania lasted for over a century. At the end of the Ancien Régime, Grimod de la Reynière was able to list 543 popular egg recipes. Louis was notorious for stuffing his pockets with sweets or candied fruit after dinner and was often seen gorging on a last hard-boiled egg on the way to his bedchamber, where two bottles of wine and three loaves of bread awaited him in case he woke up hungry in the night.

I can't help fantasizing about the invisible links between Louis and those racks of hard-boiled eggs I noticed in every Paris café in the 1970s. They were around until the dawn of the twenty-first century then poof, gone with gentrification. Were those grizzled regulars up on Montmartre wearing blue-collar badges really thinking of the Sun King with each bite? Possibly not, but hard-boiled eggs also feature in the billions of portions of crudités and egg mayo eaten then and now by generations of Frenchmen and -women royalist or revolutionary. In no other country have I seen so many eggs devoured in so many ways.

Louis also had a thing for oysters. It was largely thanks to his passion for *les huîtres* that Roman-style oyster eating became fashionable again. In 1690 he even created the official and lucrative title of Purveyor & Seller of Oysters in the Shell. For the six lucky Gentlemen of the Realm so named the world was their *huître*. So began the oyster craze that depleted wild stocks forcing the French to create ingenious commercial oyster beds. The mania may have peaked in the nineteenth century but cultured oyster gluttony continues to this day.

Louis' other cult edibles were tender green peas, figs, strawberries, and pears from his kitchen garden. Sweets weren't really his thing, but he went wild for sugary jams, as popular today as they were back then especially when stirred into yogurt or spread with butter on a split baguette to make *tartines*. The Grand Siècle saw the first chocolate fad, but Louis remained notoriously suspicious about his wife, Maria Theresa's newfangled *chocolat* shipped from

Spain. The court dreamed up a charming ditty that the queen's only passions were for the king and chocolate. It didn't work the other way around. "It staves off hunger," Louis sniffed as he marched toward his stable of mistresses, "but it does not fill the stomach."

ORDER IN THE COURT!

Filling the stomach and filling it in the right order was essential. Order, opulence, symmetry, and the precision timing of meals were a mania. Though the quantity of spice and sugar was lessened, the food at Versailles wasn't all that different from what Taillevent prepared for Charles V. As in the Middle Ages and the Renaissance, the several services included hors d'oeuvres, soups, main dishes, roasts, salads, entremets, fruit, and, occasionally, sweet desserts, cheese generally being shunned as the food of the poor. Each service featured multiple dishes brought out one by one, shown to the king then arranged in geometric patterns—the symmetry was maddeningly perfect, as in the king's parks, boulevards, palaces, and even his kitchen garden. The Taillevent-style carving of roasts or flambéing of dishes might also be part of the show, as it is today in some of Paris' traditional *grandes tables*.

"The prevailing fashion is to set four fine soups at the four corners of the table," wrote Louis' valet, Nicolas de Bonnefons, a century before the great table-planner Carême was born, "with four dish stands between each two dishes, and four salt cellars placed near the soup tureen. On the stands are placed four entrees in low dishes while diners' plates should be recessed so they can use them for soup or for helping themselves to whatever they desire eating without taking it out of the serving dish by the spoonful, since they might be repelled by the sight of a spoon that had been in the mouth of another person being dipped into the serving dish without being wiped." Good point.

With the precision of a lunatic sycophant Bonnefons details the placement of each of the dishes in each course, foreshadowing the layout of Paris' culinary topography. His books are salted with useful remarks such as "If desired, fill the middle of the table with melons, a variety of salads in bowls or on small plates to make serving them easier, oranges and lemons. Fruit preserves in syrup atop marzipan cookies might also be set there."

Each platter or dish then remained on the table while people picked at it or dipped in and licked their spoons. This was the Versailles reiteration of the famous *service à la française,* standard practice in the courts of Europe from the earliest days. Today we might call it a banquet-style tasting menu. Typically diners ate small portions of up to thirty dishes. A full menu would fill many pages. No one except perhaps the phenomenal king himself could possibly eat a big serving of each course. The reselling of leftovers was therefore a thriving business from the Middle Ages right into the early twentieth century.

Wine and the quantity of wine was the bugbear of many because it could only be poured by trusted wine waiters. Carafes and bottles were never placed on the table. No one could serve himself or others for fear of poisoning.

Louis sometimes sat alone and always sat on the long side of a rectangular table separated from others. As Princess Palatine's words suggest, he wolfed down more than anyone, eating quickly and greedily. At times he was the only person to eat. Louis enjoyed culinary exhibitionism. But he was also into watching his favorites stuff themselves. He distrusted dainty eaters.

CALORIE COUNT

So how *did* Louis XIV burn off those seven thousand calories a day? Easy: he didn't. He was grossly overweight. But he was also infernally active, walking or riding miles while touring his palace and grounds, visiting the queen and royal children, servicing his official and unofficial mistresses, transacting business and affairs of state, praying and attending mass in unheated chapels, hunting, dancing, practicing sword technique, going to war, and doing all the things hereditary oppressors, tyrants, and certain contemporary presidents do, 24/7/365.

Calories were needed. Louis' nights were short and vigorous: Once officially in bed he got up and snuck off to his mistress's bedroom for a carnal snack. He was back in his own chamber before the wake-up call. The hated Ottomans had harems and slaves. The French kings had confessors, Divine Right hypocrisy, and in the Sun King's day, about twenty million de facto serfs. In pure Louis XIV style the Parisian pattern of up late, dine late, to bed late was established, philandering optional. Though interrupted by the Revolution and altered during the nineteenth century it remains the rule today among what a populist might call "urban elites." Only tourists, boorish peasants, the working poor, and the vestigial blue collars get the early bird specials. Louis and everyone else at Versailles doubtless also burned calories by shivering—the heating was the château's worst feature except, perhaps, the toilets. There were none.

Was he as gutsy as royalists claim? Also known as Louis le Grand, the great monarch was a phenomenon of nature who lived to be seventy-seven years old (minus four days) at a time when the average life expectancy was a third that. He was a bona fide demigod gourmand, if the historic record is to be believed. Postmortem investigations revealed a stomach three times normal size. His bowels were three times the normal length. Truly he was Grand.

In Louis' day the main kitchens in the Grand Commun were several football fields away from the king's apartments. That's why hot plates and cloches were essential to fine dining.

Bubbly may not have been invented by Dom Perignon in 1668 as we used to believe—sparkling wines were around in the Middle Ages, and the first true Champagne-like bubblies seem to have been made in Normandy or England of all nonvinous places. But the refreshing, lust-inducing drink did come of age during the reign of the Sun King and was perfected just in time for the debauchery of the Regency.

HOT TO TROT

With luck you're wearing sturdy walking shoes and enjoy striding out as much as Louis XIV did. He wrote a fascinating booklet about his gardens and loved showing them off. Bring a string bag or backpack with you just in case. In case of what? You'll see . . .

There are many acres for a gastronomic quester to cross at Versailles. Start in the château by imagining those intimate little breakfasts, lunches, and suppers in the king's or queen's cozy quarters, or the joyous official state feasting in the banqueting halls and glittering galleries.

"Imagine" is the key word. As you and thousands of others shuffle heel-to-toe over the polished parquet through the Alice-in-Wonderland marvels, your imagination is required because the château's original dining rooms and the kitchens in the former Grand Commun are gone. After the purifying rack and ruin of revolutions and periodic if unneeded redecorations by idle heirs, few things culinary have survived in this sparkling soulless vastness. There is nothing culinary left from the reign of Louis XIV except the kitchen garden.

Buck up: Among the visible vestiges of Ancien Régime eating are two Louis XV–period dining salons used by this king after his happy hunting parties. The second of the two is better known as La Salle à Manger des Porcelaines because Louis XVI and his queen Marie-Antoinette displayed the latest Manufacture de Sèvres porcelains in its elaborate cabinets.

My favorite food-related parts of Versailles aren't in the château. First take a look at the handsome Orangerie of many tall windows, where hundreds of citrus trees grow—citric acid was the only way to battle scurvy in Louis' day. Then gird your loins and march half a mile or so toward the Petit Trianon and Le Hameau—the hamlet. Doesn't "hamlet" sound edible, like a ham omelet?

In the Petit Trianon's cavernous half-basement there's a yawning fireplace. Next to it is a rare *rechaud* that looks like a *potager* stove but was conceived to *rechauffer*—i.e., reheat—cooked dishes brought in from the distant Grand

Commun or Bouche du Roi kitchens. The Grande Salle à Manger is egregiously misnamed: It's an intimate dining room by royal standards, ordained by Louis XV then remodeled and used by Marie-Antoinette.

As you might expect, the décor isn't original in the dining room, either. But the proportions, natural lighting, and views are seductive. The tall second-rate canvases were intended to stimulate the appetite by showing the bounty of hunting, harvesting, and fishing. Pass the feathery pheasants and unskinned rabbits, please, and a few sea monsters and nymphs while you're at it!

Insiders know those marks on the parquet in the middle of the salon—mostly hidden by the carpet—outline a trapdoor and putative dumbwaiter. Through it "flying table" pop-ups were meant to appear fully set, candles lit, ready to go. Bingo, no bothersome servant-spies reporting to the queen. You've got to wonder how many tablecloths would've caught fire.

The same flying pop-up tables were supposed to appear in the even more intimate Petite Salle à Manger next door, but Marie-Antoinette perhaps hoping to discourage overly intimate suppers and philandering by dear little Louis XVI turned this into a billiard room.

That painting of *La Belle Jardinière* demanding your attention shows the coy, beribboned, pearl-wrapped mistress of Louis XV, Madame de Pompadour, in her grubby lace gardening clothes, ready to dig some dirt out back. Don't miss the Boudoir de la Reine, the perfect breakfast nook where during the reign of Louis XV the gallant king sipped his coffee—introduced one generation earlier during the reign of the Sun King—and admired La Pompadour's fruit baskets. It is claimed the budding botanist managed to grow coffee plants in his Trianon hothouse, rolled up his silk sleeves, harvested the fruit, toasted the beans, and made his brew with his very own royal hands. Amazing!

CAFÉ BREAK

If you are tormented by the irresistible smell of fresh java and choc, don't worry it's not the king's ghostly brew filling the Petit Trianon. It's the smell of Angelina, maliciously wafting delicious scents from a strategically sited outdoor café terrace. The Parisian maven of hot chocolate and the premodern Mont Blanc is now a franchise operation selling pastries made in a suburban plant. This is merely the Versailles location. Luckily the coffee is still good. It seems perfectly okay to me to have a café in the royal enclave: Chocolate then coffee made their breakthrough at the Louvre and Versailles during the Sun King's reign, thanks to his queen, Maria Theresa's caffeine addiction—she was a Spanish-Austrian, after all—and the Arabica-scented gifts of Suleiman Aga, coffee-drinking Turkish ambassador to France in 1669. All that's missing at Angelina to complete the holy trinity of seventeenth-century fads is the Champagne.

It is odd, don't you think, that coffee premiered not in Paris, Caffeine City, but in Versailles, which has never been known for genial cafés. Actually it makes perfect sense. For one thing novelty foods from turkey to potatoes, chocolate and bubbly transited through the royal court. That's where the money and power were: get royal blessings and your import would thrive. Second, the big bad city is where the aristos went to play and the artists and intellectuals who became France's first caffeine addicts lived, met, jawed, and plotted. The only middle class and popular retail market of any size for coffee was in Paris and that's why the first recorded coffee roaster and seller, a man of Armenian origin familiar with the brew, set up a coffee stand in the Foire Saint-Germain a few blocks from the Abbey of Saint-Germain-des-Prés. Little could he know 250 years later caffeine-driven Existentialism would be excogitated on the former abbey's grounds by Jean-Paul Sartre et al.

The year Armenian coffee hit Paris was 1672, the height of the Sun King's reign. The year the first official café, Le Procope, opened, was 1686, its founder the very French signor Francesco Procopio dei Coltelli, a Sicilian ice-cream and sorbet maker. In the seventeen years it took from the time

Louis XIV first tasted coffee to the opening of stylish Le Procope, the beverage had found weighty boosters and detractors in Versailles and Paris. Princess Palatine famously said coffee smelled like her worst enemy's appallingly bad breath. Saint Simon called it pig slop and mud. Madame de Sévigné was also not enthusiastic, though she noted the brew's powers of stimulation. "Racine will go out of fashion like coffee," she supposedly quipped (no one has ever found the letter), proof she wasn't exactly a visionary. Racine is worshipped and there are five thousand cafés in Paris alone.

Perhaps it was Voltaire in the time of Louis XV who put coffee on the Enlightenment pedestal—unless it was Diderot, Rousseau, or Beaumarchais, all habitués of Le Procope. In any case this venerable institution, now a restaurant favored by the package tour set, lived its heyday in the Age of Enlightenment. Its fancy Versailles-style décor with glittering chandeliers, woodwork, oil canvases, and mirrors became the template for all later grand cafés and eventually for Paris' first restaurants. It is now part of the same corporate group that owns Burger King France, Quick, Angelina, Lipp, and Au Pied de Cochon. Perhaps the new team will improve the food and leave intact what is left of the period décor?

BLUE MOUTHS AND GREEN THUMBS

Back in Versailles for more coffee and vegetables, in 2014 Marie-Antoinette's handsome little Jardin de la Reine kitchen garden at Le Hameau was revived and planted by Alain Ducasse to supply organic vegetables to his temples of gastronomy including the Plaza Athenée in Paris and Ore, the Château de Versailles's latest culinary addition. A paean to regal Frenchness, Ore is in the revamped Pavillon Dufour. It opened to great fanfare in the fall of 2016.

Ducasse's aspirations and pretentions are definitely Ancien Régime. The name means mouth in Latin and refers to "the pleasures of the mouth so important to French *art de vivre*," according to spokespersons, "evoking the Bouche du Roi." That was the department in charge of preparing the king's meals.

With an eye to twenty-first-century tastes, Ducasse conceived Ore to be "an elegant contemporary French café by day, and an haute-couture restaurant, available for private events by night." The goal was to showcase "magnificent royal splendor." The daytime café restaurant is certainly a classy, comfortable designer operation—leather armchairs, bronze-topped tables, gray wood wainscoting, marble fireplaces, big round mirrors, and quirky high-tech chandeliers. You see the château's other wings through the windows. By French standards the coffee is excellent.

If your budget, like mine, is less than kingly you can limit yourself to a sandwich or café, tea, hot chocolate, and pastries such as savarin cakes, *mille-feuilles*, lemon tarts, and a luscious chocolatey lingot with chocolate sponge cake and praline layers dubbed Le Louis XIV. Lunch sets you back about $50 a head sans *vin*, and my wife and I thoroughly enjoyed the experience. But was it a royal meal? I don't think so. If you were to serve Louis a taste of every dish on the menu, he might consider the ensemble a decent first course. Given his passion for things Franco-Italian his majesty might even approve of the Ducasse signature specialty, tiny shell pasta with ham, Comté cheese, and black truffle.

The royal treatment is reserved for Sun King–style private dinner events. Waitstaff wear wigs and fashionista reinterpretations of Ancien Régime garb: royal blue pants and a vest over a light-blue long-sleeved shirt with broad musketeer cuffs. It costs 15,000 euros to keep the château open at dinner-time plus $500–$1,000 per person for the food and wine. Only upscale groups, oligarchs, and monarchs wishing to emulate absolutist tyrants need apply. The stops are pulled out, the antique cookbooks are dusted off, the recipes lightened and updated, and the restaurant's richly napped tables overflow. On them are oysters, soups, freshwater and saltwater fish especially turbot (Louis' favorite), lobster, frog legs, crayfish, guinea fowl, sweetbreads, patés, and terrines, foie gras croquettes, roasts or filets of beef with foie gras (an exquisite deconstructed Tournedos Rossini, also available at lunch), or roasted poultry, and plenty of fresh vegetables from the Jardin de la Reine, particularly Louis' faves—cauliflower, cardoons, green beans, and artichokes. A meal might be rounded off by delicious roasted figs, fresh fruit, and other putative seventeenth- or eighteenth-century sweets.

Ore is a welcome addition to Versailles and the pocket-sized Jardin de la Reine is certainly charming. But the most impressive monument to Ancien Régime gastronomy at Versailles is still the Potager du Roi: Louis XIV's vast royal kitchen garden. He was proud of this practical, perfectly symmetrical, handsome walled paradise of strawberries, melons, artichokes, asparagus, figs, and pears, and Louis greatly admired his Royal Gardener and Horticulturist, Jean-Baptiste de la Quintinie, whom he raised from middling third-estate status into the aristocracy.

Standing at a safe and unsoiled distance on his viewing terraces, Louis would watch his beloved subjects toiling below, his mouth watering. You, too, can watch seasoned gardeners directing à la Quintinie while budding horticulturists from the National School of Horticulture based here do the spadework. With its central birdbath pool and walled gardens the *potager* is slightly seedier but little changed since it was created by La Quintinie in 1678. The rustic, twenty-five-acre plot is off the château's grounds due south across the street from the doleful baroque cathedral of Versailles. There are no lines to get in. Depending on the season you might be able to buy pears, melons, strawberries, figs, cabbages, pumpkins, and peas, stuff them into your capacious 1970s string bag and take them back to your temporary Paris lodgings for a feast.

"Revolutionary" is not a word spoken aloud in Versailles yet the king's kitchen garden was precisely that: It turned farming on its bewigged head. La Quintinie must have been a true homegrown French genius. Without formal training he perfected espalier techniques for growing trees against walls to protect them from wind and benefit from refracted heat. He created heat sinks and used cloches to raise fig trees and vegetables in cold weather to defy La Mère Nature—thus delighting the king who was, after all, a demigod yet very much down to earth. A man for all seasons La Quintinie's ennobled device could have run "Peas in April, Figs in June."

At the height of summer the *potager* could produce four thousand figs per day and still produces many. Were they dried and fed to eager geese to make

Louis' foie gras? Perhaps, though I suspect the king gobbled many of them himself (he was a great believer in laxatives). Ditto the pears—forty-six varieties—and peas. Like Alain Ducasse, he was mad about peas.

Thanks in part to La Quintinie, France underwent the edible equivalent of the Tulip Mania that swept Holland in the early 1600s. "The craze for peas continues," noted the Marquise de Sévigné, the ubiquitous, omniscient letter writer of the century, one of Paris' most precious chroniclers. "The impatience felt waiting to eat them, to have eaten them, and the pleasure of eating them are the three topics on our princes' tongues for the past four days."

What Madame la Marquise and the folks in charge of the *potager*, not to mention Ducasse et al, don't tell visitors is primo, those peas were brought to the king from Genoa, the maritime republic Louis XIV firebombed and humbled for its perceived arrogance, and, secondo, the genius La Quintinie learned much from the botanical gardens he made a pilgrimage to in 1656. Traveling to Turin, Pisa, Padua, and Bologna he debriefed horticulturists and watched them at work, a high-level agro-industrial spying mission. Historians speculate he also hit Rome, visiting Villa Aldobrandini, the Vatican gardens, and Villa d'Este in Tivoli.

You've already guessed it: La Quintinie's "espalier" is French for *spalliera*, the technique invented in ancient Rome and used throughout the Italian Renaissance. La Quintinie brought it to France. Funny, isn't it, how English language auto-correctors don't mess with espalier, but run a red line under the Italian original.

Also unsurprising is how two native delicacies of the Latin homeland, beloved of Caesar and Caterina de' Medici, were among the Great Louis' favorites: La Quintinie was ordered to grow six thousand asparagus and a thousand artichoke plants in the *potager* for His Voracious Highness.

Artichokes had migrated north to France from Italy in 1532 and were on the Medici queens' tables, but La Quintinie turned them into giant globe-shaped French scepters presumably with new and improved powers of sexual arousal.

As to that other peninsular aphrodisiac, asparagus, when Augustus Caesar was in a rush he demanded things get done "in less time than it takes to cook an asparagus." Jack Robinson hadn't been born yet.

In the Augustan Age, this provocative plant's phallic shape and pungent smell induced the Romans to dedicate it to Venus, goddess of amour, and ascribed to it performance-enhancing qualities. The ultimate finger food, designed to be gobbled al dente, it was perfect for greedy, impatient Louis: using a knife and fork to eat asparagus was and remains an insult in much of the Mediterranean world, indicating overcooked flaccidness. What could be worse than a limp royal asparagus? No complaints were heard from the Sun King's bedmates in that wise. It is a matter of salacious record that a generation later, Madame de Pompadour was less interested in Louis XV's greenhouse-grown coffee beans and handmade hot chocolate than in his Champagne and *pointes d'amour*—the succulent "love tips" of asparagus. Her suggestive not to say obscene recipe for *Asperges à la Pompadour* in a creamy, buttery white sauce is astonishingly popular today.

As heir to the Roman emperors and the ancient pantheon of gods, and the spiritual and perhaps genetic son of Mazzarino, there was no defeated-Gallic-warrior nonsense in Louis le Grand's self-confident admiration of Italian manners, statecraft, and food. He never spoke of the cannibalistic barbarian Vercingétorix, preferring to emulate and dress like Augustus, another semidivine winner. The finest 3-D example of Louis' imperial Roman fixation is a life-sized, highly flattering portrait by Antoine Coysevox, the Bernini of France, who also created many marble sculptures you've been admiring as you tour Versailles.

Coysevox shows a lithe, manly young Louis XIV with the attributes of Hercules and Augustus, though many-chinned Domitian, Vitellius, or Elagabalus would have been more appropriate. It's the only original bronze to have survived the Revolution and stands in a courtyard in the Marais at the Hôtel Carnavalet. Coincidentally the Marquise de Sévigné once lived in the mansion, now the History of Paris Museum, and, it's speculated, shared the king's bed. Whether she preferred the king's peas, asparaguses, or artichokes is not known. For a time de Sévigné was recklessly wild for chocolate, the beverage of Venus, but overdosed and soon swore off it.

A CABBAGE IS A CABBAGE IS A CABBAGE

The upshot of the Sun King's greedy year-round passion for certain fruits and vegetables became manifold in markets and kitchens around France: He had twenty-seven varieties of pear for winter, ten for fall and nine for summer. You might even say it foreshadowed our postmodern, eco-unfriendly demand for nonseasonal produce the "to hell with the snow! I want my strawberries now," syndrome.

More wholesomely, Louis' love for the bounty of his *potager* enticed people we'd call opinion makers or trendsetters to eschew mountains of meat and begin eating a modicum of healthful fiber-rich fresh crudités, fruits, and herbs. Bonnefons enlivened Louis' salads with pimpernel, tarragon, garden cress, watercress, saxifrage, and lamb's lettuce. Ennobled like Louis' gardener these formerly humble ingredients were gradually folded into the Grand Siècle's imperial Roman revival haute cuisine. Along with the oysters and a score of other favorites, they trickled into the recently dubbed "cuisine bourgeoise" and from there drip-irrigated the lower orders and their boorish Celtic peasant repertoire. Gastropod-paced, French cooking inched forward toward enlightened nouvelle.

Among the reasons French-eating habits didn't gallop into the Age of Enlightenment is habit. The medieval-Renaissance mold was harder to break than a petrified loaf of Pompeiian bread. For instance, in the 1600s the only root vegetables fit for an upper-class table were leeks and turnips. As ever, winged creatures, fish, and wild game were believed to be less contaminated by the soil and so continued to reign supreme. Spices, verjuice, and indigestible sauces smothering overcooked foods were as popular as ever. Of the piles of new cookbooks and manuals that appeared after La Varenne during the reign of Louis XIV and XV, many militated for reform. As French culinary historians have remarked, few delivered.

Often with a feeling of queasiness and self-loathing I have greedily pored over the prime examples of Grand Siècle cookbooks in the Mazarin Library or National Library of France, my mouth watering no matter how bizarre the recipes.

In Nicolas de Bonnefons' 1654 *Les Délices de la campagne*, for instance, the king's at times indiscreet valet de chambre pleads for simplicity, honesty, respect for an ingredient's natural qualities, avoidance of "masked flavors," and unneeded spices and seasonings, minces, and mushrooms, especially in what were known as *potages de santé*—soups conceived to restore the health of invalids. "A healthful cabbage soup should taste like cabbage," says Bonnefons, sounding like an adept of nouvelle cuisine, "a leek soup like leeks, a turnip soup like turnips, and so forth." Too bad the recipes don't correspond to the sentiments.

Similar fine sentiments are echoed in *Le Cuisinier* by Pierre de Lune published two years later in 1656. It includes the first-known recipe for boeuf à la mode, which is still a French classic. Scores of other recipes seem like they were borrowed from Taillevent or *Le Mesnagier de Paris*. De Lune's sweet-and-spicy salmon would've delighted Apicius and might also be a hit in sweet-and-spicy-loving "bold food" America today. He tells you how to prepare steaks of salmon "or whatever else you want" floured and pan-fried in butter then cooked to death a second time in a sea of red wine sauce with sugar, cinnamon, salt, pepper, cloves, and lime juice. For the "whatever you want," you might as well use canned salmon or shoe leather so smothered and suffocated is the fish's true flavor.

The same ham-fistedness runs through *Le Cuisinier royal et bourgeois* by heavyweight champion François Massialot, published in 1691 (and updated in the 1700s with "nouveau" tacked to the title). With Massialot begins the rise of so-called cuisine bourgeoise, which is one reason many of his recipes live on today albeit in modified versions, as witnessed at Ore.

A Sun King–look-alike, big bewigged Massialot first cooked for the brother and then the son of Louis XIV and is credited with inventing (among other things) that healthful, slimming delicacy crème brûlée. With a few tweaks his recipe works fine today. It's a little trickier than it appears but I like it. Why Alain Ducasse didn't make it his signature dessert at the château I do not know.

THE ORIGINAL HEALTHFUL CRÈME BRÛLÉE AU CITRON VERT RECIPE BY FRANÇOIS MASSIALOT, 1691

(With a few modern tweaks in parenthesis)

Take four or five egg yolks, it depends on the size of your serving dish. Stir them together in a casserole (or nonreactive pot maybe) adding a generous pinch of flour (I'd skip the flour and add the four tablespoons of sugar the chef forgot to mention). Pour in two cups of milk a little at a time and keep stirring.

Add stick-cinnamon (about half a teaspoon of ground cinnamon is more practical) and (about three teaspoons) minced fresh lime zests and (the same amount of) minced candied lime zests (which don't add much and might even subtract from the deliciousness). Alternatively use minced orange or lemon zests instead and call it Crème Brûlée à l'orange (or au citron).

To make your Crème Brûlée even more refined add (about five tablespoons) ground pistachios or almonds and a drop of orange blossom water.

Put the pot on a (medium-low source of heat on your) stovetop and stir gently, making sure your Crème Brûlée does not stick to the bottom of the pot. When the crème is cooked (nearly set without being scrambled), put a serving dish (oven-safe is best) on the medium-low stovetop, pour in the crème and continue stirring until the mixture starts to stick to the edges of the dish.

Remove to lower heat and sprinkle on lots of sugar (as much as you need to generously cover the top of the crème) in addition to the sugar already in the mixture (which chef forgot). Get a red-hot fire shovel (or maybe an iron rod or blowtorch) and scorch the (sugar on top of the) crème until the top is a beautiful golden brown.

This crème brûlée is a breeze compared to most of the convoluted recipes from the period parading as simplicity itself.

Sound familiar? Yes, the rhetoric and telegenic patter of the great chefs and cookbook writers then and now was set: like Bonnefons, Lune, or Massialot all you need do is say "simple," "healthful," and "nouvelle," or "terroir" and "authentic" and then go ahead with "complicated" and "overblown." Big, rich, complicated is what most diners wanted then and want today: impressive, entertaining, spicy, taste bud-stimulating, exciting, wow-wow-wow food. Turning heads and keeping up with the Louis or thrilling the bourgeoisie is anything but recent.

Most historians tell you that Louis XIV's Grand Siècle is when cuisine bourgeoise was codified and named. That's nearly a century before the supreme *bourgeoise*, Jeanne-Antoinette Poisson, i.e., Madame Fish, better known as the Marquise de Pompadour, the most famous official mistress of Louis XV, took the reins from that king and made being bourgeois chic. Actually cuisine bourgeoise predates the reigns of both kings. Remember the anonymous author of *Le Mesnagier de Paris*, a bourgeois writing for his baby bride? He forgot to christen his brainchild back in the 1390s when the cuisine of Paris' rich "third estate," neither noble, ignoble, nor ecclesiastic, was really born.

DELUSIONS OF GRANDEUR

Before contemplating a return to Paris, spare a thought for unlucky Nicolas Fouquet and unluckier François Vatel. Fouquet was Louis XIV's extravagantly wealthy Superintendent of Finance during the administration of Mazarin. Arrested on the king's orders by the real-life d'Artagnan, he wound up in the Bastille. Fritz Karl Watel, his name transmogrified into the vaguely French-sounding Vatel, was Fouquet's miracle-working maître d', France's first gastronomic martyr the one played by Gérard Depardieu in the movie. Vatel thrust himself upon his own sword—because the fish arrived late. Actually the tale is more complicated and provides a good excuse to visit the startlingly magical waterborne Château de Chantilly where the deed occurred.

First things first: travel in your armchair or swap your pumpkin from the Potager du Roi for a royal carriage then roll about forty miles southeast from Versailles to Fouquet's sumptuous Château de Vaux-le-Vicomte near Melun. It's a lovely drive and worth le detour not only because you can stop en route at Brie and buy a wheel for a picnic—you'll want a picnic, even though there are eating establishments at the château.

It would take an entire book to describe Fouquet's dreamy Grand Siècle domain with its dome and hatbox roof of slate, its moat, fountains, and reflecting pools, and its hedges of handsome outbuildings set in an unimaginably vast park predating Versailles. Designed by the royal architect and decorated by royal artists, it's not quite as big or sumptuous as the royal domain was to become but was far too big and far too sumptuous for a mere nonroyal superintendent or minister.

While others admire the grand salons and bedrooms or sip cocktails in the garden then lunch predictably at the château's restaurant, I head for the famous Salle à Manger. It's hard not to gape at the dining room's gilded coffered ceiling decorated with gods and goddesses, Tritons and naiads, splashing saucily in the waterworks. The walls are also richly decorated and gilded, there is a noticeably large and expensive mirror, and the giant fireplace is elaborately carved. Fouquet's many sumptuous ground-floor rooms were the scene of plutocratic feasting as hadn't been witnessed since the days of Apicius and Lucullus.

The story is possibly apocryphal, but Fouquet supposedly had his prestigious visitors served their meals on solid gold plates. Waiters and valets cleared them then disdainfully threw the golden wares out of an open window, to the astonishment of guests. Naturally the wily superintendent took the precaution of stretching nets below the windows. He used his gold tableware trick one too many times.

My favorite part of the spread is the austerely beautiful, vaulted cellar kitchen. No noise, mess, or smell in the sunlit rooms of the château, *s'il vous plaît*. The walls are five feet thick. This kitchen is immeasurably grander than the one in Cormatin. There is copper galore and a sprawling, quadruple-wide cast-iron stove that would not have been here in the time of Vatel. No matter.

The fundamental difference between adorable Cormatin's authentic, lived-in kitchen and the grand one in Vaux-le-Vicomte is simple: This is a perfect, polished, sanitized re-creation. Still it gives you a good idea of what life in Vatel's brigades might have been like. Nearby there's a subterranean refectory with a vast fireplace. Imagine this inferno of ovens, stoves, roaring fireplaces, and badly lit servants' passageways. Huge gray convolutions of eye-stinging smoke swirl up and out of the gullet-like vents. Vatel rushes to and fro, shouting at his crew of hundreds as he prepares the feast to end all feasts—which also happened to end Fouquet's career one fatal summer's day.

Louis XIV was a regular at the château. But he had missed a big party in July so on August 17, 1661, he and his court circled back for a little buffet whipped up by Vatel for the occasion. A thousand places were set, six hundred for the king's company of courtiers and four hundred for other distinguished guests. There were eighty tables and thirty buffets laden with food. It arrived in five separate services, each with countless dishes that would fill the rest of this book to list. The dessert course featured a novelty—something a lot like sweetened whipped cream, which, chauvinistic experts regretfully admit, was one of Caterina de' Medici's imports, much improved by Vatel. The guests wined and dined magnificently, the royal family eating off Fouquet's dishes of gold. Fountains played tunefully, their jets rising and falling to the music of royal composer Jean-Baptiste Lully.

After dinner, fireworks exploded overhead, and Louis' sometimes-favorite playwright Molière staged the premier of *Les Fâcheux*—a diabolically appropriate name for a balletic play, it turned out. Usually rendered in English as *The Bores,* the term really means "the annoying." Louis was annoyed big time—by Fouquet. Molière was merely disgusted by the spectacle of decadence and later famously had a character in *l'Avare* quip, "Eat to live, don't live to eat," a gloss of Socrates. No one was listening.

Ninety-nine-point-nine-nine percent of the king's starving subjects may have suffered from chronic ancestral hunger and been worse off than their medieval forebears: Thirteen catastrophic famines hit France during his reign. Louis suffered from ancestral envy—he was humiliated and enraged by Fouquet's wealth. Where had it come from? It outshone his own, sorely depleted by his extravagance and incessant warring.

LE GOOSE IS COOKED!

Stuffed roasted goose was a triumphant recipe in the days of Fouquet and Louis XIV. Reminiscent of the nesting-doll recipes of ancient Rome, it was relatively easy to make. Take the largest gander you can lay your hands on, stuff it with its own organs especially its fattened liver and nested, smaller game birds, whatever bits of meat you can cram in, season the stuffing with fresh herbs, and roast the goose slowly until golden brown. The stuffing went to the aristos and royalty, the tough, dry, roasted old goose meat was left for the servants or poor.

Was Louis served the stuffing or the flesh by mistake? We will never know, but metaphorically speaking the answer is clear.

So angry was the invidious king he refused to spend the night at Fouquet's château. On their way back to Fontainebleau at 3:00 A.M. the irate and possibly soused young Louis is said to have snipped to his mother that Fouquet's goose would soon be roasted. It's unlikely the former superintendent supped on foie gras, or roasted anything, during his sojourn at the Bastille. His career was finis. Terrified, Vatel fled France but soon bounced back—he was too skilled to languish in exile.

Having escaped vengeful Louis' clutches, Vatel was quickly hired by the king's cousin, Prince Louis II de Bourbon-Condé, aka Le Grand Condé. He whisked Vatel to the sumptuous Château de Chantilly north of Paris. Actually it's Vatel who did the whisking, giving the name crème Chantilly to Caterina's whipped cream he'd reinvented at Vaux-le-Vicomte. Or so the legend goes. Whipped cream is doubtless even older than Caterina de' Medici, as is Chantilly whose name and location are borrowed from the villa of the Ancient Roman potentate Cantilius or Quintilius, governor and prefect of nearby Senlis.

Who was Vatel anyway? Probably a Franco-Swiss or Swiss-French kitchen hand of low birth. He became a pastry maker and worked his way up until he appears fully formed in the history books in Fouquet's kitchens. Swiss, did you say? Why be surprised, some of history's best French chefs have been or are Swiss, Belgian, Swedish, Scottish, American, or British. Talent is not genetic or specific to one nationality though you might think otherwise by the rhetoric in France.

At least since the secular missionary Auguste Escoffier, French haute cuisine has belonged to the world, the sophisticated fare of grand hotels and grand private homes or restaurant tables. It's precisely the globalized nature of haute that has given the French the pluck to crow about their "culinary hegemony." Hegemony brings to mind kings and emperors and when they are no longer fit to rule, their kingdoms and empires crumble like cookies or cakes or Marie-Antoinette's brioche.

Following Vatel's trajectory it's time to hopscotch through time and space. Here's what really happened to him and why he did himself in. Almost exactly a decade after Fouquet's fatal feast at Vaux-le-Vicomte, the king and his six hundred famished courtiers were on their way to a new get-together, a reconciliation visit at Le Grand Condé's place in Chantilly. The Condé had picked the wrong side during the Fronde Rebellion against Louis XIV twenty years earlier; it was high time to kiss and make up. Three banquets filling twenty-five gargantuan tables and five complete services à la Fouquet were planned. They would stretch over three days and nights, from Thursday April 23 to Saturday April 25. The Condé's reputation and future depended on their success. The middle banquet was on a Friday, a lean day on the canonical calendar, so meat was out and fish was de rigueur.

Vatel was stressed, hadn't been sleeping for weeks, and was worried about the posse of unexpected aristo guests who galloped up at the last minute, plus he had to deal with the rowdy 2,400-strong contingent of the courtiers' servants. You begin to get the picture. The first banquet was only a partial success because the fireworks fizzled in fog and there weren't enough main courses to overload all the tables. Then as now saltwater fish was considered far nobler than freshwater fish. Vatel refused to serve the lowly local river and lake fish, an insult to the Condé's tables, and frantically awaited the catch sent up from the coast by overnight horse cart. The first batch was paltry and the second hadn't arrived by 8:00 A.M., so the frazzled, dishonored maître d' whose main job after all was quartermaster general, went up to his room, locked the door, and did the gory deed, impaling himself, succeeding only on the third bloody try.

The show went on brilliantly—the fish arrived shortly after Vatel was found spitted on his sword. Hushing up the death, the valets and executive chefs hustled out the food on time and in obscene abundance. The Grand Condé and Louis XIV did indeed kiss and make up. All was well. As Madame de Sévigné recorded in her inimitable precious style, "We dined very well, had collation, had supper, took walks, played, went hunting; everything was perfumed with the scent of daffodils, everything was enchanting." La-di-da, the king never knew and certainly would not have cared about his cousin's impaled maître d'hôtel.

What would France do without Vatel? Someone would need to invent him. Otherwise the books, movies, plays, and theme restaurants dedicated to his memory could not exist. If it hadn't been for his spectacular suicide, Vatel would probably have fizzled into obscurity, just another step-and-fetch-it to the royals and the rich. But Madame de Sévigné's quill saved him from oblivion with a sympathetic portrayal as "le grand Vatel," an extraordinarily capable man. She would know. She had dined with Fouquet and had met the maître d' on more than one occasion. So had Mazarin, Corneille, Molière, La Fontaine, and La Quintinie. Over a century later, Carême praised the "inseparability of honor and culinary art" Vatel demonstrated. Alexandre Dumas in an unusually heartless mood remarked that Vatel should have kept his head and figured out a work-around. Vatel was negligent, the author of *The Three Musketeers* pronounced.

Dumas may have been right. Historians agree it was iffy to get fish delivered on time hundreds of miles inland from the coast in the 1670s. Vatel knew it and should have kept live fish in tanks or brought in the catch earlier and kept it on ice. Yes, the rich had icehouses centuries ago. But why quibble? The essential thing is Vatel the antihero and his tragic or tragicomic tale is familiar to every educated Frenchman and woman. His fate touches many in their gastronomic hearts of darkness with gut-level poignancy. Honor and flawless entertainment above all! The much-abused "to die for" is at last an appropriate expression.

STAR SUICIDES CONTINUED

To die for" is not often heard on the lips of busloads of diners in the Château de Chantilly's in-house restaurant, La Capitainerie, located in Vatel's much-remodeled but breathtakingly handsome vaulted kitchens. "Okay" is the more common view. It's hard to mess up crème Chantilly, and they don't, but the rigmarole and hoopla in the preparation and service of it is kitsch enough to kill. Likewise the brand "Vatel" is so ubiquitously exploited and the descriptions of his suicide told with such relish that the overall effect is to spoil the appetite. Luckily, the setting inside and out on the restaurant's terrace compensates for these drawbacks, and if high culture tempts you, the floating enchanted-kingdom château happens to possess the second-largest fine art collection in France after the Louvre.

Way out in the gorgeous watery grounds landscaped by Lenôtre, a rustic-bucolic eatery awaits whipped cream lovers at Le Hameau. The thatched huts actually predate Marie-Antoinette's hamlet at Versailles. Speaking of which, Chantilly's pocket-sized Potager des Princes though humbler is infinitely more charming than the king's garden in Versailles—it's my favorite thing in Chantilly.

Vatel's kitchens like those in Vaux-le-Vicomte and other châteaux and palaces outside Paris offer impressive displays of copper, giant fireplaces, and unmovable nineteenth-century stoves and ovens amid which famished hordes of tourists now nosh and guzzle. Studying the decorative vintage eight-foot-long steel rotisserie skewers affixed to the walls, you understand why that particular job was for muscular toughs like Taillevent. Loaded with poultry or sides of lamb and beef each skewer must've weighed a hundred pounds or more.

It strikes me as slightly ghoulish to dwell on Vatel's tale when famous chefs dogged by debt and stress continue to commit suicide today. Vatel Syndrome is eerily contemporary. Before the volcanic, endearing three-star chef Bernard Loiseau shot himself in 2003, I happened to be among the last hacks to interview him. In hock for millions and in a panicky misguided bid to content the Guide Michelin with gold-plated luxury, disappointed by Gault &

Millau's demotion, overworked, not sleeping, worried about the excellence of his dry-hung beef and local pike perch, he succumbed.

In the run-up to Loiseau's death, when various top tables like his were facing bankruptcy because of their wrongheaded pursuit of stars, the affable longtime director of the Guide Michelin Bernard Naegellen assured me Michelin never encouraged anyone to go into the red expecting rewards. He would say that, wouldn't he? Directors have come and gone since Naegellen, the palace hotels and their restaurants have made a concerted comeback, and the official spiel remains unchanged. Stars are for the cooking. You have to wonder.

Meanwhile other celebrity chefs following Vatel and Loiseau's lead include Homaro Cantu and Benoît Violier "the world's greatest chef" according to the French government's top-thousand ranking, La Liste. Each took his life in 2015. Passionate love—the love for food and regal luxury—sometimes leads to folly.

EAT LIKE A KING

After trotting around in Louis' company you deserve to eat like a king—or a queen or at least a prince or princess. Back in Versailles there are several aristocratic haunts beyond Ducasse's Ore, foremost among them for quality and sincerity the dinky but stylish Michelin neo-one star La Table du 11. A perfect segue to your visit, it happens to be on the square facing the cathedral and Potager du Roi. Whippersnapper chef Jean-Baptiste Lavergne Morazzani works out of the requisite cool viewable kitchen, sometimes buying peas, asparagus, or fruit from the king's kitchen garden. In a one-room Spartan-chic, beige décor, juvenile staff (some from the École Ferrandi hotel-restaurant school in Paris) solicitously serve slimming nano-portions of tantalizing exquisite foamy teetering market-based artistry at upscale bistro prices. Never have I tasted more delicious tender squid ingeniously transformed into fettuccine ribbons. Gourmandizing is impossible: Louis would dispatch in a single gargantuan bite an entire three-course meal from the microscopic hors d'oeuvres to the dainty post-dessert chocolates and bonbons.

La Table du 11 is elegant. But measured in terms of opulence the only truly imperial or kingly dining experience you're likely to have in Versailles off the château's grounds is at the Trianon Palace, a Waldorf Astoria Hotel where Lavergne Morazzani once toiled. What fond memories I have of the inauguration of this palace back in the early 1990s! For the occasion, I rashly bought a tux I was unable to wear again because of my expanding girth. Still the experience of playing penguin among the peacocks and swans of Paris' beau monde was worth it and if I can keep the moths away I may yet wear that tux again in old age.

Nowadays the cuisine at the Trianon Palace Versailles is under the distant direction of that brightest of Scottish constellations, Gordon Ramsay, star pupil of supernova chef Guy Savoy, Ducasse's archrival. I'm not sure what the Sun King would make of the techy chef's table dining arrangement in the kitchen: it feels like a Plexiglas box at the opera. Given Louis XIV's passion for opera and for watching others work or stuff themselves, this brand of voyeurism might tickle the royal funny bone. Haute has always been more about entertainment than nourishment. The posh neo-*ancien* casual-chic décor and style of this palace merges Marie-Antoinette-through-the-Looking-Glass with Salvador Dalì in Miami, but hey, those royals wigged out in Louis' day and the nouveaux arriviste clients seem to love the look.

Complicated cuisine? Never! Ramsay's foie gras is cooked not in one but two ways: roasted with apple tart and pear and pressed with smoked duck and Sauternes. Rabbit replaces royal hare on the restaurant's menu. The saddle and leg are cooked in two ways and sound poetic in their convolutions. The entire menu is a triumph of surreal poetry, but that may be the translation from French into Scottish and back into something resembling English. Lyricism is a prerequisite in haute and has been for centuries.

Beyond the novel flavors and deliciousness of the cooking, what would surprise the king here and at most fancy French restaurants everywhere is the artistic plating. In Louis' day the artistry was concentrated on the placement of priceless platters and beautiful dishes onto which the dog's breakfast was mounded, piled, and otherwise overloaded in saucy superabundance. Today each dish is an edible pointillist or abstract expressionist masterpiece more gorgeous and enticing to the eye than most of the overblown *ancien* art masterpieces of monomania in the Château de Versailles. It's not that I myself particularly enjoy eating modernist daubs and swirls or deconstructing comestible skyscrapers but that's just me: I am an unapologetic gourmand and lover of authentic simplicity.

Eating like a king is actually an interesting takeaway from Versailles, one of the many entry points for penetrating the mystical Parisian love affair with food—and understanding the conflicted place French haute cuisine and stellar French restaurants have in the topsy-turvy twenty-first century.

It sounds like a fairy tale: Once upon a time everyone in his heart of hearts wanted to live and eat like royalty, right?

That's why the world's first Ancien Régime restaurants bore an uncanny resemblance to the Sun King's château or the manorial abodes of the beloved aristocracy and haute bourgeoisie. Those proto-restaurants arose during the reign of Louis XV and were entirely exquisitely Parisian in conception, a slice of Versailles served on the Seine. It's no coincidence their birthplace was only blocks away from the Louvre and Palais-Royal, residence of the Regent, the lively Philippe d'Orléans. It makes sense given the Regent's sterling example of how to entertain: lusty libertinism and stylish gluttony.

That's swell, you say, but isn't this old-fashioned regal style, taken over by the triumphant bourgeoisie and imitated in French *grandes tables* everywhere ever since, what so many young food lovers, especially Millennials who aren't genetic or cultural descendants of Louis XIV, find off-putting? There isn't a lot of excitement in the current iterations of pretentious, classically conservative, rigidly hierarchical, Ancien Régime fantasy food and décor.

Beyond the food and décor the obsequious Louis XIV–style balletic service—he loved ballet and was a fine dancer—typical in so many French luxury restaurants is comical when it's not grotesque. The global nouveaux may love it, but what about others, especially nonhierarchical youths? They are currently inheriting the earth from we wizened boomers.

Where's the shared, connected, apparently egalitarian or democratic independent dining experience in the twinkling Michelin universe? No matter what the company's propaganda says, the stars continue to go only to high-end properties. Now reverse the equation and look again. "Apparently egalitarian" is the key concept. Think about it: Even in fast foods and self-serves you're forced into a hierarchical relationship. Someone has to flip the burgers, brew the coffee, and empty the trash. Corporate chains own many of the highest-end restaurants like the Trianon Palace because corporations seem to be among the few entities able to maintain the requisite level of luxury, perfection, and excellence clients demand—or is it the guidebooks that demand it? Corporations own the fast foods, too. Corporations large and small also own most of the historic brasseries and even some ostensibly politically correct vintage indie bistros in Paris, which aren't indie anymore. Hierarchy and "no surprises" predictability are more than an imposed norm. They're what most customers want or think they want. Otherwise market forces would cause their extinction, wouldn't they?

The viral spread of American-style franchise eating in France may sound to some like the lunch bell at the French mortuary, the end of the traditional way of dining, the one UNESCO and the French Ministry of Foreign Affairs are somehow expected to safeguard. But it doesn't ring like a death knell to me—it's a wake-up call, an alarm bell. At the risk of causing indigestion among readers, I'd argue the real problem is economic decline and the simultaneous irrepressible desire felt by people across the economic and social spectrum everywhere, including in France, to widen the range of their restaurant choices, to go horizontal, so to speak, breaking away from the hallowed French traditions enforcing fixed eating hours and multiple-course meals served by uniformed pros.

Luckily this isn't a zero-sum game. Ore, the Trianon Palace, Brasserie Balzar, Angelina, and the golden arches can and do share with the surviving authentic indie properties the same ancient French civilization. All can thrive and many do so side by side. Between the regal and the infrahuman stand hundreds of likable, long-standing, democratically, and gastronomically correct cafés, bistros, brasseries, and *tables d'hôte* that haven't yet fallen into the corporate maw. The biggest threat to them is their own mediocrity, and the slow death of the middle classes that once patronized them. UNESCO and the French government can't do much about the "Uberization" of gastronomy without inventing a new paradigm.

PART SIX

Entrées, *Quatrième* Service:

Ancienne Nouvelle, 1700s

REGENCY STYLE

Sitting at a sunny table listening to the centerpiece fountain in the leafy, car-free heart of the Palais-Royal, I am often struck by the exquisiteness of the site and the historical aptness of its current occupants. Richelieu's imposing palace on the southern end is now part of the Ministry of Culture and so is one of the Revolutionary period's most famous restaurants, Chez Méot. On the north end of the compound's airy arcaded perimeter is the city's most venerable, grand Ancien Régime eating establishment, Le Grand Véfour, a worthy survivor.

Raise your glass to progress—though never a straight line, it does exist. As Catholicism transmogrified the pagan pantheon into God and his saints, French republicanism has transformed the monarchy, Revolution, and Napoleonic empires into a presidential democracy with an elected secular king. One of his duties is to glorify French cuisine, the unofficial state religion. Seated in his papal throne in the Palais-Royal, the Minister of Culture plays pontiff to the French president's king or emperor. These potentates are committed to sampling and promoting native delicacies and potables, spreading the bounty of budgets among stellar restaurateurs, as they would have in the days of Louis XIV. Some entertain as lavishly as Fouquet. Culture and food are big business, France's soft power. Unlike France's armies so far they haven't been beaten in battle.

Pry yourself off your bench and take a tour around the palace's garden courtyard. On the façade of Le Grand Véfour, lettering spells out "Café de Chartres," the name of the premises' first occupant. The café opened in the late eighteenth century when Chartres was a hereditary title owned by the Orléans branch of the royal family. Most of the Palais-Royal as we see it today dates from the tumultuous last decades of the 1700s. But the history and gastronomic significance of the site are older.

Louis XIV's nephew, the Regent, Philippe d'Orléans, lived, loved, feasted, and frolicked where the Minister of Culture now sits garlanded by contemporary artworks. The setting seems terribly grand, prim, and in some ways proper. It was grand but neither prim nor proper during the Regency, from 1715 to 1723, when Philippe transformed Richelieu's former lair into party central.

Like French haute cuisine, the country's history is an exercise in complexity. Here's a nutshell version of the Regency.

In the late 1600s, Louis XIV deeded the Palais-Royal to the titular head of the Orléans branch. In his will, drawn up in 1714, the Sun King appointed as Regent his nephew, Philippe, the great-uncle of the king-to-be, Louis XV. Louis XIV died in 1715 after reigning for seventy-two years. His great-grandson Louis XV was five years old. When the time for succession arrived, Philippe the Regent, reigning temporarily, installed the underage Louis XV in the Tuileries Palace several safe blocks away from his own residence. He then got down to the business of picking apart the most autocratic elements of the Sun King's heritage. A born dealmaker, Philippe turned out to be the proverbial skilled statesman, though his heart wasn't in the job. His heart was in his stomach and loins. Philippe seems to have inherited his prodigious and perverse appetites from his mother, the self-described suckling pig, i.e., Princess Palatine, the only creature in the realm Louis XIV had actively feared.

Princess Palatine and her son Philippe were not only unrepentant gluttons, they were also enthusiastic amateur cooks. It's ironic, given the influence the duke in particular has had on the legends of French gastronomy, that both mother and son learned to wield knives and frying pans not in France but in Spain. He showed as much alacrity for potages and partridges as he did for power and passionate sex. At an early age Philippe made an enviable reputation for himself as a fiend, molester, and Rabelaisian eater.

The tale is well-known of the duke's secret sorties to a certain farmstead in suburban Asnières, now reachable on the Paris Métro. It has been recounted without the salacious details by many including Auguste Escoffier. In deep disguise, Philippe would steal away from the Palais-Royal, appear at the farm, tie a cotton apron over his precious silk garments, and whip up an intimate supper for the Comtesse Marie-Madeleine de Parabère, his favorite of many, many mistresses. More often, however, the duke would summon the countess to his palace and feed her gilded lilies and other munchies while he cooked up succulent stews for his debauched pals.

It's for this gourmandizing and philandering plus other, darker reasons that Philippe d'Orléans is a role model to the Rabelaisian set to this day. Hagiographers politely refer to him as "an aesthete." Actually he has been more accurately described as "the most debauched and most corrupt of princes." In Paris this has long been a compliment, a sign of sophistication, especially among swingers.

Like many of his ilk, Philippe d'Orléans was drunk half his adult life, another source of pride to Parisian high livers then and now. Etymologists note the term "roué" was first used at the Palais-Royal to designate the duke's select entourage. They were fit to be broken on the wheel—*la roue*—for their outrages or were so devoted to their leader they would happily submit to that worst of all tortures. Sexual orgies sandwiched between debauched drinking and gourmandizing sessions were convened three or four times a week in good years. Most histories tell you these were refined, sumptuous feasts thrown for the crème de la crème of Paris society, gatherings where modern French cuisine and table manners were born. Maybe, but I don't think so.

After the warmongering Divine Right monomania of the Sun King and the joyless later years of his reign when the pious party pooper Madame de Maintenon was the king's mistress, the duke's bonhomie, pacifism, and libertinism came as a relief to many aristos. Royal gluttony dressed up as gourmet sophistication continued and that was the essential thing. A savvy crowd-pleaser, Philippe threw open the palace gardens to the public and before anyone knew it, the tree-lined allées blossomed with stands selling snacks and drinks and the great Sicilian novelty, ice cream.

The pleasures may have been innocent outside, but the story was different inside the duke's vast apartments.

One thing that makes Philippe so quintessentially modern and republican French is his joyous anticlericalism. His great gourmandizing partner was the Grand Prior of France, Monsieur de Vendôme, whose impiety titillates and shocks even today. Philippe praised Vendôme for forty years of continual drunkenness, ostentatious adultery and whoring, and irreligious imprecation in public. With a select circle of choice individuals the likes of Vendôme, the duke carried on behind impenetrable locked doors.

The Marquis de Sade and similarly kinky Grimod de la Reynière would've felt right at home and must've been racked by retroactive nostalgia for the Regency—both were too young to experience its pleasures. The Regent's daughter La Duchesse de Berry was a regular at the orgies, "a paragon of all the vices." She lived in the Luxembourg Palace and partied back and forth. A widow at nineteen, she died at twenty-four, apparently the willing victim of her father's incestuous passions. The duke was also molesting his other daughter, Mademoiselle de Chartres, who saved herself by becoming an abbess and living a happy same-sex life in a convent.

But orgies were only part of the picture. The duke also enjoyed tête-à-têtes. Remember those "flying tables" at the Petit Trianon? They and the concept of romantic dining were pioneered here before being perfected in Versailles. Champagne on ice in silver buckets was another Palais-Royal novelty no festive Parisian table could be without then or now. With meddlesome servants and spies safely gone, the roués and cloistered romantics roistered and roasted, served themselves lavish meals, and swilled indecent quantities of precious wines.

No wonder the beardless Louis XV upon reaching majority at age thirteen headed to Versailles: He couldn't outperform his great uncle. Not yet, at least. For the rest of his long reign—he was crowned in 1723 and died in 1774—the new Louis galloped to and fro between the Louvre, Versailles, his other châteaux, and the addresses of his uncountable lady friends. It's said his psychological development was arrested. He remained an eternal adolescent incapable of doing "a man's job" ruling Europe's most populous, powerful country, a country at war again, burdened by debt, and full of underfed malcontents who had only gruel, bread, roots, and watery soup to eat. Young Louis promptly ran France's finances into the ground and reestablished de facto theocracy, adding to the spread of common bliss while entertaining in the style of his forebears. In other words he was a fine fellow, a great king, and deserved the propagandist's nickname "Louis the Beloved."

Actually it was probably his love of food and gallantry that won over hearts and minds back then and does so, perhaps in secret and guiltily, today.

Louis XV when young and slim, 18th-century engraving, artist unknown

Was it his affectionate devotion to his aesthete Regent, and his permanent hormonal adolescence that made Louis XV so fond of feasting? Not only did he gluttonously devour entire capons for breakfast in the style of his great-grandfather, he also fashioned chocolates with his own fingers, grew and roasted coffee beans, baked pastries, distilled liqueur, organized 10:00 P.M. "*petits soupers*" with flying tables in secluded dining rooms, and maintained omnivorous mistresses by the score. The gourmandizing of Louis XIV and libertinism of the Regency became institutionalized during his reign, and continued minus the orgies under his successor, Louis XVI.

ON THE MENU

Like the fossilized bread of Pompeii, a menu for the *souper* at the Château de Choisy on September 29, 1755, has survived the centuries only slightly garbled, transmitted by Charles Monselet in his *Almanach des Gourmands* of 1862. It indicates Louis XV was every bit as greedy as the Sun King. It also shows the continuing influence of France's Spanish queens—Anne of Austria and Maria Theresa—who took over from the Medici. Note the lingering medieval and Italian Renaissance influences, and the eighteenth-century novelty.

This intimate little supper started with four soups: thick, hearty *oille* onion soup, a Spanish recipe; meaty *oille* stew à *l'espagnole,* also Spanish; light *potage de santé*; and puréed turnip potage, both seventeenth-century French recipes.

The entrées were an assortment of small pies *à la balaquine,* filets of rabbit *à la genevoise,* filet mignon of mutton with a spicy sauce, filets of pheasant in a thick matelote stew, quails seasoned with bay leaves, woodcocks *à la vénitienne,* stewed partridges *à l'ancienne en salmy,* garnished squabs, blanquette of pollard with truffles, marinated *campine* pollards, chicken wings *en batelets,* round filet of veal glazed with its own juices, minced mixed wild game *à la turque,* breaded, long-simmered sweetbreads Sainte-Menehould, Rouen ducklings *à l'orange,* and *haricot* of chunky lamb with dark *velouté* sauce.

Four *relevés* followed: roast Choisy mutton, beef rump *à l'ecarlate,* a whole sirloin, its filet minced and mixed with chicory, and Caux pullets with raw onion.

Then came four main entremets: pheasant pie, *perdrouillet* braised ham, brioche, and *croquante.*

Next up were two "medium entremets"—i.e., roasts: young, small chickens, more of those *campine* pollards, *ortolan* buntings, thrushes, migratory plovers, red leg partridges, pheasants, and Rouen ducklings.

Are you still hungry, your Highness? Make room on the table for sixteen small entremets, a mixed bag of sweet and savory including coffee-infused cream, artichokes *à la Baligouro,* cardoons *à l'essence,* cauliflower with Parmigiano, eggs with partridge jus, truffles cooked among ashes and embers (La Varenne), spinach with jus, cockscombs, sweetbreads, green beans with verjuice, ham omelet, turkey *à la duxelles* with mushrooms and onions (La Varenne), mixed ragout, chocolate profiteroles, small jalousies, and *crème à la genest* (i.e., Genoise or Genoese-style whipped cream, the kind that goes into Genoise sponge cake).

Notice anything? Two things strike me: the number of Spanish and Italian dishes or French derivations from them, and, secondo, the names of dishes and the styles of cooking are incomprehensible to most modern readers.

What pray tell are artichokes *à la Baligouro*? Are they the same as *Galigoure,* named for the artichoke-loving sidekick of Maria de' Medici, Leonora Dori alias La Galigai, or are they a misspelled version of *à la barigoule*—blanched, fried artichokes with mushrooms, garlic, shallots, herbs, and spices? Any way you spell it, the term means nothing in standard French.

That's alright: Chef-speak was incomprehensible back then, too. Only the maestros and maître d's could master the vocabulary. Was that done on purpose? Probably: Knowledge is power, poetry is more appetizing than explanation, and proprietary nomenclature is flattering to the highborn, rich, or famous. People loved and still love to have dishes named for them.

ANCIENNE NOUVELLE

At least three revolutionary gastronomical developments occurred during Louis XV's reign. The first was the advent of so-called nouvelle cuisine, the second the coming of age of cuisine bourgeoise, and the third the invention of the modern restaurant. The three are intimately connected, products of the unstoppable Age of Enlightenment. A fourth trend was the beginning of the spread of French cuisine and French chefs abroad, especially in England, where food even among the rich lacked sophistication.

Connecting the dots between the glorious gastronomical events of Louis XV's reign is an entertaining pastime I particularly enjoy indulging at table. When I'm feeling flush, I book at Le Grand Véfour and feast my eyes on slimming haute, or take a romantic garden table at Restaurant du Palais-Royal, under Colette's windows, and enjoy similarly artistic, ethereal fare.

When the royalty checks are slim, my business goes to a vintage café facing the Comédie-Française, Le Nemours. Here the crudités with Louis XIV's hard-boiled eggs and the café classics are seasoned with atmosphere, the best of all condiments. The café's colonnade sprouts from the side of what was the Palais-Cardinal. Swallow a few aperitifs or a bottle of white with your *croque monsieur* and you'll feel and possibly see the ghosts of Louis, Richelieu, Mazarin, and especially the riotous Duc d'Orléans flitting among the tables—unless those are actors in period costume escaped from the Comédie-Française?

Here's another hint to push your pen between those connectable dots. When libertines are worn out by partying, what do they need? A restorative of some kind, and that's what "restaurant" meant from the Renaissance forward. With Louis XIV it came in the form of his celebrated breakfast beef bouillon. That's precisely what the early restaurants served—quintessence of Sun King bouillon. No surprises: The first eat-in "restaurants" cropped up a few blocks from the Palais-Royal and Louvre, the royal fountainheads not of the Age of Enlightenment but of delicious decadence in need of refreshment and revitalization.

Next, what happens when the king himself is a hungry libertine and takes as mistress the *grande bourgeoise* Marquise de Pompadour? She runs rings around his royal highness, putting the aristocracy and the bourgeoisie on the same gilded footing. What kind of cooking becomes not just fashionable but de rigueur? Cuisine bourgeoise, did you say?

As Brillat-Savarin pointed out sixty years after Pompadour died, this was when refinement, orderliness, cleanliness, and elegance became watchwords. Brillat-Savarin, a gentleman and a scholar, was incapable of impoliteness. Born during the reign of Louis XV he remained incurably nostalgic for the roasts and stews, the sauces and omelets of his happy privileged youth.

Here's another pair of dots waiting for a line: What is it the libertines and nouveaux aristocratic bourgeois aesthetes crave for their worry-worn digestive systems and fashion-conscious exertions? Of course, a delicate, lightened, restorative new style of cooking, a *nouvelle cuisine* parbleu that happens to be very bourgeois and full of bouillons.

The term "nouvelle cuisine" was coined in 1734, by the way, not 1970, with the publication of Sieur Menon's *Nouveau traité de la cuisine* subtitled *La Nouvelle Cuisine* in the 1739 edition. The Enlightenment in eating and cooking had begun, sort of. The intellectualized patter of chefs and maître d's had in any case.

As the century progressed, theorists, chemists, chefs, philosophers, philologists, etymologists, encyclopedia compilers, fine artists, doctors, and even progressive Jesuit priests discussed the healthful and civilizing force of French cuisine and began the never-ending argument over the many meanings of taste, and the differences between gluttons, gourmets, gastronomes, and other varieties of eaters. For the first time since antiquity, French painters showed not only allegories of original sin, death, or vanity but also still-life tableaux of real food, the eating and enjoyment of earthly things. Think of Chardin's spectacular *The Skate* from 1738, now at the Louvre, with a cat pawing oysters and a giant skate gutted and hanging from a hook. Learned societies and dinner clubs were formed. The practice of preparing and ingesting nutrients was on the way to becoming "gastronomy"—a worthy, studious occupation that did not yet have a proper name. Cooking was now science, a branch of chemistry and medicine. The philosopher's stone of the scullery was the "quintessence"—quintessential flavor, quintessential goodness, the quintessential extract of beef. New super-bouillons made Louis XIV's morning pick-me-up seem like rainwater in comparison.

It's ironic but fitting that Jesuits leaped onto the nouvelle chow wagon. The mid-1700s is when the obscurantist mumbo jumbo of chefs and other culinary professionals began to simmer: it has boiled and frothed ever since. Just as Louis XV was breaking or burning atheists and violators of the canonical eating calendar, the hocus-pocus in kitchens and the complex jargon of recipe instructions and names of specialties placed kitchen secrets firmly in the hands of initiates—the High Priests of Haute. Remember that little *souper* in 1755 described above? From then on amateurs and home cooks would operate in a lower world, pros in another superior realm. The age might better have been called Chiaroscuro—an Enlightenment shot full of shadow, alchemy, and sorcerer-apprentice foodies swinging the incense.

QUINTESSENTIAL READING

Even more influential than Menon's book were the slightly earlier *The Modern Cook* by Vincent La Chapelle (written in English in 1733 and translated into French in 1735) and *Les Dons de Comus ou les Délices de la Table,* by François Marin, from 1739.

Chapelle's career is a dizzying zigzag. He learned to cook in Spain and Portugal, made his name in England as a French wizard in the service of the Earl of Chesterfield, and wound up as Madame de Pompadour's personal chef where he perfected among many other things the mysterious *perdrouillet* braising technique for ham and other meats. Pompadour was official mistress from 1745 to 1764, when the *nouvelle cuisine bourgeoise* ousted the *ancienne cuisine royale*. Tellingly, the last reprint edition of La Varenne's perennial *Le Cuisinier françois* came out in 1738.

An enlightened innovator who respected the ancient tradition of copying his forebears, Chapelle lifted heavily from earlier authors' works including François Massialot's 1691 *Le Cuisinier royal et bourgeois*. But he gave the recipes and presentation a new spin. This was the apotheosis of modernity in a premodern world.

Some of the most popular dishes eaten in Paris today were codified during the first wave of nouvelle. In the top ten of all time is blanquette de veau, also known as *poulette de veau,* a regular feature on the menu of Le P'tit Gavroche and a dozen other restaurants I haunted in the 1970s and '80s and just as popular today. Bucking global trends, blanquette de veau has become a cult dish in the farthest-flung cholesterol-conscious countries. I once savored blanquette at Café Boulud in New York, surprised to see it on the menu. It beat some I've had in Paris, but seemed extravagantly creamy. I learned it was made not with simple cream but with *whipped* cream. Fresh over from Chantilly, I wondered, or Genoa, perhaps?

Strange to tell, the oldest recipe for blanquette de veau I've come across has no cream and little flour and comes from François Marin's revolutionary

Les Dons de Comus ou les Délices de la Table, the book prefaced by a pair of Jesuits. Stranger still, this recipe, like all blanquette recipes I know from the eighteenth and nineteenth century, was devised as a way to use up leftovers. In the heyday of blanquette the required breed or variety of veal was "Palais-Royal," an easily recognizable reference to Paris' gourmet mecca, but also a double entendre: "the royal palate."

Precise as always, in French, *palais* and *palais* mean very different things—a palatial residence and a sensitive part of the oral taste organs rolled into the same homonymous word, not to mention a cut of beef. Palais-Royal was also a particularly tasty breed of milk-fed veal. Confusing? You bet *c'est charmant*!

FRANÇOIS MARIN'S FAMOUS BLANQUETTE DE VEAU RECIPE

(With modern tweaks in parentheses)

Thinly slice some precooked (i.e., leftover) veal (try about four pounds of shoulder, braised for several hours with herbs, carrots, and an onion studded with two cloves). Prepare (clean, strain, cut up if necessary) some (several ounces of fresh) mushrooms (preferably sweet tooth or hedgehog mushrooms—you'll see why). (Lightly flour the mushrooms and sauté them in a pan on medium-low heat.) Sprinkle in some broth (use a ladle's worth of the veal braising liquid). Simmer (until the mushrooms are tender). Add the (lightly floured) veal and season with salt and pepper. Bind the sauce (off the heat) with four (beaten) egg yolks, (two to three tablespoons) finely minced parsley, a pinch of nutmeg (and a pinch of salt), and a stick of butter, if you have it (come on chef, tell them to buy the butter if they don't have it, use half a stick at most, and avoid scrambling the yolks by removing the pan from the heat). To finish, add (a teaspoon of) lemon juice, vinegar, or verjuice if it's the right season (for unripe grapes or other sour fruit). Voilà!

Marin also gives a recipe for blanquette of lamb, but suggests adding more seasoning. Lamb and beaten egg yolks? Hmm . . . no wonder the Jesuits were interested in nouvelle, they'd probably just returned from Jesuit Central in Rome where they supped on divine *agnus dei*. I'm being facetious.

Actually lamb is the clue that tipped me to the possible origin of this most popular of French *ancienne* nouvelle dishes: Roman *agnello brodettato* or Tuscan *vitello brodettato* from the Medici's backyard. *Brodo* and its diminutive *brodetto* mean broth—bouillon—so *brodettato* literally means "brothed" or braised, i.e., cooked in bouillon as per above.

In 1570 Bartolomeo Scappi gives at least one recipe in *Opera*, Book Six, Chapter XXV, for veal in broth clarified with egg whites and tart liquid (presumably citrus). It feels like a precursor to *brodettato*: instead of using whites to clarify, use yolks to thicken and bingo, you have blanquette. Lots of other Scappi recipes combine meats, broth, and eggs, and Scappi is only one possible source of many.

But the clincher for me is early Parisian restaurateur Antoine Beauvilliers' menu from the turn of the eighteenth to nineteenth century. It includes beef *à la poulette* otherwise known as *à l'Italienne*. *Mon dieu*—everyone even a Frenchman knows that *blanquette* and *poulette* (not to mention Escoffier's rebranded sauce Allemande) are the same—with potential variants. *Poulette* sometimes has cream. The original blanquette had no cream and was in fact a *sauce Italienne* as defined by the French. Evidently *poulette* and *blanquette* got mixed up after a cook started adding cream to *blanquette*. Got it?

Like the French recipes, the Italian versions work with either lamb or veal and are light in coloration—*bianchetto* means "whitish." They use white wine plus lemon juice and fresh (not leftover) meat in small chunks, as in a modern French blanquette. Most also call for minced parsley and black pepper but rarely nutmeg. There's no butter or cream, either, except in local variations in Emilia, land of Parmigiano, butter, cream, and flour, where the luscious cooking merges Italian and Gothic.

Won't France's UNESCO militants be thrilled to discover blanquette de veau may well be bastardized *brodettato*?

VOLTAIRE REVOLTED

Speaking of culinary travesties, not every connoisseur and theorist of taste of the Age of Enlightenment was wild about *ancienne* nouvelle and its novelties. Count on my kindred spirit, curmudgeonly Voltaire, to speak disparagingly of the changes. In 1765, a year after Madame de Pompadour's death, he wrote his friend the Comte d'Autrey, "My stomach can't take nouvelle cuisine. I can't stand veal sweetbreads swimming in and smothered by salty sauce. I can't eat meatloaf of turkey, hare and rabbit I'm supposed to believe is a single kind of meat. I don't like pigeon *à la crapaudine* or bread that has no crust. I drink wine with moderation and find people strange who eat without drinking and don't even know what they're eating."

Poor Voltaire, he would find many billions of us today very strange. Who doesn't? Mystery meat abounds. Forget the hot dogs or sausages—how many retired milk cows went into your burger and frozen meatloaf, and how many battery chickens into your nuggets? What's in those red or yellow bottled sauces on every table in the land? What about that mold-proof bun and doughy bread? Funny how the bland, crustless stuff Voltaire despised is the most popular kind of bread in the Western world. Granted Voltaire wasn't always prescient. It's gratifying to see flattened, grilled pigeon *en crapaudine* on contemporary Paris menus. It can be delicious if not served bloody, as most Parisians demand it. Sweetbreads are also a classic, although, it's true sometimes served with an overabundance of salty goop.

"We sometimes see in the blundering Epicure a vitiated taste with regard to some species of viands," Voltaire also wrote, in his *Philosophical Dictionary*. And in his article on taste, "bad taste consists in being pleased only with high seasoning and curious dishes."

Voltaire was born two hundred years before his time. He was a notoriously fussy eater—and thinker. So difficult, so sardonic, he always wanted to *know* things and speak his mind. Like asking, is nouvelle really nouvelle or *ancienne* fancifully repackaged? "It is fancy rather than taste which produces so many new fashions," he opined. Click refresh and keep reading. The spin doctors of fancy French fashion and gastronomy have only begun to work their magic.

À LA ROYALE À LA CARTE

Given the glorious culinary history of the Regency and reign of Louis XV, it's fitting the neighborhood around the Palais-Royal and Louvre is where those early Paris restaurants were born about 250 years ago. For nearly a century, this was where serious roués, gourmets, and gourmands like Denis Diderot, Brillat-Savarin, and Grimod de la Reynière flocked to feed. Happily for their contemporary reincarnations, the area is now enjoying what you might call a renaissance in fine dining.

Like Louis XIV's paternity, the birth of the very first restaurant is the source of anguished controversy. According to one version of the tale, a certain Monsieur A. Boulanger, a maker and distributor of bouillons and consommés for weak, sensitive proto-Romantics and debauched roués, opened the mother of all kitchens in rue des Poulies in 1765 on a corner obliquely facing the colonnaded eastern façade of the Louvre.

Without realizing why, drawn like a salmon to the spot where I was spiritually spawned, I became a regular at a café-restaurant in what was once rue des Poulies before the street was reconfigured and renamed rue du Louvre. Le Fumoir is an upscale establishment. Since the turn of the millennium it has occupied prime corner real estate facing the Louvre's colonnade just fifty yards from the giant pepper mill belfry of Saint-Germain-l'Auxerrois. It sounded to me like a fine candidate: Was Boulanger's restaurant here, I often wondered in the days of innocence before I began asking questions and finding unwelcome answers?

Each time I sit and sip or sup at Le Fumoir surrounded by the beautiful slim beau monde of Paris, I think happily of Boulanger's restaurant and never fail to inspect the basement facilities in search of some precious vestige. Nestled on a chic black banquette on a recent visit, I happened to be reading a vestigial print version of an English-language newspaper and discovered yet another obit proclaiming French cuisine dead and Paris restaurants in need of defibrillation. I chortled and sighed.

How delicious my appealingly plated but very old-fashioned roast pork loin with mustard sauce à *l'ancienne*. How polite and professional the service. How affordable the more than potable Château Haut-Musset Lalande-de-Pomerol. For dessert, I savored the exquisitely satisfying sensation that some foreign critics are hell-bent on spitting and roasting the old French lion, which is what young lions naturally do, especially those roaring from New York or London. Surprisingly, the chef at Le Fumoir is an affable Swede named Henrik Andersson. He's a worthy heir to Monsieur Boulanger. Even more surprising, Paris has embraced him with the enthusiasm other nations usually express when embracing Frenchmen and Italians.

At about the time Le Fumoir took over the premises, a rash of articles appeared in England and America questioning the existence of Monsieur Boulanger and the original restaurant. They evoked the shocking results of research by an English professor named Rebecca Spang whose myth-debunking conclusions in *The Invention of the Restaurant* raised eyebrows and hackles. Academics, food historians, and French officials of various descriptions with a stake in maintaining the Boulanger "myth" spluttered like overheated oil in a sauté pan. Was Monsieur Boulanger a fabrication, an unsubstantiated transubstantiated fantasy? The professor pointed out she'd found no proof he or his restaurant ever existed and this despite some convincing near-contemporary testimony. She went out of her way to assure offended parties she had nothing personal against him. There were other perfectly honorable substitutes for him in any case.

The shrugs, scowls, and scoffs of the French culinary establishment may have carried the day, judging by the continued health of Monsieur Boulanger in pixilated and print form. Imagine having to correct all those dictionary, encyclopedia, and reference book entries plus a zillion websites, blogs, and social media entries while removing egg from the collective face of French historiography.

Perusing my precious personal copy of Francis Blagdon's infinitely engrossing 1802 *Paris As It Was and As It Is,* I was comforted to find the following: "In 1765, one BOULANGER conceived the idea of *restoring* the exhausted animal functions of the debilitated Parisians by rich soups of various denominations. Not being a *traiteur* (caterer), it appears that he was not authorized to serve ragouts; he therefore, in addition to his *restorative* soups, set before his customers new-laid eggs and boiled fowl with strong gravy sauce: those articles were served up without a cloth, on little marble tables. Over his door he placed the following inscription, borrowed from Scripture: *Venite ad me omnes qui stomacho laboratis, et ego restaurabo vos,*" meaning "Come unto me all you whose stomachs are in distress, and I will restore you."

This was wonderfully irreligious during a Taliban-style theocracy!

Sadly I also learned that if Boulanger did live and prosper, his establishment was not where Le Fumoir is now. Instead it occupied the short block comprised between rue des Poulies, rue Jean-Tison, and rue Bailleul. The last two streets are unchanged since the Middle Ages. Housed in a building of indeterminate age on the putative Boulanger corner is the Café du Musée, the kind of place where crusty regulars mix uneasily with bewildered tourists asking for café au lait in many languages. Somehow the café's current building doesn't look much like the Gothic house with "Restaurant Boulanger" on the marquee shown in a seductive 1831 painting by Englishman Thomas Shotter Boys, a Romantic then living in Paris.

Boulanger, if he existed, was famous not only for his beef bouillons but also a nouvelle ragout of lamb's or mutton's trotters in a creamy white sauce. That is how many scholars render *pied de mouton,* which in French also happens to denote a common variety of mushroom. Now I've encountered lots of blanquette recipes but never one for mutton's trotters. What if they weren't trotters or feet at all, but rather *Hydnum repandum* aka sweet tooth or hedgehog mushrooms, very popular in France then and now, and excellent in blanquette, as noted? Maybe Boulanger was using François Marin's blanquette recipe and decided to leave out the tired old meat? The result would be delicious, light, restorative mushrooms in white sauce.

It's the white sauce that lends credence, for me, to the whole Boulanger story, which might otherwise be counterfeit, though why anyone including Francis Blagdon (who was in Paris in 1791 and 1802) would bother to spin such a fiction is a question I can't convincingly answer. Was it an egg-yolk blanquette sauce, or béchamel—butter, flour, milk, and a pinch of nutmeg—named as everyone knows for Louis de Béchameil, a plutocrat who bore the honorific title of maître d' under Louis XIV? Alexandre Dumas uses béchamel as the base sauce for his blanquettes.

Béchamel is not a nouvelle sauce even if it sounds very *ancienne* nouvelle. The standard origin is La Varenne though it's not in the first edition of *Le Cuisinier françois* from the 1650s, at least not by that name or in a recognizable formulation. Inconveniently some Italians claim earlier versions of the same sauce—more of those undesired Medici intrusions from the 1500s—used to assemble lasagna. This origin is undesired in France for the usual patriotic reasons.

That's the power of myths and legends, and faith. It doesn't matter if they're false, it's best to assert they're gospel truth. That applies equally to the dangerous realm of gastronomy where Parisians are peerless mythmakers.

So if the founder of the first restaurant wasn't Boulanger, according to other learned sources it may have been a certain caterer and cook named Jacques Minet who also opened a restaurant in rue des Poulies in the mid-1760s then rented it to a Monsieur Marcilly who passed it on to one Mathurin Roze de Chantoiseau who is, many now agree, including the English professor, a fine candidate for the true genetic father of the modern restaurant.

Chantoiseau and Boulanger may be one and the same, a question of nicknames or business titles invented to thwart lawsuits by angry caterers. Their operation seems to have migrated in search of business across the street a block north from rue des Poulies to 123 rue Saint-Honoré where it reopened in a grand 1625 town house in the Cour d'Aligre.

THE RESTAURANT REVOLUTION

The beauty of the notion of the restaurant, whoever invented it, derives less from what it served or where it was located than how and when it served, and what the premises looked and felt like to customers.

Wait a minute. How could anyone "invent" the restaurant? Since antiquity, cities like Athens, Rome, Paris, and Lyon have been awash in eating and drinking establishments, from the *thermopolia* of two thousand years ago to the taverns and inns, *auberges*, estaminets, cabarets, and *tables d'hôte* of more recent centuries. Remember the Venetian ambassador's report from 1577—Paris had so many eateries and caterers the choice made his head spin. Some inns and *auberges* in Europe or the Middle East have been in operation since the Middle Ages. There are a number of cafés dating to the seventeenth century, notably Paris' celebrated, or perhaps notorious, Le Procope.

In modern parlance all eating places are variations on the theme of restaurant, even fast-food franchises are misnamed restaurants. Except that, before the mid-1700s, there was no "restaurant" appellation. Nearly every known kind of eatery had shared tables, narrow hours for food service, a lack of options regarding menu items, and no individual price tags attached to them. Sometimes you had to wrestle to get your portion of potluck and often you didn't get the piece or the quantity your heart desired. Eating was a free-for-all. The décor was basic, the tableware primitive, and the quality of the food iffy, according to the countless horror tales of travelers and disgruntled native commentators.

And then voilà, the Parisian restaurant swans into life, a paradoxical hybrid of reactionary Ancien Régime elitism, Enlightenment openness, medical progress, and radical social change in the run up to the Revolution. It was the rise and rise of the bourgeoisie that led to the creation of the modern restaurant and a few decades later the populist explosion of 1789.

Think of those dining rooms at the Petit Trianon or Fouquet's quaint little Vaux-le-Vicomte. Suddenly, for a price, diners can enjoy the privacy of their own plutocratic table, served by waiters who replace the hovering spying staff at home. The menu features a variety of dishes available that day. Each has a price. Each individual diner or each table is served separately from others, so there's no struggling, no stress. The dining area is almost as good as a secluded private dining room at the Palais-Royal and that's what many restaurants soon decide to offer: a main room and smaller private rooms or *cabinets*, often upstairs. Some establishments go to extremes to insure the privacy of their clients, notably the Café Mechanique, opened in 1785 on the northeast end of the Palais-Royal in the Galerie de Beaujolais. Its "flying tables" are incorporated into hollow columns out of which clients serve themselves. The quality and deliciousness of the food at these novel establishments is also a pleasant surprise.

It's not just plutocratic bankers or royal tax farmers and rich merchants who flock to the proto-restaurants, it's also intellectuals, artists, and scholars. For the first time women can dine out safely and without compromising their reputations. Parisians who don't have their own cooks and staffs can entertain guests by going out. This is the revolution before the Revolution.

When he wasn't writing entries to his *Encyclopedia* or penning pornographic novels on the side, the lusty Denis Diderot was out and about enjoying what he called not the restaurant but the *restaurateur*. "Do I ever enjoy the restaurateur!" he exclaimed to his pen pal Sophie Volland on September 28, 1767, without identifying which restaurateur. "I enjoy it infinitely. They serve you well, rather expensively, but whenever you want." Remarking on "the lovely waitress" Diderot adds that, "One eats alone. Each diner has his own little room where his imagination is free to roam. The waitress comes unbidden to check to see if you want anything. It's marvelous. I think everyone praises it."

Boulanger and Chantoiseau did the prep work but it wasn't until 1782 that the great Antoine Beauvilliers, formerly in charge of the kitchens of Louis XVI's brother, the Count of Provence, perfected the Parisian dining experience. He unveiled La Grande Taverne de Londres at 26 rue de Richelieu, a slice of Versailles, Chantilly, or perhaps the Tuileries, just blocks from the Palais-Royal. Brillat-Savarin lived nearby and also lived through these heady times. He placed the plump, triple-chinned, effervescent Beauvilliers above other pioneers.

Beauvilliers himself was a *restaurateur* not merely an executive chef. He wrote a seminal cookbook *L'Art du cuisinier,* and perhaps most impressive of all he wore a sword at all times, remembering his clients by name even if he hadn't seen them in decades. The sword was more than a mere reminder of Beauvilliers' service as maître d' of the Count of Provence: It also evoked the honored medieval *écuyer trenchant*—the wielder of the saber-like knife, whose job it was to slice the roast before the eyes of his master. In other words, it was a symbolic reference to the great wind-cutting Taillevent.

Forget the chilly marble tabletops, beef broth and pied de mouton in white sauce for crapulous partiers and weaklings, at Beauvilliers' swank establishment you were welcomed by the prodigiously smooth proprietor, sat at elegant tables draped with fine linens, under twinkling chandeliers, were served by Beauvilliers himself and his trained professionals, and ate and drank in kingly fashion. That is no exaggeration: during the Restoration the Count of Provence traded in his name and became the quivering royal whale King Louis XVIII, one of France's greatest gluttonous gourmand gastronomes, the penultimate of the Bourbons.

No wonder Beauvilliers was for nearly two hundred years the universal model for high-end restaurateurs including Paris' celebrated Vrinat and Terrail dynasties. They ran, respectively, Le Taillevent (until recently) and still run La Tour d'Argent. Why the Vrinats failed to wear Taillevent-style swords I do not know. Once upon a time it would have fit perfectly with the flambé-showmanship and atmosphere.

By 1789 there were about fifty bona fide restaurants in Paris many of them grouped around the Palais-Royal and Louvre and the nearby Grands Boulevards including legendary Méot, Véry, and Février, and by the beginning of Louis XVIII's reign in 1814/1815 the score had mounted to an astonishing three thousand. Why such a boom? Read on.

THE ORIGINAL SEE-AND-BE-SEEN SCENE

What was it like to dine in one of the early Paris restaurants? There is no need to strain your imagination. Go to seventeenth-century Le Procope near Odéon if the quality of the eating experience doesn't matter to you: Some of the décor dates to the eighteenth and nineteenth century, and the slanting walls, creaking floors, and twisting staircases might, with an effort, evoke Diderot, Voltaire, and other members of the enlightened clientele.

Better still, head back to Le Grand Véfour. Arm yourself with a thick wallet or flame-resistant plastic. Cross the gilded threshold. Take a comfortable padded chair or banquette. Raise your eyes from your elegantly laid table and gaze at the glittering walls and ceilings. On painted glass panels, nymphs and satyrs romp, the Seasons display their bounty, Flora flirts with Fauna. There are putti and cupids; griffins, garlands, and grotesques; painted urns and platters; and 3-D wall sconces and chandeliers straight out of a château. Lower but more elaborate than Vaux-le-Vicomte, the ceiling is coffered *and* mirrored.

Talk about see and be seen. Narcissus is in love with his reflection. There are mirrors, mirrors, mirrors, creating infinities of infinite regresses. In them is everyone you want to know or prefer to avoid—the beau monde has come to sup. That is how it was centuries ago and that is how it remains to this day. Especially for foreign travelers with an iffy mastery of French, restaurants were petting zoos where the tongue-tied could observe, be observed, and learn everything there was to know about France—French manners, French customs, French beliefs, politics, history, and more—instant expertise. As the celebrated French nineteenth-century wit Alphonse Karr said, the more things change, the more they stay the same. If in doubt read the online reviews.

The mirrors are suggestive of something beyond voyeurism, but what? Feasting at Versailles, of course, in the Hall of Mirrors, but also dare I say it, carnal desire? Up the carved wooden staircase you go, into a private dining room, a prim and proper contemporary version of the individual *cabinet* Diderot mentioned in his correspondence. Shut the doors or pull the curtains, travel back in time, and you, too, can get up to the same tricks as Louis XV and Madame de Pompadour or the Duc d'Orléans and the Comtesse de Parabère—at least in your fulsome imagination. For Parisians, two hundred years ago the *cabinet particulier* offered a new kind of refreshment.

Mesdames, messieurs, now the food. This is where the time warp breaks down. In the days of Boulanger, Chantoiseaux, and even Beauvilliers and Véfour, Parisian restaurants served bouillons or *ancienne* nouvelle cuisine. It would seem pretty old bistro hat to a twenty-first-century acolyte of haute.

In *Paris As It Was and As It Is* Francis Blagdon provides a complete Beauvilliers menu from 1802 that runs to sixteen pages on standard typing paper—the original was printed like a broadsheet newspaper. There were hundreds of menu items, from *potage de santé* to *pied de cochon à la Sainte-Menehould* or Voltaire's *pigeon à la crapaudine,* not to mention blanquettes of veal and lamb.

In the beginning, in 1784, the Café de Chartres served food the way Le Procope did and does—almost as an afterthought. It was one of many similar establishments in and around the Palais-Royal. There were so many, said Grimod de la Reynière, that "few could flatter themselves to have tried them all." Spurred by the duke's debauchery and lack of liquidity, the palace compound was transformed in the 1780s and '90s from a private enclave into the world's first shopping mall-cum-casino-and-entertainment-center including brothels, clubs, cafés, and restaurants. Since it was entirely owned by the latest incarnation of the Duc d'Orléans and therefore inviolable private property the law of the land could not be enforced. Anything went—the morals police and royal spies had no power; political discussions freewheeled; fugitives and rebels took refuge; clients gambled, whored, boozed, and made havoc. No wonder the area became the throbbing heart and lunging loins of the city—and remained that way for decades, a hatchery of dissidents and future revolutionaries.

After several changes in ownership, a Revolution, and the Napoleonic Empire, in the heyday of the Bourbon Restoration period the newly named Véfour opened in 1820. It offered the kind of hearty haute cuisine eighteenth-century kings and mistresses, and nineteenth-century emperors and empresses enjoyed. Grimod de la Reynière claimed it was the best place in Paris to savor "a sauté, chicken Marengo or chicken with mayonnaise." Skip to the mid-twentieth century and Raymond Oliver, the legendary incarnation of Michelin stardom. Oliver revived and ran this national monument for decades. His shadow has never darkened his current successor's congenitally sunny character and perfectly shaved face. Zen master and chef, Monsieur Guy Martin's current menu is as far from the Ancien Régime as the Ancien Régime was from an Ancient Roman roadside tavern, and doesn't have a lot left over from Oliver's heyday, either, at least not as described by Julia Child circa 1949: "little shells filled with sea scallops and mushrooms robed in a classically beautiful winey cream sauce . . . wonderful duck, and cheeses, and a rich dessert."

Memories, memories! The first time I supped at Le Grand Véfour before the digital age, Guy Martin had recently taken over and the restaurant boasted three glittering stars in the Michelin firmament. I sat at Victor Hugo's table and ate divinely in the vertical, colorful, ethereal, affected French nouvelle haute style though it would be misleading to pretend I remember the details of the extravagant march of the meal those decades ago, and my scribbled analogue notes have disappeared. One thing's certain, I did not eat Victor Hugo's celebration menu after the opening of his revolutionary play *Hernani* in 1830: vermicelli and roast breast of mutton with white beans.

The second time around in 2004 the food was equally divine: preceded by amuse-bouche and followed by a parade of desserts, tiny *mignardises* pastries and chocolates worthy of Henri III's mignons, I savored aromatic truffle ravioli in a creamy but light emulsion and stewed lamb perfumed with salsify and tuberous cervil, remarking in my write-up that the food had "never been more enjoyable." The stylized service by flocks of penguin-suited waiters shaving the tablecloths and diving for fallen napkins was flawless and the décor unchanged—it can't change, the interior is a listed landmark. Whether the great Romantic poet Alphonse de Lamartine ever sat at my table as advertised seemed immaterial.

Ditto my third time around a few years later, when I asked for Humboldt's table—members of my family were born in Humboldt County, California. Yet, *poof*, shortly after that third perfect experience of eighteenth- to twenty-first-century grand dining, one of Le Grand Véfour's stars disappeared into a black hole. Having spent nine months researching and writing an investigative piece about the Guide Michelin I had a fair idea why. The mysteries of Michelin are many, however, and my suppositions may have been wrong.

The loss was unpleasant but not fatal for the philosophical Martin. Some restaurants have lost a third of their business with the loss of the third star. Some chefs have taken their own lives. That sad observation leads me to another twenty-first-century, digital age question: Do the stars still count?

But I'm getting ahead of myself again. More on Michelin down the rocky road.

SPRING BACK, FALL FORWARD

Kings and aristocrats are not the demographic at Spring, the trendy *table d'hôte* serendipitously sited on rue Bailleul halfway between the first and second presumed iterations of Monsieur A. Boulanger's mythical primal restaurant. In some ways Spring is a reversal to pre-restaurant ways, with promiscuous dining, a fixed menu, and a fixed price. Guests arm themselves with patience. To while the time away, many immortalize their authentic, unique Parisian-American dining experience in pixilated formats. Before they've finished a meal its components are already on social media. Dinner at Spring arrives in four courses. The first three are savory, the last a dessert.

The chef-proprietor is Daniel Rose. When I first sampled his wares in 2006 he was a modest young former art historian from Chicago trained in France to cook. He had just opened a one-room *table d'hôte* in lower Montmartre, a one-man show plus a waitress. Rose made big and now rules over a multicultural New World fief in the culinary heart of Paris. He is expanding his territory by the day, snapping up property in the style of Alain Ducasse.

Rose's name sounds like the proto-restaurateur Roze de Chantoiseau, but not at all like Boulanger or Beauvilliers. He is at their antipodes, a twenty-first-century throwback to pre-restaurant days. Cheek by jowl with chummy others you do not know, you wait while, as Rose puts it, "We simply make you dinner." It is fresh, unpretentious by Paris standards, and can be outstanding, an antidote to haute yet some people find it exciting. The "people" are most often American, Japanese, rarely French—some of the same people who once flocked to the echoing Michelin mega chefs' temples of gastronomy hoping to be dazzled.

Rose's slogan is "Simple, seasonal and joyful." Who doesn't enjoy simplicity and seasonality? Joy is welcome when it's spontaneous and sincere.

The neo–*table d'hôte* concept seems swell to me, but I downright thrill at the challenge of mixing and matching menu items at my very own table shared leisurely with friends and loved ones. Call me reactionary.

Different strokes, you say, and you're right. Yet for today's diners to understand the success of the eighteenth-century restaurant as an institution when born 250 years ago, it's helpful to know about its communal *tables d'hôte,* no-choice predecessors. You realize why in its infancy in Paris the à la carte restaurant Diderot frequented was as novel and refreshing and exciting as a tradition-reversing neo–*table d'hôte* can be today.

Presumably that's why the Michelin-starred Anne-Sophie Pic set up shop around the corner from Spring on rue du Louvre in a reconverted shop front and included a long *table d'hôte* in the center of the dining room surrounded by à la carte individual tables. This was the norm for most eating establishments two centuries ago in Paris: fixed-price *table d'hôte* service and novel restaurant-style eating on the same premises.

Pic's ethereal delicacies—in the haute post-nouvelle genre—cutely infantilized and studiously "fun" and "feminine" (the chef's words not mine), regulation casual-chic ambiance, and all-white décor are garnished with that other modish requisite of the high end in Paris, a window opening onto the kitchen so diners can watch the circus performance.

Might the fact that millions of young adults grew up with McDonald's playpen-style eating have anything to do with the viral spread of silly décor, food-as-entertainment, and engineered jollity, I wonder?

For the time being, luxury *table d'hôte* dining is limited in Paris but other novelties abound. Barstools and high chairs for big babies, sometimes at shared tables, are mushrooming everywhere, inspired by the counter-style interior of star chef Joël Robuchon's famed restaurant L'Atelier, itself modeled on American and Japanese diners. Like some adult primates, I have developed an allergy to perching amid strangers atop barstools at daddy longlegs tables.

Many innovative young Parisian restaurateurs are practitioners of other cruel and unusual punishments, including the refusal to reserve tables for guests—first come, first served only. Two other spears in the flesh of paying clients are the rapid turning of tables, particularly bad for the digestion once a human has crossed the threshold of thirty, and, worse, the noise levels and hipster music played loud enough to kill conversation. This is the rule now at the self-styled gastronomic bistros serving "bistronomie" meals. Since Paris restaurants are a public extension of the private home dining room, being rousted out in a thumping ruckus to make room for the next shift of wallets feels like a betrayal of a centuries-old sacred compact.

Until recently such barbarous practices, including the measuring of spending per minute—SPM—were unknown in France in anything better than a fast-food chain restaurant or falafel joint. It's hard to see how they square with joie de vivre or how they're likely to encourage and prolong the Parisian love affair with gastronomy. Perhaps "Parisian" should be subtracted from the equation: The demographic at the new wave of gastro-bistros and SPM practitioners is mostly non-Parisian.

PART SEVEN

Entremets, *Cinquième* Service:

Regime Change, Late 1700s–Early 1800s

18th-century engraving of Parmentier, artist unknown

MONSIEUR PATATE

The one comestible you would not have seen on aristocratic or bourgeois tables in Paris during the Ancien Régime let alone on the menus of any of the original restaurateurs was the humble potato, *la patate* or more elegantly *la pomme de terre*—"earth apple." That is unless you were dining at Les Invalides chez Antoine-Augustin Parmentier, aka Monsieur Patate, in the company of his spud-eating pals Benjamin Franklin and Antoine Lavoisier, the father of modern chemistry.

First allow me to serve you some solid history, then the mashed myth. Despite the universal popularity and deserved fame of French fries, despite my learned opinion that among the world's three thousand varieties the best potatoes are grown, cooked, and served in France, the potato is not actually a French plant or even a particularly French delicacy. France was one of the last countries on Earth to embrace and swallow earth apples. As to Monsieur Parmentier, he neither discovered potatoes were edible, nor was he their first booster in France. That doesn't mean Parmentier wasn't their best and greatest promoter.

Yet another New World import, the magical root of all good, the food that conquered starvation across much of the globe, much of the time, the potato showed up in France in the late 1500s. By then it had transited from the Andes across South and Central America to Virginia, England, Spain, Italy, and Germany finding acolytes. Everywhere the potato went people loved the potato and devoured the potato. They were given potatoes, they ate potatoes, they kept eating potatoes, and still eat potatoes end of story. Not in France. No, no, no.

An unwelcome, dirt-poor migrant, the spud was shunned by French society as unfit for human consumption meaning it was fine for pigs, peasants, and prisoners, but not for the aristocracy or bourgeoisie. Consequently it couldn't be grown on a large scale because the aristos and bourgeoisie owned the land and chose the crops. Potatoes were unclean. They grew underground, rooted close to the Devil in the medieval cosmography of creatures still firmly in place during the Ancien Régime: demons and roots below, plants above, domestic animals above them, birds above hooves, humans above birds, angels above humans, and God above all creation except, perhaps, the reigning monarch. Or so the story goes. Why truffles were exempted from the Devil's table is never explained.

As has been noted earlier in these pages, the great gastronome Louis XIII did not like the potato, not even when served with roast turkey, an American bird that by the 1600s had become a French citizen and French specialty, its origins forgotten. If the king wouldn't eat potatoes, then no person of quality in France could possibly eat potatoes. None did until nearly 150 years after Louis' timely death in 1643.

Fast-forward past the Sun King and Regency into the middle of Louis XV's reign. Lusty Denis Diderot in the 1751 edition of his *Encyclopédie* notes that the fist-sized tuber is "bonne à manger." Diderot reports that potatoes thrive in many places in France, from Alsace and Lorraine to the Lyonnais, Vivarais, and Dauphiné. The recipes for cooking potatoes are many, he adds, among them meat and potatoes, potato cakes, baked potatoes, potatoes cooked in hot ashes, and boiled potatoes—there's no mention of fries. Though not delicious, he opines that they are the source of "abundant and fairly healthful" food for those who need calories. They cause flatulence, but that's of little concern to hearty peasants and workers in need of fattening.

Diderot doesn't mention hogs, the biggest French consumers of potatoes, or convicts, whose sustenance was shifting at the time from bread and water to potato slurry. He also forgets to mention the decrees from 1630 and 1748 that made it illegal to grow potatoes in parts of France for fear they caused or helped spread scrofulous tuberculosis, plague, leprosy, and fever.

The budding scientific community of the Age of Enlightenment battled this subspecies of obscurantism for decades with mixed results. The potato got nowhere. Enter Parmentier, a skinny, goofy-looking pharmacist, agronomist, proto-nutritionist, and monk-like lifelong bachelor immune to the corrupting temptations of gastro-hedonism and culinary entertainment at newfangled *restaurateurs.* Where other potato-loving do-gooders failed, Parmentier succeeded. As a prisoner during the Seven Years' War he had survived by eating spuds. Even after the delights of POW food, Parmentier actually seems to have liked his *pommes de terre.* Mostly he was one of the honest-to-god heroes of his age, a secular saint bent on saving the poor from malnutrition and death. To say he fought doggedly to promote potatoes is misleading: Hounds are not strategists nor do they produce upward of twenty thousand pages of writing on alimentary subjects.

Naturally enough, the rutted road Parmentier and the humble tuber traveled, from German prisons to Paris' temples of gastronomy, passed through Versailles and various royal enclaves Louis XVI had assigned the pesky researcher for his potato-growing experiments. Louis also gave Parmentier a pension and lifelong accommodations at Les Invalides, where he rose to Chief Pharmacist. Whether the king actually enjoyed the flavor of potatoes is unknown, but to his considerable credit he did encourage efforts to find a fattening replacement for wheat-based bread in famine years. If only Parmentier's potato-flour brioche had been a hit, Marie-Antoinette might have lived a long and happy life as a cake-baking French heroine, and July 14 would not be Bastille Day. But as the Ancien Régime rumbled toward the Revolution, potatoes still had a bad rep as "pig roots" or convict food and Parisians were reluctant to adopt them.

That's when Parmentier cooked up a plan. It was the spring of 1786. One of the royal plots of land loaned him was a sterile, sandy military parade ground at Les Sablons in the Bois de Boulogne just beyond today's Paris beltway. Where Parmentier's potatoes struggled against the odds, nowadays a petting zoo and narrow gauge train thrill Parisian kids, and the silvery silhouette of Frank Gehry's Louis Vuitton Foundation etches the skyline, glorifying a billionaire. The story goes that Parmentier cleverly posted royal armed guards around the land to make Parisians think he was growing exquisite root vegetables for the royal table. The guards left at nightfall cleverly allowing potato thieves to pilfer the patch and spread the word that the king's potatoes were delicious and fattening—this when fat was good.

The strategy worked except it wasn't really a strategy but rather serendipitous oversight, a myth mashed and served with butter and cream. The soldiers had always been posted during the day, never at night, to protect the king's parade ground during military maneuvers. So much the better, thought Parmentier, counting on the marauders to be his missionaries. Unable to keep enough potatoes in the ground because of theft, he concentrated on another plot in the Grenelle neighborhood.

Coincidentally it was near Les Invalides and the battlefield where Julius Caesar's troops defeated the Parisii in the beginning of this book. Fitting? "Let me have men about me that are fat," said Shakespeare's Caesar, and "Yond Cassius has a lean and hungry look. He thinks too much: such men are dangerous." Was that just one of old Will's fantasies? Either way, Parmentier and the king's goal was to fatten up the Parisians and keep them from Cassius-like revolt.

Despite the guerrilla marketing at Les Sablons, potatoes on the plate and potato flour in the bakeries were still a hard sell in Paris, the flash point of rebellion and riot. But what about potato flowers in a buttonhole? What better way to flatter Louis and promote the potato among the aristo-bourgeoisie classes than pluck a bouquet of beautiful mauve blooms, rush out to Versailles, and hand them to the king? On August 24, 1786, that's precisely what Parmentier did, an act of inspired genius. Louis took several potato flowers and stuck them in Marie-Antoinette's beehive wig and in her corsage. "Monsieur Parmentier," said his majesty, "men such as you cannot be rewarded with money. There is however a currency more worthy of their heart! Give me your hand and come kiss the Queen."

Before the royal embrace was over the word was out. Potatoes were beautiful, potatoes were good, the king and queen liked potatoes; they wore potato flowers, they loved Parmentier!

There was no looking back for the shy, awkward yet forceful Monsieur Patate, a royal favorite, or for spud flowers. Note: *flowers* not *spuds*. Would the Parisians finally eat their potatoes? No, ah, no, no, no!

LIBERTY, GLUTTONY, FRATERNITY!

In the fall of 1787 with less than two years left before the Revolution, the dauntless Parmentier organized a potato banquet at Les Invalides. He invited scientists, leading lights, pharmacists, eccentrics, and other willing victims like Franklin and Lavoisier intrepid enough to sup on "pig roots" then sing their praises. The royals, aristos, and bourgeois grandees demurred. The banquet menu itself has not survived, but a firsthand account of what was eaten, transmitted via various chroniclers and scribes to the Modern Age, provides an appetizing outline.

PARMENTIER'S POTATO BANQUET AT LES INVALIDES, OCTOBER 21, 1787

As Reported by Monsieur Paul Heuzé

They served us two soups, the first a puree of our roots (tubers), the other a meaty bouillon in which potato-flour bread simmered away nicely without crumbling. Afterwards came a matelote stew followed by a dish topped with a white sauce, then another dish à la maître d'hôtel and finally a fifth au roux. The second service consisted of five other dishes, no less good than the first, starting with a pâté, then a fry-up, a salad, beignets and a potato-flour cake. The remainder of the meal was not sumptuous but was delicate and good: cheese, sweet preserves, a plate of cookies, another tart, and last of all a brioche, also made with potatoes. We had the brioche after our coffee, which likewise was made from potatoes. There were two types of bread: the first was a mixture of potato pulp and wheat flour, a rather good example of soft milk bread, the second was made with potato pulp and potato starch and was labelled "hard bread."

Is it any wonder that in my fanciful gastronomic topography of Paris, the gilded dome of Les Invalides appears like a giant baked Bintje halved, set upright, and slathered golden with butter?

Did Monsieur Heuzé say "fry-up?" This may have been the original French fried potato. What about the brioche, was it delicious? Perhaps one day an archivist will discover another account of the banquet with more details and a five-star rating system.

No matter how many potatoes Parmentier lobbed into the cobbled streets of Paris, the Revolutionary juggernaut could not be stopped. Up came the cobbles, down came the Bastille. After dispatching Louis XVI and filling the Seine with blood, the Revolutionaries slowly circled back and adopted Parmentier's tuber—it was food for "the people" after all. Flower growers were made to uproot their plantations and replace them with potatoes. With a Royal Cordon of Saint Michael around his neck and the queen's kiss still burning a bull's-eye on his cheek, the fleet-footed Parmentier dodged a free shave during the Terror, returned to Paris when Robespierre had lost his head, and rose through the Revolutionary ranks, then spent the rest of his years working indefatigably while savoring spuds in the company of his widowed sister. Chroniclers neglect her. With luck she also enjoyed potatoes since she spent many decades cooking and mashing them for her inveterate bachelor brother. The funny thing is Parmentier never got fat. But he did die of tuberculosis.

Parmentier is one of those rare heroic Frenchmen whose lasting cult reaches beyond the royalist-republican political divide. He is food incarnate, remembered by everyone in the country as the father of a hundred different potato dishes, all named "Parmentier." The fact that French fries as we know them today were probably perfected, and certainly popularized, and unquestionably named as such during World War I by American troops fighting in France is immaterial and will not be admitted as evidence.

Parmentier's is definitely among my top-ten favorite tombs at Paris' leafy Père-Lachaise Cemetery. It sits in one of the oldest parts of the graveyard, high upon a hill, near the mossy cenotaphs of life-loving La Fontaine and playful Molière, mocker of kings. A handsome, stylized neoclassical temple of limestone, it's hedged by living potato plants and decorated with a carved alembic, grapevine, and basket of spuds. Like many admirers, including every graduating pharmacist and most chefs in town, I have placed a *pomme de terre* atop Parmentier's tomb, whispering my thanks.

Then I go out and enjoy a dish of *hachis* Parmentier, alias shepherd's pie, or, better yet, duck confit Parmentier, at one of the bistros on or near that

19th-century engraving of Parmentier's tomb, artist unknown

former paragon of working-class 11th-arrondissement arteries, Avenue Parmentier. Fittingly, out of this ragtag neighborhood, in 1789 the revolutionaries swept down and sacked the Bastille and today in the weave of its gritty streets, hundreds of eateries pullulate to a distinctly bobo beat. Some are great—Bistrot Paul Bert, for instance. But my golden rule before eating at any hipster hangout in Paris nowadays is to pause near the kitchen and listen for tuneful peeps. Hear them and you know the specialty is microwave cuisine—the rage—meaning seek your potatoes elsewhere. *Hachis* Parmentier, like blanquette de veau, is among Paris' best-loved processed, premade frozen foods, found on a thousand shameful menus.

Today France grows dozens of varieties of potatoes. Fries are claimed as a birthright but most are frozen and microwaved or fried a second time before being served. Every imaginable form of food containing spuds has a mouthwatering French name except, perhaps, Parmentier's experimental "hard potato bread" and his leaden potato-flour brioche or potato coffee: happily they have disappeared.

Parmentier was a regular at the Louvre, Tuileries, and Palais-Royal where he hobnobbed with the royals, but he wasn't allowed to grow his plants in the Tuileries or palace gardens. Nonetheless I have savored sublime *pommes de terre* in that neighborhood at Le Grand Véfour, Spring, Le Fumoir, and other places nearby. I've had excellent oxtails Parmentier at Café des Musées, a great corner bistro in the Marais. But the most remarkable tubers that ever slipped down my gullet were prepared by super chef Joël Robuchon at his first three-star hostelry, Jamin, in the toney 16th arrondissement, a district where potatoes still make Gallic noses rise in disdain. Jamin is no longer and Robuchon is an industry spread across continents, but his mashed fingerling *rattes* live on in cookbooks, on the internet and countless Parisian tables, and in the memories of former fans. Why so good? Beyond the excellence of the succulent, firm little *rattes* each serving probably contains an entire stick of butter and half-pint of cream. As I savored them in the intimate, relaxed dining room of that simple little restaurant in those golden, all-expenses-paid days a quarter-century ago, I spared a thankful thought for Antoine-Augustin Parmentier.

PIG'S TROTTERS, ROAST CHICKEN, AND SALTY BLOOD

Before saying adieu to the Ancien Régime, its monomaniacal monarchs, and overfed prelates, there is the question of Louis XVI and Marie-Antoinette's downfall, trial, and death. Not an appetizing chapter of Paris history, you say? Actually, the bloody end of Absolutism whetted Parisian appetites and popularized modern gastronomy, giving birth to the genres of food writing and restaurant criticism. It also ushered in the kind of democratic, accessible daily mode of marketing, cooking, eating, and dining out that persists today despite Americanization, globalization, and digitalization.

Revolutions don't come from nowhere. Could the royal family really have been so purblind despite the warnings of Parmentier and a host of enlightened others? You know the answer.

Travel by armchair from the Palais-Royal back to Versailles for one last Ancien Régime feast, courtesy of that supreme mid-nineteenth-century food chronicler Charles Monselet and his *Almanach des Gourmands*. Mysteriously, the last sixteen desserts and other entremets are missing from the lineup. But the pattern of gross gluttony during a time of repeated crop failure, famine, and civil unrest is clear. Needless to say, there are no potatoes on the menu (unless they were among the "lost" *petits entremets*).

DINER DE SA MAJESTÉ

Le jeudi 24 juillet 1788, à Trianon

QUATRE POTAGES

Le riz

Le Scheiber

Les croûtons aux laitues

Les croutons unis pour Madame

DEUX GRANDES ENTRÉES

La pièce de boeuf aux choux

La longe de veau à la broche

SEIZE ENTRÉES

Les pâtés à l'espagnol

Les côtelettes de mouton grillées

Les batelets de lapreaux

Les ailes de poularde à la maréchale

Les abatis de dindon au consommé

Les carrés de mouton piqués à la chicorée

Le dindon poëlé à la ravigote

Le ris de veau en papillotte

La tête de veau sauce pointue

Les poulets à la tartare
Le cochon de lait à la broche
La poule de Caux au consommé
Lé caneton de Rouen à l'orange
Les filets de poularde en casserole au riz
Le poulet froid
La blanquette de poularde aux concombres

QUATRE HORS-D'OEUVRE
Les filets de lapereaux
Le carré de veau à la broche
Le jarret de veau au consommé
Le dindonneau froid

SIX PLATS DE ROTS
Les poulets
Le chapon pané
Le levraut
Le dindonneau
Les perdreaux
Les lapreaux

SEIZE PETITS ENTREMETS
C'est le mystère, au revoir!

Now imagine smiling Marie-Antoinette one year later, almost to the day, dressed as a shepherdess in her enchanted hamlet surrounded by gentle lambs and organic vegetables. She snacks on brioche of purest white wheat flour, sips her hot cocoa, and yawns luxuriantly. Back at the château, His Majesty, the sixteenth Louis of the Bourbon line, glorious descendent of Hugues Capet, bumbles, stumbles, and struts, scattering herds of courtiers while attempting to digest another one of those thirty-two-plus-sixteen course meals. He, too, yawns, eructates, contemplates a well-deserved nap, and pauses to inscribe a single neatly scripted word in his diary: *Rien.*

Nothing? But sire, it is July 14, 1789. *Rien, trois fois rien!* Louis repeats.

Meanwhile the restaurants near the Palais-Royal are full to capacity, the blanquette de veau is bubbling at Véry, the *lièvre* simmering at Méot, the wine and conversation flowing at Beauvilliers. But there is no flour in Paris, no bread, no brioches or cakes, not for the populace. The wheat *and* potato crops have failed.

Now fast-forward past the heads on pikes and the burned out Bastille, to the nighttime "Flight to Varennes" of June 20, 1791. This is not a red-eye special for those with lots of miles. The flying object is a carriage. Why? Louis doesn't like being crimped by the post-1789 constitution and feels threatened by the mobs in Versailles and Paris. Egged on by unwise advisors he adopts the scheme of fleeing the country, joining up with monarchist allies in Austria, overthrowing the constitutional monarchy, and reestablishing Absolutism.

If you haven't seen Ettore Scola's fabulous movie *That Night in Varennes,* starring Marcello Mastroianni as Casanova, Michel Piccoli as Louis XVI, and Jean-Louis Trintignant as Monsieur Sauce, do—the fiction is more colorful and riveting than the real history. Casanova, the great oyster-devouring gourmand who transformed every meal into a seduction scene! He was nowhere near Varennes in historical fact, but who cares? Historical reality is totally relative in this case: There are a dozen conflicting eyewitness accounts of what happened during the Flight to Varennes. Take your pick. Some are told by republicans with guillotines to grind, others are hagiographies, still others are more or less reliable. The king's daughter, Madame Royale, Duchess of Angoulême, tells it straight with few details and, disappointingly to gastronomes, makes no mention of food and drink in her narrative, but then why would the terrified young girl?

"Madame de Tourzel [the dauphin's governess] would travel under the name of Baroness de Korff," writes the young Madame Royale, "my brother and I were to pose as her two daughters, with the names Amelia and Aglaë. My mother [Marie-Antoinette] would be Madame Rocher. Our governess, my aunt, a lady's companion named Rosalie. My father would pretend to be our valet de chambre named Durand."

The king posed as a valet? No wonder they were caught.

There is an apocryphal variant of the tale believed to this day by millions of Frenchmen. It runs as follows: After a tense all-nighter in the rumbling carriage, the frightened Louis was ravenous by the time the family arrived in Sainte-Menehould, 140 miles northeast of Paris. He had the conveyance stop for logistical reasons and during the halt ordered the town's celebrated *pieds de porc à la Sainte-Menehould*. These long-braised pig's trotters are breaded, fried, and eaten whole, bones and all. When chewed, the bones burst like bonbons flooding the mouth with warm, liquefied marrow. They were made famous by Beauvilliers. Who can blame the king for stopping? The snack proved, literally, to die for.

Louis paid with a silver coin bearing his effigy—or an assignat, a fifty-pound banknote, portraying the king, according to some versions of the tale. He was recognized by Jean-Baptiste Drouet, the postmaster. Drouet, a patriotic revolutionary, promptly rode ahead to the village of Varennes, alerted the republican authorities, and the royal family was arrested.

The mythical foodie variant continues at Varennes. The Deputy Mayor

A Bone to Pick: Louis XVI arrested while dining, 19th century, unidentified artist

of the village, a grocer named Jean-Baptiste Sauce (wonderfully played by Jean-Louis Trintignant in the movie), was pressed into action by riotous revolutionaries. These patriots were boozing at the Bras d'Or, an estaminet. Rushing out into the street they forced the royal family to leave the carriage and accompany Sauce to his house. Some versions of the tale have the arrest take place at the Bras d'Or or upstairs in Sauce's house while the fugitives are feasting.

A guy named Sauce, right, could it be true? Funnily, Monsieur Sauce is one of the few characters in the episode who is a known quantity.

Serious historians don't swallow the pig's trotter story or the part about the family being arrested while dining. In reality Drouet had lived in Versailles and recognized both the queen and the king. But does it matter? People then and many now are persuaded of the tale's truth. Sainte-Menehould has been a pilgrimage site ever since for gutsy French republicans. In my gluttonous days in the 1990s, I myself was a regular at Le Pied Rare, a café-restaurant in the then working-class 11th arrondissement: Its owners were from Sainte-Menehould and excelled at preparing this peculiar porcine dish, which I savored many times.

In Louis' case, royal gluttony was temporarily not a great idea. That's what the moral of the story seems to be on a first reading. In actual fact the lesson learned is this: Pig's trotters are irresistible and it's only human to be hungry; therefore, Louis wasn't semidivine and probably not such a bad guy after all.

As Alexandre Dumas put it, when Louis XVI ate he did not carry out an intellectual, reasoned act, but rather a primitive, brutal one: when hungry he had urgently to eat.

To his credit Dumas discounts the story of the king's arrest due to pig's trotters. But he acknowledges that hunger and gluttonous behavior proved the monarch's ultimate downfall during his incarceration and trial. Louis' main complaint about his detention at the Temple Prison in the Marais was the inadequacy of the food—not good and not enough of it. Too many boiled potatoes and little roast capon we presume?

When Louis was at last put in the dock in December 1792, he was so famished and so used to bossing his subjects that he insisted on being served a roast chicken on the spot. What's amazing to me is the tribunal complied. He gobbled the whole bird with unprepossessing relish before the hostile assembly, clearly not thinking what impression he was making. Marie-Antoinette had tried to dissuade him. Dumas quotes Descartes saying, "I think therefore I am" and adds that Louis XVI thought, "I am so I eat."

The king wolfed not only every scrap of poultry, but the many precious loaves of bread brought to him. The verdict was pronounced: of 721 "voters" in the convoluted Revolutionary "jury" system, 361 voted for unconditional execution, one of them being the king's cousin Philippe, Duc d'Orléans, owner of the Palais-Royal, alias Philippe Égalité. The National Razor was sharpened and on January 21, 1793, the king was trundled to Place de la Révolution—now Place de la Concorde—and given a close shave as the crowds roared.

It was then that someone standing below the basket, a Revolutionary citizen or perhaps an aristocratic foreign observer dipped his finger in the king's blood and pronounced it particularly salty. How did he know to compare? Was it cannibalism, again? I can't help wondering whether this same grisly commentator also dipped his handkerchief into the blood and carried it back to Italy where it has been preserved, a precious relic, ever since—and given geneticists and royalists ammunition in their struggle to prove the royal paternity of the Sun King and his gluttonous descendants.

A TALE OF TWO GASTRONOMES

It was the best of times and the worst of times for French food and the French people: by upending everything economically, politically, and socially, destroying centuries-old guilds, revoking the canonical calendar of lean and fat days, and blending the social classes more violently than at any time since Attila, the Revolution of 1789 reset France. Nothing would or could be as it had been. Or so the tale goes.

In actual fact once the Terror ebbed, the aristocrats and bourgeois

The Penultimate Bourbon King: Louis XVIII, gourmet, gourmand, glutton extraordinaire, 19th-century portrait, artist unknown

royalists trickled home and many of the church's properties were returned to the Vatican. A new normal began. It took a decade of paranoid revolution and fifteen years of Napoleonic belligerence but voilà the Bourbon monarchy boomeranged back, Louis XVIII fork in hand.

Deep readings of the period suggest that, as ever, the more things changed, the more they proved unchangeable—except for the costumes, titles of nobility, and the names on deeds and marquees. The hats sat on nouveaux heads, the gloves and reins were in nouveaux hands, but the Parisian beast's soul and appetites remained the same.

Wearing the getup of citizens, the hungry republican bourgeoisie emerged triumphant. Feasting and gluttony among those who had the means went hog wild, a rebalancing act after the Terror. "Paris was gay, wildly gay," Victor Hugo recalled, and he was no slouch when it came to partying. "An unwholesome joy overflowed. The frenzy to die was followed by the frenzy to live . . . There came among us a Trimalchio whose name was Grimod de La Reynière."

His full name was Alexandre Balthazar Laurent Grimod de La Reynière, Grimod for short, but he preferred to be known by another name from antiquity, Amphitryon. Grimod promptly proclaimed that "the heart of Paris had become a gizzard."

To Grimod's delight, a thousand new restaurants sprang up, as tavern keepers, café and cabaret owners added "restaurant" to their shingles and offered à la carte meals at individual tables. A handful of the original reconversions still exist: Le Vieux Paris on the Île de la Cité where we started out, and La Petite Chaise on rue de Grenelle, both former taverns, Le Procope, of course, and Le Grand Véfour, the ex-Café de Chartres. That's the simple explanation of why between 1789 and 1815 the number of "restaurants" exploded from one hundred to three thousand.

But the Parisian love affair with food has always extended beyond restaurants and cafés. The city's markets were packed with produce, fish, and game as never before. Constant war brought famine and horrors, but also wealth and an unquenchable thirst for hedonism and debauchery. Meanwhile the peasantry especially Paris' urban poor continued in misery and ate as they'd always eaten—little and badly. Boiled old meat and potato-everything was the refrain. As the new century dawned, Napoléon did the Bourbons one better by crowning himself not king but emperor. In the old châteaux and old palaces of the new court, the little Corsican emperor, indifferent to food except as fuel, watched his minions devouring the conquered wealth of Europe.

The truth is Ancien Régime table manners, recipes, restaurants, purveyors, cooks, valets, maître d's, and patrons emerged from the gastronomic wainscoting in surprisingly large numbers. Two of the ductile survivors were the quirky, provocative Grimod de la Reynière and the stolid Brillat-Savarin. They were contemporaries, colleagues in the legal profession, and they shaped French gastronomy in lasting ways. Without Grimod and his *Almanach des Gourmands,* there would be no Brillat-Savarin and without Brillat-Savarin the self-consciously highbrow element of French gastronomy would lack intellectual and philosophical or "physiological" foundations.

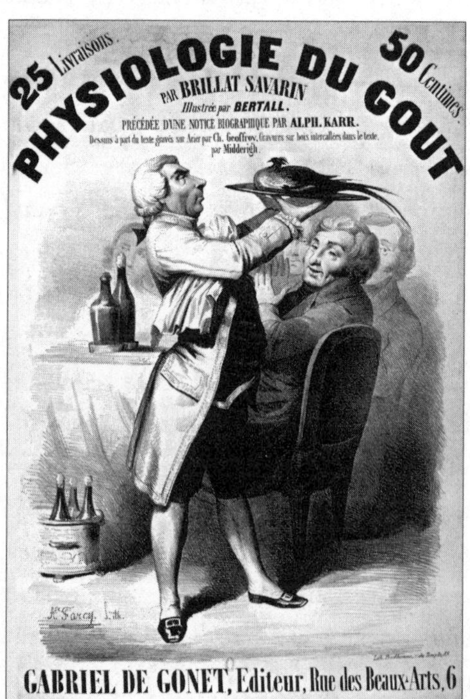

19th-century poster by Bertall for Brillat-Savarin's Physiologie du goût

Of the pair, Brillat-Savarin was the sleeper, his gifts revealed shortly before he died in the mid-1820s. His fame is greater today—*The Physiology of Taste* has never been out of print—and he was the more personable of the two. "Brillat-Savarin eats to live," noted La Duchesse d'Abrantès, who met Grimod and Brillat-Savarin over dinner chez Talleyrand. "But since he likes to live well he pays special attention to this highly important task. Having read the *Almanach des Gourmands* [by Grimod] I was no longer hungry . . . Having read Brillat-Savarin I ordered my dinner."

Still, the coruscating author of the almanac was the real groundbreaker, the "most gourmand of the literati and most literate of gourmands," as his admirer and early biographer Charles Monselet put it. In Grimod's own words, he was the father of "gourmand literature." Coming across his books back in the 1980s when working for the Gault & Millau guides, I remember thinking "Aha, this is where they got their ironic, persnickety, smart-ass style." Where Brillat-Savarin's legacy is joyous daylight, Grimod's shadowy nighttime influence on the psyche of modern French gourmands and snarky critics is inky and profound. His adepts are known as *Grimodiens* and are often virulently *anti-Savarins*, his detractors, equally numerous and passionate, are the *anti-Grimodiens* who consider him a prankster, crook, and parasite.

"As a poet, lawyer and philosopher I am triply entitled to not be humble," Grimod said speaking of himself tongue-in-cheek, sort of, but not really. To his boastful titles of noblesse he might have added "heir to an ill-gotten fortune," "womanizing theater critic," "orgiastic libertine," and "mildly sadistic misogynist sexist." In his defense nearly everyone who could was a libertine and sexist back then, both men and women, and he can't be blamed for the rapacity of his forebears, either.

Grimod was the proverbial man-about-town: while authoring his long-running gourmand almanac, he not only broke ground, he covered it on foot daily, inspecting, tasting, and requisitioning. The exercise is possibly what allowed him to eat and drink imperially and live mischievously into his eightieth year, burying Brillat-Savarin, Napoléon, and Louis XVIII. His stomping grounds were the Palais-Royal, the Les Halles district, the Louvre, Tuileries, and Champs-Élysées.

One question dogged me for years as I trotted across Paris in Grimod's footsteps: How did the smart-aleck, irreligious, antimonarchical son of a filthy rich tax farmer survive not only Ancien Régime theocracy but also the Terror? The quick answer is he lived by his wits. He was a genius.

You might well be breathless by the time you cover the easy mile separating Grimod's table at the Café de Chartres—Le Grand Véfour if you prefer—and the family mansion on Avenue Gabriel off Place de la Concorde, at the beginning of the Champs-Élysées. Your lack of breath would come not just from the exercise and incessant banter but also almost certainly from the sampling sessions at multiple gourmet stops. A prankster with a dark sense of humor and wicked tongue Grimod's unrepentant sardonic gourmandizing propelled him on what he called "semi-nutritive" sorties during which he would solicit samples for his celebrated Wednesday and Saturday "philosophical dinners" and the monthly "tasting juries" that determined who and what would be included in his guides, articles, and other publications.

Head north out of the Palais-Royal to busy rue des Petits Champs and reconnoiter. Wonders lie in many directions. Nearly all the businesses and eateries of Grimod's day are gone, but others have replaced them. Now that the nearby Marais is a certified bobo paradise the time has come for the Palais-Royal, Les Halles, and the adjoining Montorgueil former market districts to enjoy blanket gentrification. The merry-go-round of shop fronts spins as you walk by.

For decades I sensed Grimod's presence at my elbow, slumming, sipping, and feasting at the much lamented century-old Aux Bons Crus, a cozy wine bar-bistro on rue des Petits Champs that served hearty classic fare. Patrons tall in stature brushed the tacky, yellowish ceiling with their hair. But the place disappeared under new paint emerging with a new name, new owners, and a banal new menu in the winter of 2016, another neighborhood icon sanitized for yuppies.

"Sanitized" is not a word I associate with Grimod de la Reynière. Beyond his fearsome wit and shocking capacity to eat he had wild hair, but was neither tall nor prepossessing. Paunchy, with a bird beak of a nose and a long, slanting brow, he wore gloves day and night not as a fashion statement but rather to hide his prostheses. Born with a claw for a hand on one side and a webbed goose's foot on the other, the rare defect horrified and embarrassed his dreadful parents, providing a pop-psych explanation for his bizarre, chipped personality and behavior.

If you'd like to see Grimod before spending time in his tyrannical company, detour to the Marais and the history of Paris museum at the Hôtel Carnavalet—Madame de Sévigné's old roost, where Coysevox's bronze of Louis XIV greets you in a courtyard. Grimod's effigy is here, too. It was painted in 1801 on the wooden sign of Corcellet, one of the Palais-Royal's celebrated specialty food shops. Or so it is claimed. The sign hangs on the museum's ground floor near the main staircase. It portrays a ravenous diner with brushed-back white hair and bulging eyes with a tongue licking lasciviously at his lips as he attacks a platter of seafood. He's not wearing gloves, but after all Corcellet's goal was not to sell portraiture but to stimulate the appetite.

Walking west from the Palais-Royal on rue des Petits Champs, within a hundred yards of the dearly departed Aux Bons Crus, Grimod would certainly be drawn in by the excellent vintages and culinary artistry at long-running hipster hangout Willi's Wine Bar and its similarly tony neighbor Macéo. Grimod may look to modern eyes like an untidy madman, but in his day he was known as "the most polished man in the realm," a dandy on the cutting edge.

Speaking of which, at the corner of rue Méhul, Grimod might make a stop to pick up—probably without paying—a handmade knife at Coutellerie Courty et Fils, the mecca of Laguiole-wielding contemporary boorish Celts. Still waiting to be gentrified, the shop has been in business for the better part of a century. Given the neighborhood trend you'd better rush to see its displays, including maps pinpointing sites in France where knives are or were manufactured. Grimod was famous for his knife technique, the quintessential skill of a proper host, as posited in his 1808 housekeeping and entertainment bible *Manuel des Amphitryons*, a paean

Presumed portrait of Grimod de la Reynière on 1801 shop sign, artist unknown

to "the good life" and dissertation on "the dissection of meats." The title was quintessential Grimod, a learned nod to Molière's play *Amphitryon*—a comic send-up of the perfect host—itself named for earlier plays by Plautus and Sophocles.

By the time he'd dragged rue Danielle Casanova, rue des Capucines, Place Vendôme, rue Royale, and Place de la Concorde, a modern-day Grimod would be teetering under pastries, macaroons, and other baked goods, wines, cheeses, and possibly jewelry and wristwatches, too. His usual method was to have deliveries made to his town house, obsequious purveyors bowing and scraping. He had a roguish way with merchants and restaurateurs, and an ingratiating patter to solicit advertorials. His methods eventually put him in the dock for fraud, forcing him in 1812 to discontinue his publishing ventures and the freeloader tasting juries after an impressive run of 465 sessions. By then Grimod had inherited the family mansion and what was left of the fortune. He no longer needed to scrounge to indulge his gastronomic habit. But the institution of the freeloading reviewer survived him and thrives in France today.

The Library of a Gourmand: Frontispiece from Grimod de la Reynière's early-1800s Almanach des Gourmands, artist unknown

As an alternative, you could click and drag Grimod's itinerary from the Palais-Royal around the glassy new Marché Saint-Honoré and its ring of bobo hangouts, down to Le Rubis, a century-old touchstone bistro with wine barrels out front, a zinc-topped counter, worn wooden chairs and tables, and the classics of the French comfort repertoire served from 7:00 A.M.

to 2:00 A.M. Heading south then west from there on rue Saint-Honoré or rue de Rivoli, Grimod might have stopped at the Galignani bookstore, founded in 1802 and still doing analog business today, to see if his almanacs were in stock.

Just west of Galignani facing the Tuileries is the original Angelina location where Coco Chanel would hang out in the mid-twentieth century, watching the world reflected in the salon's many mirrors. Angelina is now a chain operation for Japanese-American selfie-shooters, but also remains a haven for bona fide hot chocolate and Mont Blanc lovers like Grimod. In his day, on the tony, leafy Terrasse des Feuillants edging the Tuileries Garden the famed Véry operated its smaller spin-off restaurant La Tente des Tuileries where, mostly at others' expense, Grimod threw dinners and held tasting jury sessions.

Beyond Caterina de' Medici's royal garden now known as the Tuileries, facing Place de la Concorde, pause on the corner of rue Saint-Florentin and gaze up at the handsome ochre-toned Hôtel de Talleyrand, for decades home to the U.S. consulate. In pre-terrorism days the mansion was easy to visit, including the ornate eighteenth-century neoclassical rooms where Talleyrand, the ultimate noncommittal diplomat, entertained red-blooded republicans, kings, queens, emperors, empresses, plutocrats, and lawyers, among them his near neighbors Grimod de la Reynière, Brillat-Savarin, and the Duchesse d'Abrantès.

Since Talleyrand was an inveterate gourmet it's no wonder he bought this architectural landmark: seen from his windows the square looks like Louis XIV's symmetrical dining table with the Obelisk of Luxor as centerpiece. That first exemplar of modern celebrity chefs, an architect manqué, Antonin Carême was Talleyrand's cook and pastry chef (though as far as I can deduce he did not work on these premises). While Grimod perambulated, snacked, and scrounged, Talleyrand and Carême were busy carving out a place for themselves in French history, respectively as the great ductile diplomat who used the table to seduce rivals, and the torchbearer of artfully rebranded and artistically served Ancien Régime aristocratic cuisine.

Fifty yards west of the square is the hallowed site where the odd-bird Grimod was born and grew up in a splendid town house. Why are there armed guards on the street in front of it, and why does 4 Avenue Gabriel sound so familiar? Perhaps you've been there to get a visa or renew a passport. Grimod de la Reynière's family mansion is now the American Embassy. The address is correct, the buildings are not; sadly the originals were destroyed, but imagine a grand Parisian palace like the French prime minister's nearby residence at the Hôtel Matignon and you won't be too far off. So splendid was the interior décor of the Hôtel Grimod de la Reynière that the painted woodwork wound up at the Victoria and Albert Museum in London where you can see it to this day.

The property was what some might call a class act. Except that Grimod's gross, gluttonous, classless father was the nouveau-riche tax-farmer heir of a gluttonous pork butcher-*charcutier*-turned-tax farmer ennobled by the crown for his services. The Grimod clan had made millions by wringing money out of the middle and working classes. One novel way to raise revenues as the city grew was to place tollgates on the Wall of the Farmers General, built in the 1780s, when Grimod was at the height of his partying mode. Each time merchandise came into town, the tax farmers creamed something off; another provocation leading to the Revolution. Where the wall once ran, a ring of boulevards now runs—those at the base of Montmartre, for instance, or fronting Père-Lachaise Cemetery in the Faubourg Saint-Antoine, launching pad for the storming of the Bastille.

Grimod's paternal grandfather was also a notorious gourmand. By heavenly retribution he choked to death while gobbling an entire pâté of fatted goose liver. That's why the newborn heir's goose-foot hand had struck terror into the superstitious hearts of his parents. They mistook him for a demonic reincarnation sent to punish them for hereditary gourmandizing. No, I am not making this up.

ALIMENTARY, DEAR GRIMOD!

Food and sex obsessed, unloved, a pariah, during the Ancien Régime, the budding gourmand Grimod de la Reynière delighted in tormenting his parents. Chasing demimonde skirts across stages and doing pro-bono advocacy for the poor was bad enough in their eyes, treating pigs like man's best friend and hiring out the family carriage as a taxi after his allowance was cut were unbearable. A prodigy and a prodigal son in one package, Grimod declared himself a "gourmand" not an epicure, gourmet, or connoisseur at a time when, to his Catholic parents, gourmandizing was a capital sin. With these and other tricks he reminded them of the family's pork butcher past. A lengthy book would be needed to recount his rebellious antics. My favorite episodes shed light on today's mordant modern Parisian sense of humor. Outsiders often mistake it for gratuitous aggressive nastiness when actually it's merely sophisticated caustic arrogance shared à la Grimod.

An apocryphal story has it that Grimod in his early twenties waited for his parents to leave town then organized a feast dressing a pig as a guest and seating it at his father's place at the dinner table. This filial impiety prompted his father to get a lettre de cachet to incarcerate Grimod in a distant abbey. The legend is not unbelievable: Young Grimod was infamous for enthusing about a condiment that was so good "one would eat one's own father with that sauce." Late in life the eccentric Grimod did dress pet piglets and feed them in an armchair at his table. His porcine pets slept on cushions like Parisian dogs and were served hoof and trotter by baffled valets. He also liked conversing with herds of swine and in his writings praised the pig as "the encyclopedic animal par excellence," meaning it was the supreme food, essential to French cuisine, and everything in it was edible. But that's not why he was exiled and locked up.

One of the real reasons was Grimod's sentimental attachment to at least one actress he threatened to marry, a no-no for a lawyer and ennobled tax farmer's son. Secondo, he did organize a scandalous banquet but no pig was involved. He'd lost the only person he'd been fond of in childhood, his parents' friend Jeanne-Françoise Quinault, a lifetime boxholder of the Comédie-Française. Quinault had encouraged him to be a theater reviewer. His parents barely acknowledged her death. So when they left town he put together an unusual "funeral dinner" in her honor. Known as the *Fameux Souper,* it has been recounted by Grimod's biographers and other chroniclers, including the notorious novelist and police informer Rétif de la Bretonne.

Like Caterina de' Medici, Grimod was a numerologist—or pretended to be. His lucky number was seventeen, bad luck in most Catholic countries. There were seventeen members of his Wednesday Society dinner club, each required to drink seventeen cups of café au lait upon arrival (and never more than twenty-two). Grimod's funereal invitation printed on a black-rimmed card with a cross and a catafalque went out to seventeen guests, sixteen men and one woman disguised in men's clothing. She was his mistress, Madame de Nozoyl. Guests were to arrive, without nosy servants or valets, at 9:30 P.M. to sup at 10:00 P.M. They were a mixed bag of noblemen, butchers, construction workers, and other artisans who in normal life would never meet at a dinner table. Dozens of invitations went out to a second group of guests not to dine but to process across an elevated gallery, viewing the supper as the public viewed Louis XVI's suppers in Versailles. This mockery of royal ritual was *lèse-majesté.*

True to Grimod's lugubrious character, the dining-room décor evoked a cemetery or catacomb: skulls and crossbones, a tombstone table bristling with candles, glinting gold and silverware, and crystal glasses in the shape of funerary urns and weeping-vessels. Under each napkin was a wreath of funerary cypress woven with roses. The self-styled "King of the Feast" Grimod de la Reynière ordered his guests to wear the wreaths as they dined. Nine multi-partite services of food were served on plates showing erotic death scenes—lust among tombs and suchlike—the kind of kinky behavior of which the last Bourbon king, Charles X, was fond. In deep disguise and still known during this time as the Count of Artois, this disastrous future king was among the dinner guests.

Grimod's banquet cost the bagatelle of $30,000 in today's money. Sadly the menu has been lost. Luckily one guest had the perspicacity to record that the fifth service consisted entirely of pork "cooked in every way" imaginable. Taking a final jab at his pretentious father, Grimod announced that a relative of his still in the charcuterie business had supplied it. The evening's success was such that a reenactment—minus the funerary trappings—was staged three years later. It wound up in Rétif de la Bretonne's racy novel *Monsieur Nicolas.* Some sources claim the Count of Artois' eldest brother, Louis XVI, secretly wangled an invitation to this second supper in disguise, but that's almost certainly apocryphal. The dinner also featured in J. K. Huysmans' 1880s classic novel *À Rebours.* In 1958 the banquet was served up again by a Parisian hotel and restaurant school celebrating the bicentennial of Grimod's birth. In this and other ways generations of French food professionals have been exposed to Grimod's peculiar genius.

The irreligious banquets got him exiled, thrown into the Abbey of Domèvre in the Lorraine three years before the Revolution. Cut off from the family purse he went from practicing the law and writing theater criticism to inventing a career as an anonymous provincial grocer. He made good with specialty foods in the boondocks of southern France. Lying low through the Terror then returning to Paris when safe, he combined his skills as a writer and purveyor to exalt the burgeoning new world of gastronomy.

Born of the Enlightenment, the term gastronomy meant more than "gastro science." Its adepts understood it to embrace everything from the longstanding Parisian passion for food to the art of eating, decorating, and entertaining. "Gastronomy" appeared in print for the first time in 1801 in a poem by the long-forgotten Joseph Berchoux. The time had come. The job of Chief Executive Gastronome and Chairman of the Amphitryons was crying to be filled. The crass nouveaux riche of Paris needed expertise to help them pick the right restaurants and suppliers and learn home entertainment tips while mastering the finer points of this new science. A food lover, gutsy gourmand, certified intellectual, and successful grocer suckled on the gluttonous ways of the Ancien Régime, cunning Grimod de la Reynière was their man.

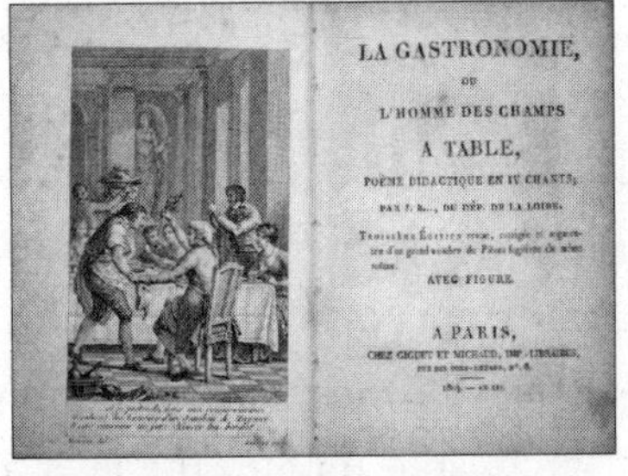

LA GASTRONOMIE,

OU

L'HOMME DES CHAMPS

A TABLE,

POÈME DIDACTIQUE EN IV CHANTS;

AVEC FIGURE.

A PARIS,

The birth of "gastronomy," Joseph Berchoux's 1801 La Gastronomie, *artist unknown*

SANCTIFYING THE DEVIL

Some of his admirers tell a slightly different version of the tale. They think Grimod was a heroic subversive, a revolutionary prankster who put on an act, subtly mocking, bilking, and roasting his readers and wealthy fellow gastronomes, the petroleum pashas and high-tech or finance billionaires of his day. His admirers may be right. There are umpteen examples of parody in Grimod's books. One is his "recipe" for Rôti sans Pareil—the ultimate roast of nesting-doll meats, one placed inside another inside another—published in the *Almanach des Gourmands*, in the 1806 and 1807 editions. It runs to four pages.

The recipe name means nonpareil, i.e., "peerless." Grimod gives it a refined, learned, unassailable spin by identifying the nesting-doll cooking technique as something used by the Ancient Romans. But his formulation of the recipe actually comes from a comic play written in 1730 about a lovesick butcher making his mistress a Mardi Gras feast. In his cooking instructions Grimod pokes fun at society ladies, comparing a young tender succulent bird to a certain Mademoiselle Volnais, for instance, and calling a fattened hen "as white as Madame Belmont and as plump as Mademoiselle Devienne, as fat as Mademoiselle Louise Contat."

Whether subversive or reactionary, to give gastronomy intellectual street cred among the oligarchs and nouveau nobility, in 1803 in the first edition of his almanac Grimod raised the new science above literature and the visual arts. He describes a dream feast, "Uniting in the same coarse of roasts thrushes, quails, red partridges, young Rouen ducks, chickens and fattened hens from Normandy, not to mention carp, smelt and trout, a tableau illustrating the most refined notions of autumn that no poetic description can match, appealing to the eyes and heart, the taste and soul, the palate and nose."

No modern writer anywhere before Grimod de la Reynière—not even Montaigne—had dared to intellectualize the culture of food and entertaining or place them on a par let alone above the beaux arts. Could Grimod have been serious? Possibly not and we may never know for sure.

The reign of Louis XIV and the Regency were ancient history in the minds of most 1 percenters of the early 1800s, yet for Grimod and his acolytes they represented the pinnacle of regal gluttony shrouded in a misty golden light. In one of his springtime menus Grimod includes the evergreen crème brûlée with orange flower water from La Varenne's *Le Cuisinier françois*. But spring and summer were the worst time for gourmands, Grimod opined, fall and winter the best.

GRIMOD'S AUTUMN MENU FOR FIFTEEN GUESTS

From the *Manuel des Amphitryons*, 1808

"In the fall one begins to enjoy the most precious gifts providence gives gourmands."

TWO SOUPS

One with Italian pasta

One a potage à la Brunoy

TWO RELEVÉS DE POTAGE

Garnished pièce de boeuf

Bayonne ham skewered and roasted

EIGHT ENTRÉES

Fattened hen à la ravigote

Partridge cutlets

Hot pâté of pheasant cooked in its own juices

Filets of sole with mayonnaise

Quails à la mirepoix

A ripe Saint-Florentin cheese

Pomegranates with chicory

Eel sausage with truffles

TWO LARGE PIÈCE-MONTÉES

Rhine carp braised au bleu

Baba

TWO MAIN COURSES OF ROAST

Six farm-raised pigeons

Two young wild rabbits

EIGHT ENTREMETS

Cucumbers à la Chevalier

Cauliflowers with mayonnaise sauce

A platter of white pastries

An upside-down jelly of white currants

Peas with butter

Fried artichokes

Rye bread rolls

Cakes à la maréchale

If you think this was a lavish feast, compare the last "tasting menu" of the last "tasting jury" Grimod organized, in 1812: It filled five full pages and included no fewer than fifty-two food courses, fifteen wines, three types of coffee, and—the magic number to wind up the last of the last of the last—*seventeen* types of liqueur.

SOMETHING IS ROTTEN IN PARIS

The following gastronomic fantasy is grounded in fact. It features Grimod de la Reynière, Brillat-Savarin, and yours truly. Bear with me.

"Do you smell something?" I ask.

"The proverbial rare bird," Grimod answers with a knowing smile.

Under the arcades of the Palais-Royal, we pull abreast of a tall loose-jointed, pot-bellied gentleman dressed in Ancien Régime style strolling slowly with his hands thrust into his coat pockets. Others give him a wide berth.

"Monsieur," says Grimod with exaggerated reverence.

"Monsieur," replies Brillat-Savarin, the corners of his fleshy mouth uplifted with pleasure.

They bow. Grimod does not offer his gloved hand. Out of delicacy neither does Brillat-Savarin. Instead from his coat pockets he pulls two small thrushes, dangling them by the claws. The stench is acrid. The birds look disconcertingly like Grimod de la Reynière.

"Not ready," remarks Grimod.

"No," agrees Brillat-Savarin. "Only when the feet detach will I roast them."

Grimod indicates his approval, bows again, and takes his leave, promising to catch up with us later, perhaps at La Halle or, an unlikely shrine of gourmandizing, the church of Saint-Eustache.

As Brillat-Savarin tucks the birds away he adds, "You know, without the odor perceived in the rear of the mouth the sensation of taste would be obtuse and imperfect."

This I recognize as one of his celebrated aphorisms, proof of the chemist and medical man's brilliant, intuitive understanding of the mechanics of taste years before its mysteries could be revealed by modern science.

"You know Canon Charcot's recipe for roasted birds such as these, I am sure," he says affably, leading me north toward rue de Richelieu and his sprawling Louis XV–period flat at 11 rue des Filles Saint-Thomas near the former stock market. "Start by removing the gizzard, then hold your nice fat little bird by the beak, sprinkle it with salt and pepper, stick it carefully in your mouth, without it touching your lips or teeth, bite it off close to your fingertips and chew vigorously. The jus thereby produced will be abundant enough to envelop the entire organ of taste and while chewing you will experience a pleasurable taste sensation unknown to the vulgar."

Am I destined to remain among the vulgar? Devouring semi-putrid roasted songbirds, bones and all, is not my thing. Brillat-Savarin's words send my thoughts back to Grimod de la Reynière. They are opposites physically and temperamentally and their backgrounds and outlooks are, too. Yet I can't help hearing echoes, hearing the same stories told from different perspectives.

"If my reading of your mind is correct," Brillat-Savarin says to me with bonhomie as we pass among café tables under the echoing arcades, "you are wondering if certain elements of my *Physiology* originated with our illustrious friend Grimod." He holds up a hand to prevent me from protesting. My cheeks go the color of a cooked lobster. "Allow me to answer with rhetorical questioning," he continues. "Did Homer write the *Iliad* and the *Odyssey*? Did Shakespeare write Shakespeare? Did our dear Mozart write Mozart or was he at least part Monsieur Haydn? Did our charming friend Grimod mention all the many minds who thought similar thoughts to his own before him, or the conversations at our dinners and tasting juries? One of us told a tale, another suggested a rule of thumb, a third provided a recipe, and voilà, soon enough Monsieur Grimod de la Reynière had his books."

Affably guiding me up the rue de Richelieu under a Pig Pen cloud of rotting bird, the gangling elderly magistrate shows me where the best bakery in town was in his day and regrets that he is destined to die before the croissant is invented and the concept of breakfast revolutionized. "There, at number ninety-two, Count August Zang of the Boulangerie Viennoise in 1838 baked the first one," he says proudly. "We see all from where we sit. Have you read Dante?"

I have read Dante and have not drunk Kool-Aid in fifty years. But even I wonder if this encounter isn't fantastical nonsense. I suppose it is, but at the risk of quoting myself and Alexandre Dumas in a single line, "I have no vices but plenty of fantasies and they cost more."

For decades Grimod and Brillat-Savarin loitered daily at the Palais-Royal chez Corcellet or Chevet, the great specialty food boutiques. They hung out at the Café de Chartres and the same restaurants, knew the same people in part because they had worked in the same profession. They certainly knew each other and dined together or perhaps separately at Talleyrand's famous table and elsewhere. Who knows, Brillat-Savarin may well have been one of the anonymous members of a tasting jury—their names were kept secret and only a few are known to this day—or a guest at Grimod's Wednesday or Saturday dinners. The rotting bird story, Brillat-Savarin's aphorism, and "recipe" are legit, lifted from *The Physiology of Taste* and biographical sources from the period. The modern croissant the world loves appears to have been baked for the first time, as noted, in rue de Richelieu in Count Zang's modern steam oven, the first in Paris, a type of oven probably also at the root of the modern baguette, and certainly led millions everywhere to reconsider their boring bouillon or brioche as breakfast. The bakery was a few steps away from where Brillat-Savarin once lived.

The Aphorisms of Brillat-Savarin, early 1900s postcard by Jean [Paris]

THE DICTUMS OF GRIMOD DE LA REYNIÈRE AND THE APHORISMS OF BRILLAT-SAVARIN

Grimod de la Reynière, from the *Almanach des Gourmands* (1803–1812), *Manuel des Amphitryons* (1808), and *Journal des Gourmands et des Belles* (1807).

1. "We would never recommend talking politics at table . . . Literature, entertainment, gallantry, love and art are a deep vein to be mined for happy topics."
2. "The gourmand is not simply a being Nature has endowed with an excellent stomach and huge appetite, but rather he who to these gifts adds the faculty of enlightened taste whose mainspring is a singularly sensitive palate matured by long experience."
3. "The most important thing is to eat each food at its ideal moment . . . Everything in a kitchen is determined by clockwork."
4. "By taking precautions one can eat a lot and eat for a long time without being discomfited and this is what a gourmand should desire above all else."
5. "It's just as important for a gourmand to know the strengths and weaknesses of his stomach as for a general to know the morale and strength of the army he commands."
6. "Of twenty guests who praise a ragout, who stuff themselves to their heart's content, whose lips twist from voluptuousness, not a one would dream of asking for the name of the cook who made it."
7. "One cannot be a good cook without also being a chemist, botanist, physician, designer and draftsman. One must additionally have a subtle sense of smell, refined taste, piercing eyes, sensitive hearing and a practiced sense of touch . . . an extreme delicacy of all the senses and in all the sensory organs."
8. "It is just as impolite to leave wine in your glass as

to leave morsels of food on your plate."

9. "Cheese is the drunkard's biscuit."
10. "The soberest gourmand when placed before the most frugal of dinners cannot remain at table for less than two-and-a-half hours."
11. "Potage is to dinner what the porch or peristyle is to a building."
12. "A good potage is the dinner of the poor and a joy often envied by the most opulent of men."
13. "If the entrées make us think of the beautiful rooms on the first floor of a vast townhouse, the hors-d'oeuvre may be seen as those little cabinets, boudoirs, and corridors that add to the appeal of a floorplan."
14. "In general true gourmands pay little attention to hors-d'oeuvres, which they view as useless fillers."
15. "Dessert must speak to the soul and above all, the eyes . . . A well-ordered dessert may also on its own make the reputation of a table."
16. "The dessert-makers' art, like all the other arts, made very slow progress in France and has in common with all the other arts the fact that everything in it is owed to the Italians."
17. "For the gourmand the winter is the season par excellence."
18. "Let us leave the petty ignoramus maestros, the beardless gourmands and inexperienced palates the petty glory of eating the first truffles of the season."
19. "Great chefs are never great pastry chefs too."
20. "It is easier to find sensible women than tender lamb gigot."
21. "Great rôtisseurs are rarer than great cooks."
22. "*Du cochon tout en est bon*—everything in a pig is good to eat."

Brillat-Savarin, from *The Physiology of Taste* (1825).

1. "Tell me what you eat and I'll tell you what you are."
2. "The discovery of a new dish gives humankind more happiness than the discovery of a new star."
3. "A wine lover was offered grapes for dessert. 'Thanks,' he said, setting the plate aside, "I'm not used to taking my wine in pill form.'"
4. "To receive guests is to take responsibility for their happiness the entire time they're under your roof."
5. "Cooking is among the oldest arts and of all of them has rendered us the greatest service in civilian life."
6. "The pleasures of the table belong to all ages, all conditions, all countries, and all parts of the globe, mingling with all other pleasures, and remain to the last consoling us for their departure."
7. "The universe is nothing without life and everything that lives eats."
8. "The destiny of nations depends on the way they feed themselves."
9. "The Creator in forcing mankind to eat in order to live also invites him to do so with appetite and rewards him with pleasure."
10. "Gourmandizing is an act of judgment by which we give preference to things that are good tasting over those that are not."
11. "The table is the only place where you don't get bored within the first hour."
12. "Those who give themselves indigestion or get drunk don't know how to drink or eat."
13. "The order in eating is from the heartiest to the lightest . . . The order of beverages is from the most temperate to the fullest-bodied and most flavorful."
14. "To insist that you mustn't change wines is heresy: the tongue becomes saturated and after the third glass even the best wine awakens only the sensation of dullness."
15. "A dessert course without cheese is a one-eyed beauty."
16. "One becomes a cook but one is born a rôtisseur."

17. "The most indispensable quality of a cook is punctuality: the same is true of the guest . . . Waiting too long for a late guest shows a lack of regard for those who are present."
18. "He who receives guests and makes no personal effort in the care of the meal he prepares for them is unworthy of having friends."
19. "The mistress of the house must always ensure the coffee is excellent and the master must ensure the liqueurs are the highest quality."
20. "Animals feed, humankind eats but only the spirited thinking man knows *how* to eat."
21. "One of the privileges of the human race is eating without hunger and drinking without thirst. This can't apply to animals because it is arises from our reflecting on the pleasures of the table and the desire to prolong them."
22. "Skinniness isn't a major drawback for men . . . but it's a horrible curse for women because beauty for them is more important than life and beauty lies in a rounded figure and graceful curving lines . . . Women born thin but with a good stomach can't be more difficult to fatten than spayed hens."

SAVARIN CAKE WALK

Three years older than the dapper diminutive Grimod de la Reynière, Jean Anthelme Brillat-Savarin was twice his size, perennially unfashionable, a provincial gentleman of the upper middle class from the aptly named town of Belley in eastern France. His studies in chemistry and medicine took him abroad, the perils of the Revolution forced him into exile in Switzerland and America (where he discovered Welsh rarebit), and his successful career as a lawyer and magistrate deposited him in Paris. There those who knew him found him eccentric, avuncular, charming, affable, courteous—and dull. A lifelong bachelor like Parmentier he seems to have enjoyed the company of his family, maiden aunt, and unremarkable, uncontroversial old friends.

Where Grimod ordained and disdained, Brillat-Savarin rejoiced and suggested. Grimod provoked, Brillat-Savarin smoothed wrinkles and came up with solutions—for everything from obesity to excessive skinniness and indigestion. Grimod chased skirts, Brillat-Savarin, unlucky in love, savored chaste solitude.

Opposites they may have seemed yet they agreed on nearly everything and certainly had one attribute in common: neither knew how to crack an egg, typical of French restaurant critics then and now (François Simon, alias Anton Ego in *Ratatouille,* boasts that cooking isn't his thing). They concentrated on theory, experimentation, and bodily sensation and left the nitty-gritty to the servants.

Read them in chronological order and *The Physiology of Taste* sounds like an echo chamber of Grimodian wit and wisdom. Grimod was the first champion not just of his chef but of chefs in general, the first since antiquity to list best provenances and insist on the excellence of sourcing, the first to demand that a wine's terroir be announced, the first to obsess about perfect timing in the kitchen and the punctuality of guests—that has not stuck in Paris where fashionable lateness and insouciance are the rule. He was also the first to adopt and promote dish-by-dish *service à la russe;* the best way, he rightly thought, to ensure the food would be perfectly cooked and served hot. Brillat-Savarin picks up and amplifies Grimod then adds his own.

So what is it that makes the avuncular Brillat-Savarin universal and perennial? Many things: his invention of gastro-psychoanalysis, for a start. "Tell me what you eat and I'll tell you what you are" is a clever reformulation of Aristotle, eerily topical and deserving of book-length scrutiny. Applied collectively to our current age of everything-and-its-opposite it might point to fear, nostalgia, infantilization, and self-destruction, but also curiosity and open-mindedness.

The familiar, vulnerable, confessional tone of voice in Brillat-Savarin's book may be the key to his popularity. He admits he, like his readers, overindulges, struggling to eat properly and stay reasonably slim and fit. "The art of eating too much thrives more luxuriantly by the day," he quips.

To combat the obesity epidemic of his day, he recommends his genial "antiobesity belt"—a weight lifter's belt worn day and night to keep the paunch, bowels, and other squishy organs in place, distribute weight to the stressed spine, and keep the skin from sagging. Less bedtime and more exercise, such as strolling through a vast Louis XV–period apartment like his own, is just the thing—try it, he suggests.

Brillat-Savarin's goal of trimming weight slowly by changing the quantity and way people eat while simultaneously increasing calorie consumption is thoroughly modern. This at a time when there were no hormones in beef, no GMOs, no pesticides, no fast foods, no frozen TV dinners, and nothing to artificially alter the endocrine system. There were no elevators or escalators; no cars, trains, buses; people walked, climbed stairs, shivered in the cold burning calories—and still got perilously fat. Why?

For Brillat-Savarin it was simple: overeating and too many carbs. "Carnivores never get fat—look at wolves, jackals, birds of prey, crows, and so on," he wrote. "Herbivores fatten only slightly unless old age forces them into repose. By contrast they fatten quickly when fed potatoes, grains and flours of all kinds."

If only he'd factored in the obscene quantities of alcohol and sugar consumed in his day by the rich along with the starches—in pastries, cakes, and other sweets—he might've helped his gluttonous fellows and descendants avoid the twin curse of obesity and diabetes. But he like everyone back then thought sugar beneficial. He also didn't get what happens when carbs combine with animal protein—another great fattener of omnivorous primates. Needless to say, obesity was an epidemic among the wealthy. The poor worried about getting enough calories. Nowadays things have flipped. Fifteen percent of French adults are obese. The rate is significantly higher among adolescents, and the socioeconomic spread of obesity-sufferers mirrors America and other industrialized countries.

THE HEAVYWEIGHTS

Unlike Brillat-Savarin, Grimod de la Reynière never fussed about obesity and his mid-nineteenth-century successor and spiritual heir, Charles Monselet, actively vaunted the virtues of fat, a sign of prosperity. This was also the heyday of the Boeuf Gras festival in Paris: France's biggest, heaviest bulls and oxen were paraded across town adorned with flowers and ribbons like neo-pagan gods. The following appeared in the February 21, 1858, issue of Monselet's *Le Gourmet* newsletter. Bear in mind the average height of Frenchmen at the time was less than five and a half feet.

Under the title "Subscriptions by some fat literary men," Monselet noted that "The institution of the starving writer is disappearing by the day. As proof we provide a list of new subscribers signed by the heaviest pens in Paris." Names and weights followed: Émile Solié (100 kg/220 lbs.), Louis Ulbach (110 kg/244 lbs.), André Thomas (90 kg/198 lbs.), Hippolyte de Villemessant (100 kg/220 lbs.), Albéric Second (100 kg/220 lbs.), Gustave Bourdin (94.3 kg/207 lbs.), Eugène Woestyn (102 kg/225 lbs.), Émile de La Bédollière (85 kg/187 lbs.), Amédée Rolland (100 kg/220 lbs.), Roger de Beauvoir (90 kg/198 lbs.), Guichardet (100 kg/220 lbs.). Writers who were merely stout included Armand Barthet, Guillaume Joseph Gabriel de La Landelle, Charles Asselineau, Henry Murger, Balathier de Bragelonne, Angelo de Sorr, Alfred Busquet, and Henry de La Madelène.

The heaviest of all French gastronomes of yesteryear was Maurice Sailland, alias Curnonsky, the Brillat-Savarin of the twentieth century (1872–1956): He peaked at 126 kg/277 lbs.

THE PLEASURE PRINCIPLE

Beyond the serious stuff in *The Physiology of Taste* there's also the pleasure the author takes in sharing, the inclusiveness, the seamless merger of good times, good eating, proper health and popular science, the contagious enthusiasm, the unpretentious love of food and wine, and perhaps most essentially to the French ear, a beautiful writing style. Some translations of *La Physiologie du goût* into English are perfectly okay, but it's hard to do justice to the playful, lyrical, airy beauty of the original.

The writing contrasts with the man, by some accounts. Not everyone liked Brillat-Savarin including affable Alexandre Dumas. But probably his earliest and most formidable enemy was Antonin Carême, a chef with a nasty streak and knives to grind. "He was a big eater, spoke little and not with ease," Carême remembered. "He emanated heaviness and looked like a country priest. At the end of a meal his digestion absorbed him. I have seen him fall asleep."

Did Brillat-Savarin fall asleep at Talleyrand's table, or was it chez Rothschild? Did Carême ever serve Brillat-Savarin and Grimod at the same table? The great chef didn't specify and no one at the time thought to ask.

PART EIGHT

Hors d'Oeuvres:

Dining Out, 1800s

HAUTEUR CUISINE

You have to wonder about chipped, resentful Antonin Carême, a natural-born reactionary like many French chefs today who depend on the wealthy and powerful for their prosperity. Tell me what you do for a living and I'll tell you of what cruelties you are capable. Did Carême start the trend or was Taillevent nasty, too? Food professionals everywhere, then and now, are notorious for their ability to flay, skewer, and broil enemies. I wonder if Carême was envious of Brillat-Savarin and his astonishingly successful chef d'oeuvre. It was published the same year as one of Carême's cookbooks. Critics went wild for the transcendental physiologist's high-mindedness and some dismissed the lumpen practical labors of professional chefs like Carême as unworthy of notice.

But Carême also had it in for Grimod de la Reynière, remarking that "La Reynière has had nothing to do with the rapid progress of modern cooking." Offed in a single sentence! That makes sense: Grimod pushed rule-breaking *service à la russe*—the antithesis of Carême's decorative cuisine—and he mocked the power brokers Carême revered. For the superstar chef there was only one man to credit for culinary progress: himself. In his books he makes it clear the golden age of French cuisine began and ended with him.

Carême had every right to be chippy, case-hardened, and egomaniacal. An abandoned preteen from a dirt-poor family of fifteen (some biographers say twenty-five, but why quibble), Carême was born in a construction yard five years before the Revolution. He saw the Terror firsthand, started toiling in a kitchen at age eight (twelve say some), and began his rise to fame and fortune in the Palais-Royal neighborhood, as pastry maker at upscale Bailly in rue Vivienne. By then he was seventeen and a recognized prodigy. Grimod and Brillat-Savarin must certainly have tasted his famous savory tarts. Talleyrand spotted and recruited him chez Bailly. Down the street from the pastry shop was and still is the National Library of France where the ambitious genius feasted on books of architecture, his real passion.

If he were alive today, the angular Carême might love his old neighborhood. Nowadays rue Vivienne and its adjoining landmark covered passageways and nearby Bourse—the former stock exchange—host the nineteenth-century-style Le Grand Colbert, big on atmosphere okay on food; a shop front of Paris' longest-established, excellent chocolate maker Debauve & Gallais, purveyors to Marie-Antoinette and Napoléon (and Brillat-Savarin and Marcel Proust); a branch of star chef Yannick Alléno's Terroir bistros; and one of the world's top wine shops and wine bars, Caves Legrand, perfect for sipping while reading some vintage Carême on handheld media—a print book for instance.

If tea isn't your cuppa, there's also Le Bistrot Vivienne, a prototypical Parisian café-bistro from the 1820s, gussied up for bobos and beloved of many, including me, despite the sometimes snarky service, always mediocre coffee, and uninspiring food. Kitty-corner is local hangout Bistro Le Régent, a classic corner café with lousy coffee but very good housemade grub including seventeenth-century-style onion soup plus fresh mayo with boiled eggs the Sun King would love.

For revisited, epicurean bistro fare in another scrubbed, refitted, bobo-chic 1820s interior there's Daniel Rose's hit restaurant La Bourse et la Vie where the neo-rustic food and outstanding wine genuinely outshine most everything served in the neighborhood and you feel startlingly like you're not in Paris, but rather in the Village in NYC or Boston's Union Park or maybe SoMa in SF. No mastery of French is required.

Better still since you are in theory in Paris, Chez Georges on rue du Mail, a block beyond the Galerie Vivienne and its elegant arcades, is entirely authentic. Of the dozens of atmospheric Paris bistros from centuries past, the moleskin banquettes, wooden tables, Haussmann-era plasterwork, chalkboard menu, pewter wine pitchers, traditional delicacies, and professional service at Chez Georges are hard to beat. The kind of herrings Hemingway ate in the 1920s are here, so is the "life-changing" filet of sole sautéed in butter Julia Child savored in the 1940s and the duck breast, steaks, profiteroles, and *mille-feuilles* a nineteenth-century traveler would have adored. Who says progress doesn't run counterclockwise sometimes?

CHEF À LA KING

Oddly enough, given that he grew up in the heyday of dining out, Carême never cooked in a restaurant yet became the world's first kitchen celebrity, the "chef of kings and king of chefs" lionized by Dumas among others. He was "the Raphael of cooking," a hero capable of untold technical feats, an artist not a lowly artisan. Why? Reactionary perfectionism: Carême systematized French cuisine but wasn't innovative at the stovetop, copying then surpassing his masters while looking backward rather than forward. It was a winning formula at a time of collective nostalgia for a lost, mythical aristocratic Ancien Régime golden age of eating. A century later, Escoffier would copycat Carême across the board.

Clearly Carême had charisma, unassailable skills, and a light touch, excelling in pre-Revolutionary *ancienne* nouvelle and, crucially, creating artistic displays worthy of the table of Louis XIV. I can't help wondering whether at the National Library he wasn't also poring over the entertainment manuals of the Sun King's valet, Nicolas de Bonnefons, a past master of symmetry and vertical displays. They were what pleased the kings, emperors, and czar Carême wound up cooking for during his brilliant career.

It sounds like apostasy to his acolytes, but Carême's most lasting contribution to gastronomy wasn't his mastery and codification of the four "master sauces" and hundreds of spinoff "petite sauces"—saucy sorcery had been done before him and was done again, better, afterward by Escoffier et al. It wasn't even his magnificent books on cooking and entertaining, or his invention of exquisite, timeless tournedos Rossini—a recipe that still inspires the masters of haute. It was the creation of the edible architectural plinth, rotunda, tower, and colonnade, among other culinary construction-site features, especially popular in neoclassical desserts made to look like opera houses and conceived to wow nouveaux guests. He called them *extraordinaires*. The extraordinary wow-factor of French cuisine reached new heights with Carême.

Leaving aside possible influences by Bonnefons, I'm not sure Carême's architectural inspirations and metaphors-made-tangible were particularly original, either. Remember Grimod's famous comparison: "If the entrées make us think of the beautiful rooms on the first floor of a vast townhouse, the hors-d'oeuvre may be seen as those little cabinets, boudoirs, and corridors that add to the appeal of a floorplan." Grimod's writing was built on solid architectural foundations and is rife with architectural motifs reason enough for Carême to have disliked him out of sheer envy.

Carême's early illustrated cookbooks, *Le Pâtissier pittoresque* and *Le Cuisinier parisien*, were beautiful to behold, a novelty no one can deny him. Picturesqueness is quintessential in Carême. Dining chez James de Rothschild, the indefatigable traveler and gossip Lady Morgan raved about the chef, his ethereal cooking and artful, elegant table settings and constructions, judging them more meritorious than many works for the theater. What credentials Lady Morgan had as an epicure are unknown and in any case what really won her over was the chef's clever carving of her name on a column of sugar, plus his personal charm offensive while they sat tête-à-tête in the Rothschild garden.

Before dying in 1833 at forty-nine of sheer exhaustion—burned out and poisoned by coal-fired stoves—the martyr-hero Carême had become the unrivaled master of "decorative cuisine," creator of the pan-European feast for the eyes. Like his spiritual heir Escoffier, the other great internationalist missionary of French cuisine, French sauces, and French culinary constructions, Carême's influence lives on, albeit in altered forms. A zillion hotel and restaurant schools in France and across the globe still pay as much attention to aesthetics—the outsized designer plates and impractical designer flatware—as they do to flavor and practical considerations like getting hot, digestible food to guests, inculcating outdated silly old-haute notions of verticality, symmetry, dazzling color, and architectural line in budding chefs.

It's no longer Carême's plinths and colored aspic borders, but rather the high-end tableware and flower arrangements, the décor, luxe, and especially the artistic plating of food that Parisians prize. Like many artists, Carême's fame grew postmortem: The term "haute cuisine" usually associated with Escoffier was actually used for the first time at the end of the nineteenth century to describe Carême.

Perhaps the chef's most lasting achievement is facetious, residing in my fulsome imagination: the remaking of Paris as a gargantuan banquet table filled with gimcrack cake-box buildings on marzipan plinths with sugary colonnades and meringue domes and éclair spires laid out on symmetrical boulevards, in other words, the rebuilding of the City of Light engineered by Napoléon III and Baron Georges-Eugène Haussmann. Who knows whether the tin-pot tyrant and his ham-fisted prefect really were guests at a Carême banquet or merely studied his cookbooks of tabletop architecture? Either way they did a hell of a job transforming Paris into a multiple-course cityscape.

Despite Carême's fame and his successful harking back to pre-Revolutionary times, food appreciation in Paris gradually shifted from royal palaces to restaurants and bourgeois homes. The entertainments of modern emperors and kings were passé. Dyspepsia dogged Napoléon, who ate fast and disdained gourmandizing. Louis XVIII may have been a throwback glutton but he lacked charisma and absolutist authority. His kid brother Charles X was a nonentity ousted after only four years. Louis Philippe, the human bowling pin, reincarnated his forebear, the Regent Philippe d'Orléans, but times had changed and flamboyant piggery seemed grotesque not grandiose. Wily, horny Napoléon III preferred his mistresses to even the most sumptuous meal, using food as a means to stun rich backers and tame the starving masses. By the time the Third French Republic arrived in 1870 the modern Parisian love affair with food and wine was in full swing. Swap out the décor, clothing, and carriages and in myriad ways it continues to this day, sometimes in the same venues.

THE HOLY HOG

Imagine a chapel in one of the greatest flamboyant Gothic temples in Paris. The notes of Couperin or Lully dance from a giant pipe organ above the nave, jostling dusty motes in a fandango of orange, red, and blue light. Sun slants through a tall stained-glass window, picking out the figures of Saint Anthony and his pig, and Saint André, patron of pork butchers, caterers, and charcuterie makers. Overhead, an heirloom porker emblazoned on a regal shield is framed by laurels and the words "Corporation de la Charcuterie." On the lower left, a whole dressed hog hangs from the smoke-blacked rafters and a happy peasant cooks in an Ancien Régime–style fireplace. It's winter. The peasant is thankful. Blessed be the Charcuterie! To the far right, a proud pork artisan wrapped in the elaborately knotted apron of his trade presents a chef d'oeuvre of charcuterie to a lordly looking master in robes, a cross dangling around his neck.

Is this another jaunt into fantasyland? No: The Chapel of the Corporation of the Charcuterie—a guild—is near the apse in the monumental church of Saint-Eustache on the Right Bank in central Paris at Les Halles, a ten-minute walk northeast from the Palais-Royal. Nowadays the church faces the outsized new "canopy" of the rebuilt former central marketplace, the great, greasy guts of Paris made famous by Émile Zola, a "gigantic modern machine, some engine, some caldron for the supply of a whole people, some colossal belly, bolted and riveted, built up of wood and glass and iron."

The new glass and steel "canopy" at Les Halles is bloodless and cold in comparison. It looks to me like a Jurassic-era manta ray made by Tupperware—a catastrophically poor post-postmodern perversion of Chardin's *The Skate*. True to the gritty reality of Zola's day, the stench of fries, burgers, and sugary grease escaping from the skate's gaping maw is nauseating 24/7. This is not a propitious setting for the new hoping-to-be trendy Restaurant Champeaux where Alain Ducasse is a consultant and the prices bar entry.

A few football fields west of the skate, quiet reigns year-round inside the stratospheric nave of Saint-Eustache—until thousands of pork-loving faithful pack in on the third Sunday of November to attend the annual charcuterie mass, held here since the days of Louis XIV. Speaking of the Sun King, the elaborately carved tomb of his minister Colbert is only a few chapels away from the shrine of the holy hog. The church is a must-see, a savory historical hodgepodge. Here Richelieu, Molière, and Madame de Pompadour were baptized and the bereft Louis XIV bid farewell to his deceased mother, Anne of Austria, beloved of Mazarin. Coincidentally all were enthusiastic eaters of pork and boosters of *la cuisine française*.

Built for François I starting in 1532, Saint-Eustache originally faced Paris' ragtag medieval market district and its shingle-covered La Halle. The famous ironwork-and-glass complex Les Halles designed by Victor Baltard for Napoléon III came later, in 1853, and survived a mere 116 years, long enough for Zola to immortalize it and for a thousand others to bewail its passing to this day and probably until kingdom come.

Holy or secular, no matter how you dice it charcuterie is sacred in Paris. *Chair cuiterie*—"flesh cookery"—was the fifteenth-century name given to a Parisian guild that had been around since at least the twelfth century, when the crusader king Philip Augustus created Paris' market district. No, *ma chérie,* it was not *chère cuiterie* as some suggest—that would be *bonne chère* cannibalism of the kind Grimod, and, coincidentally, Balzac favored, the metaphorical devouring of women.

I long wondered why the charcuterie guild's chapel was in Saint-Eustache and not in the much older church of Saint-Jacques-de-la-Boucherie a few blocks southeast. Saint-Jacques presided over Paris' slaughtering and butchering area, *la boucherie,* from the twelfth century onward. Though they share patron saints, butchers of "raw flesh" and charcuterie "cookers of pork" have always belonged to rival corporations. Saint-Jacques, i.e., Saint James, patron of pilgrims, wanted nothing to do with porkers—sea scallops were his specialty. Predictably enough, the pilgrimage church of Saint-Jacques was demolished during the Revolution. But its statue-studded Gothic tower still stands in a park on the rue de Rivoli, a Paris landmark.

The streets, alleys, and squares between the Saint-Jacques Tower and church of Saint-Eustache once teemed with food and wine retail businesses, taverns, inns, cabarets, estaminets, and restaurants; streets scented by blood and guts, rotting fish and produce, and overrun by rats. Some streets still are. Exiled to suburban Rungis in 1969, now almost fifty years later the memory of Les Halles is fading. One telling survivor is Auroze, a pest-control specialist founded in 1872. The ghoulish window displays feature creepy-crawlies and desiccated rats from Les Halles trapped in 1925.

It wasn't just rats that scrambled when the markets closed. A haunting work of pop art by sculptor Raymond Mason in the chapel of the Pilgrims of Emmaus at Saint-Eustache commemorates the exodus of greengrocers, butchers, caterers, cheese and fishmongers, and the members of a dozen other food-related guilds and corporations. In Mason's tableau they push pop art vegetable carts or heft and haul their pop art delicacies, tragedy writ in their expressions. The livelihoods of about 300,000 Parisians were upended. But what if the central market had stayed? Chaos guaranteed: tangled traffic, noise, a sanitation nightmare 24/7/365. Why the striking Baltard pavilions weren't repurposed is a question answerable in three words: real-estate speculation.

The demo job wound up in 1972. By the time I hit Paris for the first time in 1976, Les Halles was a yawning seven-story deep hole. Once movie director Marco Ferreri had finished filming *Don't Touch the White Woman!*, his farcical spaghetti western starring Catherine Deneuve and Marcello Mastroianni, the hole was filled with France's busiest underground commuter train and Métro station and a multilevel shopping center so ugly and badly built it was demolished and replaced by the giant Tupperware canopy inaugurated in spring 2016. Boy, oh boy, do I love skate with black butter and capers, but I do not love the graceless seven-thousand-ton skate canopy.

There are times when you have to wonder whether Les Halles has been hit by a neutron bomb engineered to annihilate the authentic and useful, leaving behind a wasteland of faux, pseudo, neo, and retro franchises where frenzied commuters, dazed tourists, and pimply suburbanites feed on trans fats and other toxic substances.

With their florescent halos around their heads, the secular saints of the Pantheon of Gourmandizing, what would Brillat-Savarin and Grimod de la Reynière—not to mention Zola or Balzac—make of the district today? The jury is out. Leaving aside the dispersed central market of centuries past, I'm not sure how many outstanding places to dine there were in the neighborhood 150 years ago. Soup kitchens and taverns were everywhere and a scattering of higher-end spots. Then as now you had to cast wide to find excellence. The great gourmands of yore might surprise a modern wanderer and rejoice in sampling the area's restaurants deserving their business.

For instance, a block east from the Saint-Jacques Tower since 1912, the luxury bistro Benoit has been a neighborhood magnet for the well-to-do. The plush, comfy décor, woodwork, etched glass and private upstairs dining room are unchanged; the prices have always flirted with outrageousness, and the service sometimes seems affably out of step with the century. Voltaire might groan at the Michelin-starred *ancienne* nouvelle cuisine, but Louis XV, Grimod, and Brillat-Savarin (and Hugo, Balzac, and Flaubert) would smack their lips. The casserole of sautéed sweetbreads, cockscombs, cockerel kidneys, foie gras, and truffle-infused jus is the kind of dish Grimod's granddad might choke on in ecstasy.

Who eats at Benoit and are they fit to judge food? That's what Grimod would ask and it's the eternal question: for great cooking to thrive, discerning palates are required. Here you find the usual Ducasse crowd, i.e., French is also spoken. And if the décor looks strangely familiar, maybe it's because you've already been to a Ducasse ersatz Benoit in New York or Tokyo.

Upstairs, a painted panel shows the great chef—though he hobnobs with Louis XIV at Versailles he has not yet mastered ubiquity and time travel. Perhaps one day a live broadcast hologram of Ducasse will animate his ever-expanding Paris properties, among them Allard, Aux Lyonnais, Rech, Le Jules Verne, Le Meurice, and the Plaza Athénée. Allard and Aux Lyonnais are better since he took over, if you ask me; ditto Le Jules Verne. So is he a savior or predator? Maybe neither: try "businessman." Add in other locations around France starting with Versailles, then fold in Asia and America, and Ducasse far outdoes Escoffier as the French global gastronomic icon. That would be reason enough for him to rally the UNESCO troops.

West of the Chapel of Charcuterie is the green shop front of E. Dehillerin founded in 1820, the most famous and labyrinthine of several kitchen supply emporiums still operating in the area. The window displays on rue Coquillière—where shellfish were once sold—glint with copper pots. A few professionals still give it their custom.

Half a block away is Au Pied de Cochon, a temple to neon-lit piggery open 24/7 since 1947 and outwardly unchanged: think vintage diner-deli with fresh shellfish and oysters tossed in. Nowadays as with many other historic properties in Paris, it's a corporate franchise. The house specialties are best appreciated when the whistle is wet and the taste buds dormant: "the Temptation of Saint-Antoine" is the breaded and fried tail, ear, snout, and trotter of hog, served with caloric sauce Béarnaise and fries. As if Saint Anthony could be tempted to devour his pig—it's hideously irreligious, right up Grimod's alley.

For another session of Gastronomy 101, head due south across the cement "gardens" of Les Halles to La Tour de Montlhéry-Chez Denise, a pre-exodus holdover certified free of Parisians other than the occasional peripheral table of nostalgic wizened boomers. If you're into red-check napkins and shouting while noshing cheek by jowl at what feels like an endless table, served by central-casting Parisian waiters, and if you'd like to savor the chunky *ancienne* nouvelle "haricot" of lamb featured at Louis XV's Château de Choisy in September 1755, this is the place. Talk about perennials: His Highness—and Grimod and Brillat-Savarin—would love the menu and wouldn't balk at the outlandish prices.

The liveliest remnant of the old central market district lies on and around rue Montorgueil and rue de Montmartre north of Saint-Eustache. Before setting out to explore it, I suggest you embrace syncretism, read some Balzac, Flaubert, Dumas, and Maupassant, and maybe some *luxe-calme-et-volupté* stuff from Baudelaire, too—*La Fanfarlo* or *Le Spleen de Paris*—then reread those early chapters of Zola's *The Belly of Paris* you know by heart. Sure, the novel is overwritten like most of Zola's books but the photographic minutiae are compelling. The bacon fat and onions, the pig blood and fish, the overripe cheeses, the hunger and yearning of the underfed and unloved etch every page. The action swirls in slow-motion around the Pointe Saint-Eustache, the triangular tip of the church marking the fork of rues Montorgueil and Montmartre. This was one of the great gourmand stamping grounds of yore.

THE BELLY OF ZOLA

In 1867, years before he cooked up the gritty, gutsy novel, the undiscovered Zola called Les Halles "the great daily orgy of Paris" where before dawn, butchers readied the city's "quotidian attack of indigestion." Poetry and naturalistic squalor played cat's cradle in the warren of streets then as now.

By Zola's heyday during the Second Empire and early Third Republic, the bounty of France reached Paris as never before. Up to a thousand different types of vegetables flooded markets compared to fewer than a hundred today. Drovers still herded their cattle and sheep into the city, and truck farmers in the outer arrondissements and suburbs like the heroes of *The Belly of Paris* filled the capital daily with super-fresh greens, Montreuil pears, grapes and wine from Argenteuil and Suresnes, and fresh fish and crayfish from the Seine, Marne, and Oise. "Locally grown" meant just that, though prized foodstuffs also came from farther afield then as now, by rail and riverboat.

Rue Montorgueil and rue de Montmartre were lined, Zola says, by "tempting-looking grocery stores and restaurants wafting appetizing odors with glorious displays of game and poultry, and shops selling conserves, open kegs by their doors overflowing with yellow sauerkraut looking like old lacework."

Subtract the kegs and the lacework and today you'll find the other items on Zola's list—plus great pastries, chocolates, fine wines, foie gras, truffles, herbs and spices, and cooking tools galore. Astonishingly one pastry shop and two of the restaurants frequented by Zola—and others who wrote enticingly about food, drink, and dining in centuries past—are still in business.

Rally your favorite French literary ghosts and rewind to 1832 when famed restaurant L'Escargot Montorgueil served its first gastropod, a native snail no doubt for unlike now there was no shortage of snails then. Grimod de la Reynière was still alive in 1832, playing with his piglets and may well have dined at L'Escargot perhaps sharing a table with Alexandre Dumas. That's about when they met. From the scarlet velvet banquets downstairs, the restaurant's snail-shell staircase spirals up to the Sarah Bernhardt salon. Did

Victor Hugo really seduce her here, under the painted ceiling? Probably not, but she was one of the dirty old genius's last amorous conquests. The restorative—not to say aphrodisiac—properties of snails and frog legs were well-known back then: Carême prescribed a pick-me-up bouillon made from them.

Would the adulterous pair have noticed whether the snails and frog legs had French passports or were imports from Poland, Turkey, or Indonesia? Nearly all escargots and *cuisses de grenouille* in France are non-natives today. Live specimens are flown in on jumbo jets and "French-ified" for six weeks in pens or ponds before being shipped to better restaurants. The microwave class of Paris eatery serves frozen snails and frog legs direct from freezer cases filled at the ends of the earth.

The giant golden snail on L'Escargot's sign was regilded a few years back and the place's current owners have regilded the reputation. Among other initiatives they farm their own salmon and have tapped into the Millennial-bobo markets by serving snacks and a limited menu throughout the day—a novel approach to dining pioneered by the early Paris restaurants of the 1700s and perfected in New York delis a century ago.

A few blocks north of L'Escargot, the street's other celebrated restaurant, founded in its first iteration in 1804, is Le Rocher de Cancale, where Grimod held tasting juries in 1809. It thrives albeit in an 1846 reiteration, created when Le Petit Rocher de Cancale outlived the original Rocher de Cancale and took its name. Easy to recognize, the restaurant's elaborate pastel-blue-and-white façade is encrusted with carved wooden lumps depicting oysters clinging to rocks. Nowadays this is a super-bobo hangout with fresh seafood and could-be-anywhere cooking. Its prized outdoor terrace is masked by a blanket of tobacco smog and populated by the requisite preening, smoldering cyborgs who've colonized the neighborhood.

The original Rocher was a grand gourmet institution founded by Alexis Baleine, the oyster's worst enemy. Baleine caused millions of bivalves to be massacred, serving them fresh year-round even in months without an "r" for the first time since the Roman Empire. Not even Louis XIV had done better.

Climb upstairs to the dining room to see the faded, stained wall paintings from 1846 by Paul Gavarni showing, among other scenes, a ravenous diner with a wine bottle, Grimod's cousin, by the looks of him. Sit down, order a bottle and a filet of sole, and squint, imagining the Rocher de Cancale two hundred years ago. Its vast menu lists ten lamb or mutton entrées, seventeen (for Grimod's sake?) of veal, eleven of beef, and twenty-two of poultry, twenty-seven entremets, and thirty desserts. The myth is they were all available daily, like the endless menus of microwave cooks today. The reality is, in all Paris' early restaurants a limited selection was served. Still, the bounty was impressive.

Poster by Alphonse Farcy advertising Eugène Briffault's Paris à table, *1846, illustrated by Bertall*

In his engrossing, whimsically illustrated 1846 *Paris à table,* Eugène Briffault recalled the "glory of the Rocher de Cancale whose perfections were such and where the quality of the food and wines was such that even the most opulent of private tables could not surpass them." So why maintain a costly kitchen staff? Prestige, a sign you'd made it to the top. But many Parisians didn't, even rich, successful Parisians, either to economize or to keep their opulence below the radar. Riots, revolts, and revolutions were regular features of Paris life in the 1800s and a flashy Ancien Régime lifestyle could be risky. This was just one of many reasons restaurants were so popular among the rich.

Curiously, Briffault's three-tier ranking system for restaurants, with "faultless" at the top for the Rocher de Cancale and others, feels like a visionary precursor to the three-tiered Michelin star system instituted nearly a century later.

With its faultless, unsurpassable food and service no wonder Balzac—when flush and eating—was a regular guest at the Rocher, inviting fellow greats like Victor Hugo to sup with him. It's hard to exaggerate the importance even today of Balzac's adoration of food: like Hugo he was and is a national hero and therefore a role model. As Jean Cocteau said a century after the novelist's death, Paris "keeps watch from her towers and, with her sewers, digests the monstrous nourishment described by Balzac, from which she draws her strength and her enchantment."

A barrel on legs with a marble column for a neck and a bull's shaggy head, Balzac binged between deadlines, in the brief intervals between his hundred-plus novels. A worthy heir of the Ancien Régime, he was capable in one sitting of ingesting an entire goose slathered with sauce plus multiple meat dishes (also saucy), vegetables, and dessert—washed down with three or four bottles of Vouvray, his favorite wine.

The Balzac binge pendulum swung the other way, too. When on deadline, he wrote on average fifteen hours a day, week in week out, subsisting off fifty or so cups per diem of industrial-strength coffee, piles of pears and pounds of grapes, congealed cold cuts and other potentially toxic snacks—shocking behavior for a son of the bourgeoisie.

Everything about Balzac was shocking, outsized, bizarre, and compellingly noir. That's why he's as popular today in Paris as ever. His quintessentially Parisian characters were misers, pikers, spendthrifts, dysfunctional bourgeois, or transplanted hayseeds, peasants forced into the big, bad city—real, live, neurotic people nearly all of them sharing troubled relationships not only with money but also food and drink. Balzac himself was no gourmet, not even a gentleman gourmand. I'd call him an ecstatic, compulsive gorger and borderline glutton—except when it came to his coffee, pears, and wines. Then he became fanatical, a proto-food bore of galactic proportions.

CARNAL DELIGHTS

If Grimod raised gastronomy into the realm of the beaux arts, Brillat-Savarin transformed it into transcendental digestive philosophy, and Balzac put food eaten by flesh-and-blood Parisians into popular literature. He paraded a pair of his best-known characters across the Rocher's culinary stage: debauched, perverse Henri de Marsay, and the provincial Lucien de Rubempré, a naïve bourgeois resembling Balzac, bankrupted on his first day in Paris by dining at very expensive Véry.

Véry was the place everyone just *had* to experience, the Ducasse or Robuchon of its day. The Rocher was rougher-edged than Véry, with great food and atmosphere and less haute cachet, and it appears in four Balzac novels. Other restaurant scenes shot elsewhere crop up in something like three dozen of his books, all set in Paris, proof that by the 1830s and '40s—the reign of the bowling-pin "Citizen King" Louis Philippe—dining out had become a peculiarly Parisian passion.

Was Balzac, like Brillat-Savarin, borrowing material from Grimod de la Reynière? Balzac killed off one villain by having him choke to death on a pâté de foie gras, as Grimod's grandfather had choked and died in real life—a "counter-punishment" straight out of Dante. Similarly the novelist's cannibalistic urges for edible damsels seem lifted from the *Almanach des Gourmands*. Describing his fellow Frenchmen and -women as succulent roast geese or hams, ripe fruits, satiny soups, sturgeons, lobster claws, and avaricious oysters clinging to rocks, Balzac and his antiheroes are ready to gobble or be gobbled alive—what we'd call dog eat dog.

Always in debt and ravenous, Balzac also used one of Grimod's famous scrounger techniques, writing novelistic advertorials for his favorite restaurants, especially the Rocher de Cancale and Flicoteaux on Place de la Sorbonne. What better way to get special treatment and rates?

For both men the act of eating and the manner of entertaining reveal personality traits, social status, and sexual appetites, shining candlelight on the insatiability of Parisians, a theme later reflected in the class-conscious Zola.

Hunger and lust are twined, gourmandizing and winey bacchanalia sometimes supplanting sometimes stimulating adulterous pleasure or moral bankruptcy and financial ruin. It was this vintage frisson of aromatic decadence that I sensed forty years ago and it lingers deliciously in Parisian nostrils to this day.

Forget being Caput Mundi—if it wasn't already the world capital of gastronomy of the eighteenth century, Paris became *Stomacus Mundi* in the 1800s. "Unquestionably the place in the universe where you eat best," Grimod boasted, as if he'd gone intergalactic. Carême was more lyrical: "In our belle France we are served to our heart's desire by Providence: everything that constitutes fine eating is here at hand." Carême helped spawn contemporary French notions of destiny, mission, innate greatness, and God-given superiority.

Read the fine print about the city's putative golden age of dining as told in Balzac's novels and you realize the incidence of indigestion and lethal food poisoning today is much lower than it was then; the variety, quality, and freshness of the ingredients greater, and the number of fine restaurants multiplied severalfold. In Balzac's day there were about three thousand places to eat in town. There are over ten thousand now. Even if four in five were unworthy that would leave two thousand keepers out of which a thousand or several hundred are good to outstanding. What other city does better? "After Paris the city that has the most restaurants is San Francisco," wrote Alexandre Dumas in 1869, amused by the rats and cats on Chinese menus. By a per-capita reckoning that may still be the case. I was lucky to be born in one and have lived in the other most of my adult life.

Beyond the restaurant scene today Parisians still entertain loved ones at home in nineteenth-century Balzac style—outsiders are rarely invited. If they have the means, the *chère* can be very *bonne* indeed because skimping is an unforgivable no-no despite the notorious native penchant for parsimony. Every French gourmet knows Brillat-Savarin's dictum: "He who receives guests and makes no personal effort in the care of the meal he prepares for them is unworthy of having friends."

NILE CRUISE

Plenty of other savory and sweet temptations on or near rue Montorgueil beckon. Herd your literary ghosts half a block to Stohrer, an address they'll recognize, opened in 1730 by Marie Leszczynska's pastry chef. Marie was Louis XV's queen, daughter of King Stanislas of Poland. The father-daughter pair of gourmand Poles brought the baba to Paris, where rum was added, and Stohrer, though not exactly on the cutting edge these days, continues to make a mean baba. They also construct a spire-like, triple-tiered pièce montée of vertical éclairs—among their most successful period pastries—worthy of a Balzac feast or Carême's architectural fantasies.

The real house specialty is *puits d'amour,* a scandalous Louis XV–era tête-à-tête pastry adapted by Stohrer from Vincent La Chapelle's 1735 *ancienne* nouvelle cuisine cookbook. The name means "love well" for good reason: *puits d'amour* are pâte feuilletée orifices filled with unctuous, erotically suggestive vanilla-flavored pastry cream sealed on top with caramel, like a crème brûlée.

North of rue Montorgueil is unprepossessing rue du Nil as in Nile Street—nothing to do with nullity or void. Were they alive today on rue du Nil's single short block, you would find Grimod and Brillat-Savarin cruising like famished crocs plus the slavering gourmands Balzac, Dumas, Hugo, Flaubert, Zola, and Maupassant. It's bobo a-go-go, meaning the prices at the artisan coffee boutique, butcher's shop, sustainable fishmonger's, bakery, deli, wine bar, restaurant, and farm-to-table produce boutique are beyond stratospheric. So were the prices at Corcellet and Chevet in the nineteenth century and their contemporary equivalents Fauchon, Hédiard, La Grand Épicerie de Paris, Le Bon Marché, and Lafayette Gourmet, to name a few. Gourmandizing has rarely embraced egalitarianism.

The transformation of the rue du Nil from low-end ragbag to gastro ghetto started in the early 2010s with the return from America of enterprising Grégory Marchand, chef-owner of Frenchie, hailed for its modern classics. Brillat-Savarin loved his exile in America during the Terror and I'm confident he especially would enjoy the Reuben sandwiches at Marchand's deli. Given that it now takes months to get a table at Frenchie, the great physiologist of taste might have to settle for corned beef and pastrami on the hoof, or maybe a snack and a bottle at Marchand's wine bar.

PART NINE

Dessert:

Modern Times, Mid-1800s–Late 1900s

La Grande Taverne, Faubourg Montmartre, 19th-century postcard

GRAND BOULEVARDIERS

From the days of Louis Philippe through the Belle Époque right up to World War I the *moderne* dining scene slowly migrated from the increasingly seedy Palais-Royal—the haunt of prostitutes—and roughshod rue Montorgueil to the broad streets and boulevards linking Place de la Concorde and the church of La Madeleine counterclockwise as far as Place de la République and Place de la Bastille—Paris' celebrated Grands Boulevards. During the Second Empire, Haussmann's redevelopment and slum clearance schemes pushed the comfort range of the bourgeoisie farther, to new and wider boulevards between the Opera, train stations, and churches of the 8th, 9th, and 10th arrondissements—and beyond. By the mid-1860s Paris had reached its current arrondissement count of twenty and its city limits: The 1970s Péripherique beltway marks the nineteenth-century no-man's-land outside the last ring of city walls.

In this modern, leafy, luminous part of town the fashionable boutiques, theaters, restaurants, and cafés thrived—Tortoni, La Maison Dorée, Café Riche, Vachette, Le Banquet d'Anacréon, Le Cadran Bleu, Café Anglais, Café Hardy, and Café de la Paix, which is still in business, as tony and fin-de-siècle as ever.

The first three faced each other across a corner on Boulevard des Italiens. Soon the lions of literature and their fictional characters were prowling the boulevards, transforming novel haunts into backdrops for drama, gourmandizing, and seduction. As Eugène Briffault reported, you had to be hardy to eat at Riche and rich to eat at Hardy. Balzac was both, but he sent his doppelgänger Lucien de Rubempré to dine at the Maison Dorée. Dumas moved his office to the Maison Dorée building to be near the kitchen, while

Café de la Paix, 19th-century postcard

the unlikely gastronome, Marcel Proust's hero Swann, swans in looking for Odette—not for madeleines dipped in linden blossom tea but as a prelude to passion. A closet carnivore, Proust loved the Boeuf Mode at Maison Dorée (though he preferred it homemade by Françoise, the life-transforming cook in *Le temps retrouvé*). Flaubert, Maupassant, and a hundred lesser scribes also got in on the act.

In the style of Beauvilliers, at these preternaturally Parisian institutions, the endless menus presented tabloid-sized versions of gastronomic philandering—infinite carnal variety, provided you could pay. More than ever, sex and food made amorous pretzels. As explorer-author Jacques Arago said of the Rocher de Cancale, "It's where you make a clandestine rendezvous with the mistress of an intimate friend or your neighbor's wife, because in this blessed restaurant the private rooms are quiet and dark, the waiters discreet and the proprietor blind and deaf to morality."

Connoisseurship and the excellence of the *chère* took a backseat to opulence except, perhaps, at Tortoni where star chef Urbain Dubois cooked for a time. In the social scheme of things, money provided a means to entertain and through entertainment came power and conquest, sexual and otherwise.

During the days of the Consulate, Napoléon I's second-in-command, Jean-Jacques-Régis de Cambacérès may have invented the Napoleonic Code, but he's more famous for echoing Montaigne with his quip that a country was "governed from the dining table." This still holds true in France. By the second half of the nineteenth century it wasn't only statecraft but day-to-day business, dealmaking, networking, adultery, prostitution, and lovemaking that played out around dinner tables in the homes and restaurants of the bourgeoisie, petite and haute.

The beat goes on: old venues have morphed, Frenchwomen are now alpha players, but fundamentally not a lot has changed in Paris since the 1800s. Food, wine, and entertaining remain the true religion in this most secular of republics.

One of my favorite literary descriptions of the boulevard dining scene is in Gustave Flaubert's sprawling coming-of-age novel *Sentimental Education*. Stout of body and mind, Flaubert enjoyed his food and drink as much as chasing skirts, notably of feisty proto-feminist poetess Louise Colet, his muse for nearly a decade. She wound up as Emma Bovary, but also inspired other characters including Rosanette in *Sentimental Education*. A well-to-do Norman landowner, Flaubert kept apartments in Paris and moved easily among the grand restaurants including the Café Anglais on rue Royale, observing rituals with cinematic sweep.

In the Café Anglais' luxurious private upstairs dining room the novel's increasingly debauched hero Frédéric, a transplanted country squire, is eager to be alone with Rosanette, alias the Maréchale, a courtesan he is pursuing. Encountering Cisy, a viscount, she invites him to join them, much to Frédéric's chagrin. A regular at the Café Anglais, like Flaubert, the Maréchale immediately orders oysters then peruses the menu, "stopping at every fantastic name." She's tempted by turban of rabbits à la Richelieu, pudding à la d'Orléans, and turbot à la Chambord, but winds up ordering a simple filet of beef, crayfish, truffles, a pineapple salad, and vanilla ices.

"That will do for now!" she exclaims. "Ah! I was forgetting! Bring me a sausage—sans garlic!"

Flaubert describes her as positively edible. "She nibbled at a pomegranate, her elbow resting on the table. The candles of the candelabrum in front of her flickered in the wind. The white light penetrated her skin with mother-of-pearl tones, gave a pink hue to her lids, and made her eyes glitter. The red color of the fruit blended with the purple of her lips, her thin nostrils dilated, and there was about her an air of insolence, intoxication, and recklessness that exasperated Frédéric yet filled his heart with wild desires . . ."

Mystification of the kind the Maréchale experienced was commonplace. By the mid-1800s the proliferation of "fantastic names" à la whatever had made it all but impossible for the uninitiated to know what they were ordering without lengthy explanation. As Eugène Briffault noted, "To truly feel at your ease in the restaurants of Paris you must understand the language of the waiters: their kitchen-French often sounds sarcastic or insulting." Briffualt recounts one restaurateur's failed attempt to attract attention by naming his specialties after waitresses or bestselling novels, "sprinkled with argot."

The free-for-all of nomenclature prompted one enterprising journalist to gather menus from leading Paris restaurants and translate them into comprehensible French. Someone ought to do that today with the haute and molecular crowd. Sauce names in particular were maddeningly confusing. Later authors deciphered recipes and names for chefs, waiters, and maître d's listing equivalents, redundancies, techniques, and ingredients. The first books of this kind I've come across are from the 1820s, but my favorite is Gabriel de Gonet and Alphonse Karr's delightful *Répertoire de cuisine simplifiée* from 1872. The best known was and remains *Le répertoire de la cuisine* by Théophile Gringoire and Louis Saulnier, published in 1914 and meant to be a companion to Auguste Escoffier's ciphered, monumental *L'Aide-Mémoire Culinaire* and *Le guide culinaire.*

Crib manuals still sell like hot crêpes in Paris because guess what? The confusion, opaqueness, and redundancy are worse than ever. In 2015 a new one came out, *La Cuisine de Référence.* Professionals everywhere have to master a guesstimated seven thousand à la something names. The poetic diction of haute and regional cuisine lends itself to obfuscation, serendipitous surprise, and double entendre.

Perhaps inspired by Grimod or Brillat-Savarin, Flaubert chose another famous boulevard hotspot, the appropriately named Café Riche, as the H.Q. of an epicurean society that he, Zola, and other "Booed Authors" founded in 1872. Flaubert's gourmet club wasn't the first. Like men's clubs in London,

Parisian dinner clubs and epicurean associations had been around since the 1700s. They boomed in the nineteenth century as the aristocratic .1 percenters grew to .5, then 1, then 2 percent of the population.

Some of the early gastronomic societies still thrive including the Club des Cent, founded in 1912. You'd think the genre was too fuddy-duddy for the twenty-first century, but think again. The wealthy, connected members of the Club des Cent, among others, are moons determining the tides of media, causing waves of TV, radio, magazine, and guidebook reporters to fling themselves upon worthy restaurants. Ducasse and Robuchon belong to the Club des Cent and so, too, do Paul Bocuse, Jean-Pierre Vigato of Apicius, and Bernard Pacaud of L'Ambroisie plus at least one prince and a former prime minister, actors, writers, politicians, and some of France's richest men. Like Flaubert's epicurean society it is definitely a man's club.

One unforgettable food-seduction scene in Guy de Maupassant's *Bel Ami* is also set on the boulevards at the city's most celebrated, expensive restaurant, Café Riche—the equivalent of a Michelin-starred temple today. Like the Café Anglais it disappeared long ago, though Au Petit Riche, a nineteenth-century holdover located a few blocks from the original, still does a roaring business—for good reason. A proud indie with décor from the 1880s, penguin-suited waiters, private dining rooms upstairs, and a *très riche* menu to match—buttery garlicky snails, whole fried whiting à la Colbert, cheese-breaded veal chops, calf's head with tart *sauce ravigote,* baba and *île flottante*—Au Petit Riche makes a perfect perch while you riffle the pages of *Bel Ami.*

Haute cuisine wasn't Guy de Maupassant's thing. Known in his day for quirky habits he famously lunched daily atop the Eiffel Tower, a monument he loathed, to avoid seeing it on the horizon. What he ordered isn't recorded. Given his propensity to skive off to Normandy feasting on country fare chez La Belle Ernestine, an *auberge* in Saint-Jouin serving tripe, omelets, roasted fish, or stew, Maupassant probably didn't indulge in the kind of haute Alain Ducasse surrogates serve nowadays at the tower's Michelin-starred Le Jules Verne. The prices are stratospheric, the view from on high as splendid as ever. Forget the tower: If Maupassant were alive today, he couldn't escape Ducasse whose ubiquitous marquee symbolizes syncretism from bistros to haute-haute and designer chocolates.

Meanwhile, in the nineteenth century far below in the unreconstructed parts of Paris among the poor and working classes, a different scene prevailed. As in earlier days, even in the mid or late 1800s, most Paris apartments weren't equipped with kitchens. Working people ate at soup kitchens, cheap cabarets, and *auberges*; or bought cooked food from caterers, rôtisseurs, bakers, and street hawkers of tripe, bouillon, and savory pastries. Jacques Arago explores this "other Paris" in his book *Comme on dîne à Paris* where "what is natural seems strange and what is strange is incredible."

Flaubert's *Sentimental Education* is set in the same city, taking place partly during the 1848 revolution, but if you want to understand where that revolution and the Commune revolt of 1871 came from—the population was reduced to eating horses, mules, dogs, cats, rats, and zoo animals—or why the ancestral hunger of the poor pulsed menacingly in a time of plenty, read Arago's bizarre food-and-travel book.

POTLUCK

"Way up near the summit of rue Rochechouart, to the left, down a blind alley," writes Arago setting the scene for his chapter titled "Fishing Dinner," "there's a big house with a courtyard and garden where the Auvergnats of Paris nest and perch . . ."

The roughshod Rochechouart neighborhood was home then to Auvergne provincials—the future masters of Paris' cafés and bistros. Nowadays it's where non-European immigrants live in firetrap tenements. In Arago's book, day laborers, rag-and-bone men, factory workers, clochards, and others at the bottom of the scale meet in the courtyard of what Arago calls "the Auvergnat's place" clutching five-centime pieces, the price of a fishing expedition. "A monstrous cauldron half filled with revolting bouillon holds shreds of beef and mutton or more likely, old milk cows and Billy goats, bubbling up to the greasy surface."

That's the unchanging menu of the last three generations, served starting at 5:00 A.M. at the Auvergnat's place. The "perpetual cauldron" has boiled away 24/7/365 for decades. Meat and liquid are added to top it up.

It's the cruel and unusual method of dispensing the boiled meat that fascinates Arago whose travels took him around the globe among Stone Age tribes and cannibals but never astonished him the way Paris could. Standing before the cauldron, diners pony up, armed with long three-pronged wooden forks. Plunging the forks in fast and deep, if they spear meat, they eat. If they don't, they pay and try again. And again, until they "catch a fish" or run out of centimes. Regulars who miss three times get the fourth or fifth try gratis, "charity" doled out to the desperate by fellow bottom-feeders.

Across town in the Marais—then a slum—in today's rue de l'Hôtel de Ville, Arago visits another bizarre eatery for a "syringe dinner." Judging by the sludge on the ground in the unpaved dining room "you'd think you're standing in the street on a rainy day," Arago says. Rounds cut out of a long wooden table hold tin basins roughly nailed down. Stools face the basins—the precursors of the perches in today's bobo joints and haute "ateliers," I wonder? The requisite "perpetual cauldron" bubbles away. Hefty waitresses wield a giant syringe sucking up bouillon to squirt into the basins. Those who don't pay watch their broth sucked up and squirted back into

Le bouillon Duval dans le parc du Champ-de-Mars.

Bouillon Duval at 1878 Paris World Fair, from L'Exposition de Paris by Adolphe Bitard, illustrator unknown

the cauldron. Then they're thrown out. Pay, and you get a hunk of stale bread to toss in your bouillon. Leaning over, you suck down the liquid and scarf the sops. The second course is boiled beef. The waitresses hand out forks "de-greased with their lips."

From the Sun King's table and the dining rooms of Palais-Royal roués, by the 1840s bouillon has become the restorative of the urban *misérables* soon to be portrayed by Victor Hugo.

Other "perpetual cauldrons" were more appetizing. Disappearing during the Second Empire they were missed by Alexandre Dumas, nostalgic for the excellence of broth derived from constant boiling, the "restaurant" beloved of kings, the quintessence of French cuisine without which there would be no French cuisine, he opined. Replacing these eateries were the famous Bouillon Duval, Paris' first restaurant chain, founded in 1855. The bouillon is dead; long live the Bouillon!

BUBBLE, BUBBLE

Two historic eateries in Paris whisk you at least partway back to the Gilded Age of boiled beef: Bouillon Chartier and Bouillon Racine.

Chartier is off the Grands Boulevards. Not much has changed since the 1890s at Chartier let alone since the 1970s or '80s when I was a regular. Since we've spent time among boulevardiers and had aperitifs at Chartier several hundred pages ago, we might happily hit the Latin Quarter, settling onto moleskin banquettes at Bouillon Racine, founded by the Chartier family in 1906. Gray-hairs remember the locale's nadir as the staff cafeteria for university professors—the Sorbonne is two blocks east. Reprivatized and restored in the mid-1990s, it's a Paris fixture again. Downstairs or up, the pistachio-green décor is dizzying, a registered Art Nouveau landmark. Wall-to-wall mirrors reflect forests of wavy wooden frames, mosaic or parquet floors, and enough curlicue ironwork to satisfy pretzel makers.

To be clear, you didn't and don't go to Paris' bouillons for gourmet cuisine, *au contraire*. Order something safe: pumpkin soup, rib-eye steak with fries, and maybe some crème brûlée, then imagine la petite bourgeoisie of a century ago flocking to the Racine and hundreds of other similar eateries designed to dazzle with décor and comfort with reasonably priced, reasonably good food and cheery *bonne chère*.

The first Bouillon was born in rue de la Coquillière near Les Halles' wholesale meat market, where master-butcher Pierre-Louis Duval, purveyor to Napoléon III, served broth to workers and local white collars at tiny tables packed side by side facing crowded banquettes. The boeuf was fresh, the premises clean and modern. This was the original fast food. Waiters and waitresses provided brisk service, wearing the white aprons of the butcher's guild. The outfit stuck, becoming iconic of France with penguin-like variations across Paris and the world, particularly in cafés, bistros, and brasseries.

Bouillon Duval in 1893, from Tableaux de Paris, *illustration by Pierre Vidal*

Within a generation, Duval and son had 8 then 33 Bouillons across town. By the early 1900s the Bouillon count had risen to 250-plus, including other knockoff chains like Duval's main rival, Chartier.

As you sup on beef at Bouillon Racine, enhanced by Monsieur Parmentier's spuds, you might mirthfully reflect that the world's first fast-food chains selling boeuf and sometimes fries were Parisian. And you might chortle over certain natives' righteous wrath concerning the burger joints proliferating across gastronomy's holy land. Is it envy, because the New World burger beat out boiled beef and bouillon?

Voting with the wallet, like laissez-faire economic theory, isn't a concept current Parisians seem comfortable with. Witness the surprising factoid that the world's second-biggest market for the golden arches is France. Those nearly 1,300 franchises aren't filled uniquely by traveling Yankees. The French inhale burgers and fries—at a leisurely pace, slowing the notion of "fast" and stretching French conceptions of "food." McDonald's restaurants are often physically hemmed by rival French or European chains and cheapo eateries. All told, in 2015, an estimated 1.1 billion hamburgers were served, worth well over $2 billion. Three-quarters of restaurants in France serve burgers today, and in eight out of ten of them, burgers are the hottest item. Le Dali brasserie at the five-star Hôtel Le Meurice raises the stakes and stats with its palatial luxe patties priced at about $45. As of fall 2016 the informal French consumer price index known as the "Jambon-Beurre"—ham and butter on a baguette—has been supplanted by the "Burger Index." There's only one food more popular in France than burgers and fries: pizza.

A final satisfying beefy bite at Bouillon Racine before your Louis XIV–era Massialot crème brûlée while you savor another historical nugget: Steak *frites* is a French national culinary ID card. "Steak like wine is a basic building block of France," wrote chain-smoking philosopher Roland Barthes in the mid-1950s, "it is a French possession (but encircled by invading American steaks) . . . fries are the alimentary symbol of being French."

Too bad Barthes, genuinely brilliant, couldn't get beyond the tragicomic boeuf chauvinism, failing to comment on the peerless French capacity for appropriation and revisionism. That traitorous old Vincent La Chapelle way back in 1735, in the service of Lord Chesterfield of England, had the effrontery to give a recipe for "beef steak *à l'anglaise*," among his boss's favorites, devoured since the days of Robin Hood. Translated from English into French the cookbook revolutionized French cuisine. But *bifteck* really only caught fire in France post-Waterloo thanks to the Brits (les Roast-beefs) or so Alexandre Dumas claimed. The French have been enthusiastic carnivores since antiquity, but steak or *steack* or *bifteck*, as you please, served with fried potatoes really only went viral in the 1900s thanks to pesky Brits and Doughboy *amerloques* who seemed strangely familiar with the combo long before fast food arrived. Citing legitimate fears of GMO feed and growth hormones used in American beef production, contemporary French cattle ranchers continue to lobby the government and European Union to get French beef declared a "cultural exception" worthy of UNESCO protection. The bottom line is always the bottom line.

As to *les* fries, Parmentier and Grimod mention potatoes fried in butter. But since the French were about the last nation to embrace *la pomme de terre*, who's to say spuds weren't being fried in oil or grease or butter in Germany, Spain, and Italy in the 1500s or in America in the 1600s or 1700s? Who, you ask? Why nativist Frenchmen of course to whom the fried potato belongs as a birthright.

BOIL, BROIL, BRAISE, AND BREW

Having digested your boeuf while waddling two blocks east to Balzar for some parachute reporting, or ridden back to the Marais to Bofinger, or perhaps having explored Montparnasse or Saint-Germain-des-Prés and just about any other neighborhood in Paris in search of *ancien* novelty, you are now ready to experience that other perennial mid-nineteenth-century Parisian invention, the brasserie. On the books it outdates the bistro and is nearly as ubiquitous.

What is the difference between a restaurant, bouillon, brasserie, and bistro, not to mention café, which can double as any of the four? There's no clear answer. In theory at a restaurant you eat multicourse sit-down meals served between specific hours on specific days, there's a printed menu, you have your own table draped with some kind of cloth, there are trained waiters or waitresses, and the main alcoholic beverage served is wine. Bouillons are few nowadays and have merged with restaurants and brasseries.

Again theoretically brasseries are open daily, continuously, also have a menu and private tables with tablecloths and a professional waitstaff, are large and spacious, but in addition to multicourse meals, offer single all-in-one specialties like *choucroute* or shellfish platters accompanied by as much beer as wine. "Brasserie" sounds brassy and most brasseries are. Because everything is politicized in Paris, brasseries are often associated with the bourgeoisie and the political right. Bistros and cafés are often indistinguishable, especially faux and retro bistros that are cafés serving unambitious selections of food. By definition, bistros and cafés have a counter, usually topped with zinc or tin and serve drinks not just food. Bistros don't always have menus or tablecloths or individual tables or professional service, focus more on wine than beer, and their opening hours and square footage vary crazily. Once upon a time they were working class and politically left of center.

To keep clients guessing, plenty of restaurants call themselves bistros and vice versa, some brasseries are little more than cafés and cafés can be anything. None of the traditional brasseries brew their own beer anymore. French bureaucrats group all establishments with category IV licenses—liquor licenses—serving food and alcohol in the same statistical category.

How to recognize an indie café? If they serve artisan or Italian coffee, that's a sign their lease and short-and-curly parts probably aren't held by the so-called Auvergnat mafia, a lobby or "mutual aid society" supplying four in five Paris cafés and constituted mainly by Frenchmen and -women originally from the Auvergne region of the Massif Central. For a century or more the Auvergnats, or Bougnats (as they're also called), have "helped" café, bistro, restaurant, and other food-and-beverage operators to start or finance their businesses, conveniently also supplying much of the factory farmed food and second-rate wine and all of the rough coffee and tea.

Explanations engender thirst and hunger. That's why I have just spun through the revolving door, taken a table dressed with starched white linen, ordered a platter of *choucroute* and sausages and a bottle of Alsatian Pinot Noir and am ready to roll again. If you guessed Brasserie Bofinger, you were right. In 1864 less than a decade after Duval founded the first Bouillon Duval an Alsatian named Frédéric Bofinger started serving braised *choucroute*, sausages, and homebrews in rue de la Bastille near the city's small Alsatian quarter where woodworkers thrived. Bofinger was possibly France's first brasserie.

The word derives from "braise" and "brew" as in beer, beergarden, and brewhouse. Historical precedence is claimed by rivals including the notorious La Mère Catherine on Montmartre, which also claims to be the first bistro and is, indisputably, the mother of all culinary tourist traps. Be my guest.

Bofinger is unquestionably the first to have served beer on tap. The current brass-railed, colorful, tiled Art Nouveau décor downstairs dates to 1919. Jean-Jacques Waltz alias Hansi, the Alsatian patriot and celebrated illustrator, created the "Hansel and Gretel" look upstairs circa 1930. The great Curnonsky, a regular, lunched with Hansi and others, many times, in this décor, but where did he not lunch many times on the way to growing triple chins and reaching nearly three hundred pounds?

Ironically, in 1981 Socialist President François Mitterrand, the man often blamed for initiating France's ongoing economic decline, bucked rightist brasserie trends and celebrated his election victory at Bofinger. Most guests prefer dining under the stained-glass cupola, but I find the acoustics challenging. Though Bofinger is a chain operation now, the same chef has been at his piano—i.e., the stovetop—for over a decade, a good sign.

Steaks and fries may be a French ID card, but toss a coin in Paris and if it doesn't strike a bistro or café, it will land on a brasserie. At Saint-Germain-des-Prés where the monks made fine wine and mustard a millennium ago another famous Alsatian brewhouse opened for business in 1880, Brasserie Lipp. Forty-odd years before Hemingway had his herring epiphany in the freshly redecorated Art Déco interior, the place was already a hive of politicians, power brokers, artists, and writers. Tourists were given rough treatment and still are. There's nothing like consistency. Upstairs is still "Siberia" for hayseeds and other undesirables with accents. The service was famously snarky—it still is—the food okay—ditto—and the attitude entertainingly pompous and arrogant, cultivated perhaps to justify the outlandish prices and nonsensical exclusivity. These advantages do not prevent the self-lacerating from throwing themselves with a *merci* on the mercy of Lipp.

Of the dozens of vintage Parisian faux brewhouses, I give my business to a select few, scattered, like Paris' modern gastronomic history, geographically with no apparent logic. They're proof that time stood still in the City of Light about 150 years ago. Wealth trickled and spread during the Second Empire and Belle Époque—the "empire without an emperor." With it so did dining across all genres in all neighborhoods. The sole common trait of vintage brasseries is their location on Haussmann-era or later boulevards.

Bonne chère lives on at evergreen upscale Le Stella, facing the spot where Victor Hugo lived in the tony 16th arrondissement. At Place de Clichy in the north, Wepler is an islet of well-worn cheer in a maelstrom of agitation. Brawny Zeyer presides over dull Alésia in the south of the city, and at self-admiring Montparnasse, there's Le Dôme, Le Select, La Rotonde, and La Coupole. They were interchangeable when founded in the 1890s or early 1900s and to an extent are today. Picasso, Hemingway, Soutine, Fitzgerald, Gershwin, Debussy, Stravinsky, Satie et al shunted back and forth, to and fro, following the sun, skirts, and temporary fashions and friendships.

Le Dôme was a bistro that morphed into a restaurant with excellent fish but still feels like a high-end brasserie. Le Select has always been a café-restaurant doubling as a clubby bar. The last two are full-blown brasseries defined not by the excellence of the *chère* but by décor, mood, and clientele. La Rotonde feels more Parisian than the others, for whatever that's worth. La Coupole, the latecomer, from 1927, is yawning, vast, an entertaining circus, its echoing dining room packed with foreigners and held aloft by columns painted, mostly in the late 1920s, by nearly twenty different starving, forgettable, and forgotten artists. For birthday parties, waiters assemble, the lights go out, and everyone sings "*Ça c'est Paris!*" Okay, if you say so.

There are scores of other likable, casual, unpretentious brasseries in town, an antidote to haute. Already mentioned, Le Grand Colbert, off rue Vivienne near the Palais-Royal, incorporates decorative tidbits from 1828 before it was a brasserie, and a good deal of detailing from 1900. It was handsomely restored in 1985 in time for my arrival. It doesn't evoke Jean-Baptiste Colbert, Louis XIV's stern minister, or Antonin Carême, who almost certainly passed through the premises before it was an eatery, but rather comic operas, farces, and bygone bordellos.

Of all Paris' antique brasseries, Julien, north of the Grands Boulevards, must have the most astonishing décor compacted into a smallish space. Claim a moleskin banquette or an armchair and prepare for vertigo. A registered landmark of Art Nouveau, purple-and-green grapevines and arbors tangle the stained-glass ceilings and ceramic wall tiles. There are wiggly frames around mirrors everywhere and blossom-like wall sconces, steel hat racks and coat racks, and colorful broken-tile floors. If the food seems an awful lot like the food at Bofinger, Balzar, La Coupole, and so forth, it's because they're all part of the same corporate group. An ungenerous critic might call these time capsules of culinary history "theme parks" of a peculiar style of Parisian gastronomy. That's true. Among many things, Paris is also Main Street France.

A final brassy salute goes to Le Train Bleu at the Gare de Lyon, not officially a brasserie but a buffet. Filling the station's broad upper floor it was the biggest eatery in town when it opened in 1901 a year late for the World's Fair and Paris Métro. Forget Art Nouveau, the revived Second Empire fin-de-siècle style showcases here with enough gilded plasterwork, brass racks, and crystal sconces to fill a museum of eclectic neo-baroque. The giant paintings of travel destinations allow you to remain in Paris while visiting the country—preferably over coffee or tea. The food is too banal to recommend.

THE ORIGINAL WINE BAR

Have you ever noticed that bistros, real gritty bistros and not faux neo-bistros or chic petit restaurants disguised with a "b," grow thickest and fastest on narrow shady streets, in neighborhoods better known for greasy garages, furniture repair shops, and plumbers' warehouses than for jewelry or haute couture? Bistros defy Napoléon III's Second Empire symmetry and sanitization. There's a reason. It's a conjoined binomial: industrialization-cum-Haussmannization.

Where the bobos and beautiful people now hang, the displaced peasants, provincials-become-factory workers, street sweepers, hucksters, conmen, muggers, and burglars of old Paris once roamed—the streets of Paris' unwashed blue-collar ring, damaged but not entirely destroyed during the Second Empire when the boulevards thrust gleaming blades into the city's medieval heart. Between the bleeding wounds and in the peripheral scar-zones bistros were born amid clouds of smoke, boozy vapors, and misery, their birthday some unknown point in the second half of the raucous nineteenth century. Until the bobos took over in the 1990s, bistros remained bastions of the poor on the pink side of the spectrum.

Like cafés, bistros are the soul, heart, stomach, and loins of the city, but they're recent by Paris standards. Grimod de la Reynière, Brillat-Savarin, Arago, and Briffault never mention them and neither does Balzac, Flaubert, or Dumas. Not a single cookbook, guidebook, traveler's memoir, or novel I've read from the early or mid-1800s includes the word "bistro" or anything remotely like it.

Etymologists say the first time anyone used "bistro" in print was in 1888 in the strangely fascinating *Souvenirs de la Petite et de la Grande Roquette,* a history of life in Paris' main prisons, by Abbé Moreau. It's an eye opening cure-all for retro nostalgia. *"La frangine travaille dans le faubourg et mange chez le bistro,"* says one inmate to another, meaning, "His sister works in the *faubourg* and eats at the wine merchant's." Bistro means "a seller of wine." Moreau provides the endnotes.

Prison lingo and Parisian argot remain incomprehensible to most French people and foreigners. Bistros were wine shops, some of them serving food, in blue-collar districts outside the Grands Boulevards though they could also have hidden in the historic core, in the cracks. Since the Grande Roquette prison was on rue de la Roquette in the outer 11th arrondissement the *faubourg* mentioned might have been Saint-Antoine, where the pig tripped up the prince in the 1100s and the revolutionaries of 1789 stormed down to the Bastille. The district has been lousy with bistros from the get-go, especially the Auvergne heartland of rue de Lappe, now a hipster theme park. Parisians think it engendered the genre.

Ironically, the original word doesn't include the useless silent "t" natives get belligerent about. "Bistro" is for foreigners, *"bistrot"* for Parisians. It's a vestige of *bistroquet* or *bistrotier,* argot for wine seller or bar, cabaret, café, or tavern keeper. No serious scholar believes the propaganda orchestrated by La Mère Catherine atop Montmartre. A plaque on the restaurant claims "bistro" was coined there when hurried Russian troops entering Paris during the ouster of Napoléon I in 1814 shouted *vistro* or suchlike indicating speed and demanding fast service. Other origin-myths from regional dialects have also been discarded.

The most convincing explanation for the post-Haussmann bistro boom is slum clearance, poverty, and alcoholism, the theme of Zola's best book, *L'Assommoir,* from 1870. Intramural Paris had nearly 3 million inhabitants then, most of them living without kitchens, heating, or bathrooms, and 11,500 warm, welcoming cabarets, estaminets, and *buvettes* with grub and facilities. Many morphed linguistically and today we'd call them cafés, bars, clubs, and bistros. Intramural Paris currently has 2.3 million residents and greater Paris five times that, with 10,000-plus liqueur licenses tallied by the national bureau of statistics, INSEE. Half the 10,000 are restaurants that fall under the *bistrot* rubric no matter what they are. No reliable stats exist for intramural Paris alone. *L'Assommoir* unfolds in such places but the b-word never appears as the novel's heroes and heroines keel over, blitzed by booze swilled to mitigate unbearable reality and avoid polluted drinking water—the origin of those green Wallace "temperance fountains" you see around town.

Something sinister beyond slum clearance also accounted for dangerous drinking and the bistro explosion: Phylloxera, alias *Daktulosphaira vitifoliae* or wine blight. This intrepid American aphid entered France in the 1860s devastating vineyards, driving up wine prices, and sending tens of thousands of ruined winegrowers and merchants to Paris seeking work. How to cheaply and conveniently replace lost wine? Answer: with moonshine, white lightning, concocted in Paris' boozers like Prohibition-era bathtub rye. Eventually winegrowers grafted French vines onto resistant American rootstock. Wine production soared but the cabarets and estaminets rebaptized bistros stayed.

BISTRO À GO-GO

Bistros are about life-enhancing experiences, so I'd skip the Zola, choose a favorite indie with good grub, and settle down to read upliftingly noir crime novels by Georges Simenon instead. I do this at one particular Simenon hangout in the Marais where author and inspector had the table with the brass plaque near the kitchen. Family run, down a dead-end alley in what was a slum but is now the most fashionable part of Paris, Le Gorille Blanc wasn't "the white gorilla" when Maigret dined there in the '50s and '60s. The old owners left their mortal coils. But the place still has rough stone walls and tiled floors, exposed timbers, and the requisite wooden tables and bistro chairs made to bruise your tailbone. Everything is still—or once again—homemade from scratch. I go for the thick chestnut soup or pureed sweet peas with arugula and powdered almonds followed by fresh-baked codfish or the daily roast or stew, though I suspect tough-guy Simenon-Maigret would prefer the chunky country pâté, peppery blood pudding, rustic fricasseed rabbit, crispy duck confit, or regulation steak—and lots of the inky house Bergerac.

Another vintage Marais bistro with solid food, atmosphere, and décor is Café des Musées north of Place des Vosges—there's an open kitchen in the bar area and no microwave on the premises.

Somewhere you haven't been before in these pages? A classic dog-eared corner café-bistro like lovable Les Caves de Bourgogne, near the fine, unsung food shops on and around rue Mouffetard in the 5th arrondissement? Not upscale enough? Then how about a revamped old-timer in the formerly cruddy Faubourg Saint-Antoine, fief of hipsters, bobos, and other professional poseurs: Le Chardenoux. It's the quintessential *ancien* neo-bistro and as such instructive and entertaining. Le Chardenoux calls itself a restaurant perhaps because Chef Cyril Lignac is Michelin-star trained, handsome, and ambitious. Diners swoon over him, the tile floors, zinc counter, and etched glass and tables from 1908. They also seem to enjoy Lignac's lightened neo-bistro fare: bittersweet strawberry relish on foie gras or heirloom Cantal pork with *saté* sauce that doesn't cost peanuts.

When feeling cannibalistic in the style of Grimod or Balzac, I go to a retro-revival bistro, Les Marches, on a dead-end alley near the Palais de Tokyo in the nouveau-riche 16th arrondissement. Beyond the décor, part of the draw for fashionista-foodistas is the young and beautiful staff with attitude and matching clientele. Les Marches serves self-styled "buttery bistro fare," the kind truck driver's supposedly ate: beef-cheek terrine with horseradish sauce or calf's kidneys served pinkish and sauced with creamy Dijon mustard. You're more likely to encounter guests with limos and Uber accounts than delivery trucks.

Across the Seine, passing the battlefields of Julius Caesar, the beau monde seems to dog your steps. Within blocks of each other are four vintage bistros equipped with banquettes, broken-tile floors, stars, starlets, journalists, and politicians in love with themselves: La Poule au Pot (winey *oeufs en meurette* and veal tenderloin or Henri IV's *poule au pot*), Le Petit Tonneau (another Simenon-Maigret upscale dive, with red-check tablecloths and classic blanquette), Café Constant (Michelin-starred Christian Constant's affordable retro address), and La Fontaine de Mars (Barack and Michelle loved everything about it, reportedly, and so do I, except the prices).

All are on or near rue Saint-Dominique. Along with rue de Grenelle, it's one of the best feeding areas in the classy 7th arrondissement with bakeries and pastry shops, butcher shops, and wine shops galore—like other longtime Paris market districts along rues Saint-Antoine and Montorgueil or Poncelet in the 17th (home to legendary Fromagerie Alléosse), des Martyrs in the 10th, and Mouffetard in the 5th arrondissement.

I could go on but won't because as mentioned above there are officially about five thousand bistros in the Paris area. It's also risky: faux, retro, and neo-bistros beloved of glossy magazine writers pop up and wizen like the proverbial champignons de Paris, which are Parisian only in name (think button or Portobello—same fungus). Included in the bistro count are the infinity of clever self-consciously cute variants with suffixes like *bistrôtisserie* and "gastrobistro," the progeny of the haute-trained, well-intentioned chef Yves Camdeborde who began the *bistronomie* movement at Le Comptoir de l'Odéon in 2004. Many will be ancient history by the time you finish reading this page. That's one reason to play oyster and anchor on the bedrock bistros. Their essential qualities it seems to me are authenticity, affordability, and good food, something enjoyable, roistering, or romantic, not rarefied or reverential.

RAREFIED AND REVERENTIAL

The literature, correspondence, and memoirs make clear that in the days when Grimod de la Reynière, Brillat-Savarin, Balzac, and company wined and dined in the city's best restaurants the prevailing mood was unstarched, irreverent joyfulness, even at palatial Beauvilliers or Véry. When did the grand daunting dining experience at the grand restaurants with the grand chefs and peacock grandee guests begin? That's hard to say. It certainly became the norm during the Second Empire when the tin-pot tyrant Napoléon III handed out titles of nobility the way his uncle Napoléon I had handed out Legion of Honour insignia declaring "it is with baubles that men are led."

Catering to the pretentious socialites, neo-aristos, and gilded oligarchs was a certain Auguste Escoffier. The young, driven Provençal, born in 1846 in Savoy near Nice, had a mother with the highly French maiden name of Civatte. It's comical to watch French hagiographers contort explaining how Escoffier's birthplace wasn't actually Italian but rather Savoy, forgetting the famous Savoyard patriot Giuseppe Garibaldi of Nice and the reality that the Savoy kings ruled what later became United Italy. Luckily for Italian cuisine, Escoffier was *not* Italian.

While still beardless, he wrote a book on the art of artificial flower arrangement and theorized about the necessity of poetic nomenclature for food—an indication of what was to come.

As if in a fairy tale, the humble Escoffier began sautéing his way to fame and fortune in the 1860s at the Petit Moulin Rouge in Paris in the swank Champs-Élysées neighborhood. He rose to become the gray eminence of haute, monsieur amour-propre, a punctilious dandy with imposing mustaches. Given that his life was about conquest, money, power, glitz, and glam and reached cruising speed in Paris' Golden Triangle near the Champs-Élysées, and since we've already been to Le Taillevent in these pages, why not reserve at the palatial Bristol or George V hotel for a meal? Escoffier patented the so-called cuisine de palace starting with the Grand in Monte Carlo then moving via the Savoy in London to the celebrated, some would say notorious, Paris Ritz, where (some scholars think) George Orwell slaved in the underground kitchen, a vision of Dante's *Inferno* and prequel to *1984*.

Coincidentally I was never a fan of the Ritz's stellar restaurant L'Espadon but have eaten divinely at the Bristol's Epicure and the George V's Le Cinq as a guest and on an expense account, respectively. Both may be heartily recommended in part because their ethereal cuisine, though infused with poetry and inspired by sculptural art, is otherwise utterly un-Escoffier.

Pick up a biography of Escoffier or a copy of his surprisingly dull memoirs, plus a paperback of Orwell's *Down and Out in Paris and London,* and leaf through, alternating, following with fingers and eyes the procession of jewel-like tiny bites airlifted to you by these establishments' winged waiters. Speaking of poetry and flower arrangements, you might also try historic Ledoyen, now Pavillon Ledoyen, Alléno Paris, to honor the self-effacing chef, Yannick Alléno. A former hunting lodge set in a leafy park on the Champs-Élysées it has perfectly preserved Second Empire décor and guests to match. Before Alléno took over, as mentioned, I witnessed sleeve dogs feeding surreptitiously here on foie gras, in the style of Elagabalus. And don't forget Pierre Gagnaire, a poet and philosopher of the haute-haute, famous for serving not mere food but "emotion." His eponymous, angularly modern luxury hostelry just happens to face the palatial address where Balzac died. I have had the honor to experience these two establishments under similar all-expense-paid circumstances and with similar reactions to the sophisticated, effete excellent culinary performance art. Once in a lifetime is plenty for me.

The sum total of the four's Michelin stars is twelve. The check will sting accordingly, a fitting tribute to Escoffier. Funny all four are within waddling distance of Grimod's family mansion and a mile or less from the modest apartment on Place Henri-Bergson where Maurice Sailland aka Bibendum or Curnonsky lived for decades.

If Escoffier had not existed, someone French would've had to invent him. A star was needed then as stars are needed now. Like Carême, Escoffier became the alpha rooster crowing the greatness, supremacy, and hegemony of French cuisine, herald of a nativist golden age. Escoffier was more Carême than Carême, a sauce sorcerer and master of aesthetics and décor, pomp and circumstance *à la française*. His boosters borrowed Carême's sobriquet "chef of kings and king of chefs," napping Escoffier with celebrative verbiage. Carême was an architect manqué, the impoverished autodidact who set the style for the elites of Europe and conveyed the Ancien Régime into the new. Escoffier was a sculptor manqué, the working-class provincial who became the tastemaker of the world's Gilded Age nouveaux, conveying Carême's revived Ancien Régime aesthetic and elitism into the twentieth and, battered and bleeding, the early twenty-first century. As a reward for his services to the motherland, Escoffier was made a Knight of the Legion of Honour, the first chef to be so distinguished, and he wrote the introduction to the first edition of the evergreen *Larousse gastronomique*—the official version of everything Franco-gastric. The stage was set for the arrival of the providential French super chefs of the last thirty years.

The many-sided Escoffier heritage is impressive, celebrated by among other things the Escoffier Foundation and the Museum of Culinary Art in his birthplace, Villeneuve-Loubet. Beyond transforming the opera diva Nellie Melba into a peachy dessert and writing a dozen perennial cookbooks, Escoffier also pioneered wine-pairing menus, perfected canned tomato sauce, and revived the antique or medieval flambé technique as a form of thrill-the-bourgeois-bread-and-circuses showmanship. It lives on in Paris at Le Taillevent and La Tour d'Argent, thriving in entertainment-starved provinces and in French circus-style restaurants worldwide.

Some say Escoffier's front-line experience as cook in the Franco-Prussian War of 1870 led him to reorganize specialized kitchen "brigades" and impose military chains of command, but this culinary management technique probably derives more from Taylorism, piecework, and the assembly lines of the factories of Escoffier's heyday. Wherever it came from, thanks to the great chef of kings, hierarchical assembly-line cooking became and remains the modus operandi of high-end, high-turnover restaurants everywhere.

Dare I say it? The unassailable godhead Auguste Escoffier and his five "mother sauces" actually caused Carême's already overly abundant sauce repertoire to be multiplied to infinity. If you've ever listened to a concerto with basso continuo, you have an aural notion of Escoffier's food—the same base note masking flavors, suffocating natural goodness, and following you from dish to overblown dish. That recognizably French *ancienne* haute is what emperors, kings, presidents, exchequers, and starlets adored then and now.

A merciless name-dropper and flatterer, Escoffier was the ideal man for his flimflam age and his teachings still find acolytes. The sauces have been lightened but the spirit remains. Might that be one of the many issues certain twenty-first-century eaters have with French cuisine and the French way of eating?

In retrospect, Escoffier was just possibly the worst thing that could happen to French cooking. By streamlining and systematizing while preserving its indigestible Ancien Régime, Carême-inspired pretentious Second Empire ways, he allowed it to swan unchallenged into the twentieth century on a sea of sauce and silly decoration. Tireless, talented, and prolific he may have been, but reading between the reverent lines of hagiographies it's also clear Escoffier was tyrannical and tough, cynical, smarmy, and disarmingly charming, the prototypical smug international superstar and missionary of French haute. He trained something like two thousand chefs to spread the gospel worldwide.

If alive today, Escoffier would probably militate for UNESCO and French government intervention to set the clock back to Paris Hegemony Time; he'd run palace restaurants and constellations of baby bistros, gourmet and sandwich or chocolate shops, slap his name on frozen foods and first-class airline menus, and sport a halo of Michelin stars. He died four years after the three-star rating was introduced in 1931, too soon to assemble a twinkling galaxy.

Incongruously, despite wealth and honors, Escoffier was crooked, the spiritual heir of Grimod de la Reynière, with lunch bells tied on. He and his main partner César Ritz confessed to fraud, but because they knew everyone everywhere, they managed to squelch the bad press. Few fans even now confront the shady chapters of a sainted life.

PRINCE VERSUS KING

It's time for fantasyland again: take a sip and a bite, imagine Laurel and Hardy transformed into Frenchmen, set them at each other's throats, then choose sides. Curnonsky leans over, pulls Escoffier by the white walrus moustache, flattens his toque, then flings a Peach Melba over the chef's shoulder into the dining room of the Ritz where Nellie Melba, a czar, and a field marshall are dining. Meanwhile the King of Chefs kicks Prince Curnonsky's massive shins and whacks his huge belly with a lethally heavy copy of *Le guide culinaire*. The outcome is a foregone conclusion: a draw.

Satisfying?

Definitely!

Possible?

No, absolutely not. Curnonsky, the gentle giant with brilliant blue eyes and a vulture-beak nose, was no bully. Twenty-five years younger and at least half a foot taller than dapper little Escoffier, he would not have roughed him up. Also, the Prince of Gastronomes probably liked Peach Melba, one of the King of Chefs' simplest and therefore perennial creations.

Metaphorically the kerfuffle did take place—via newspaper and magazine articles, books, comments made during interviews, and in letters. The Prince's personal feelings for the King are not well documented and vice versa, but their philosophical mutual antipathy is absolute. One negative detail tells all: Escoffier was not invited to join the Prince's Academy of Gastronomes and no chair was named for him. That honor was accorded instead to Escoffier's main rival, the jovial cookbook-writing engineer Henri Babinski better known as Ali Bab, author of the sprawling thousand-page *Gastronomie pratique*—coincidentally the first culinary bible Julia Child discovered in the late 1940s.

Opposites don't attract. Grasping, Escoffier was joyless, born without a funny bone, the slave-driving missionary of haute. A journalist, novelist, critic, and bon viveur, the jolly wastrel Maurice Sailland founded the French Academy of Humor and called himself "Curnonsky" for fun: *cur non* means "why

Restaurant Le Boeuf à la Mode, Curnonsky's kind of place, early 1900s postcard

not" in Latin, the "sky" was tacked on because things Slavic were the rage before the Bolshevik Revolution. The nom de plume is a question: "Why not adopt the name Sky?" He signed his first article as a junior reporter—about a Russian banquet—with the pseudonym "Prince Curnonsky" and never looked back. Curnonsky lived to regret it. He was no Stalinist *au contraire.* The nickname became an unshakable brand. Luckily for Curnonsky his other nickname was Bibendum: He came up with the moniker for Michelin.

Vain and venal, undereducated Escoffier resembled, envied, idolized, and mercilessly pilfered Monsieur Hauteur, chippy Antonin Carême. Curnonsky-Bibendum was anti-Carême, a highly cultivated, sensitive, slavish acolyte of his "master" Brillat-Savarin and lover of refined *cuisine bourgeoise.* Before and after *cuisine bourgeoise* he identified three other distinctly French cooking styles: *la grande cuisine* aka haute, regional cuisine aka terroir, and peasant or poor people's cuisine. A poet, Curnonsky penned verses under the lilacs on the terrace of Au Lapin Agile, the cabaret on Montmartre, as Escoffier kowtowed to no-account counts and imposed martial rule in his kitchens. The Prince's professional life was dedicated to the establishment of the academy Brillat-Savarin had envisioned, a French Academy of Gastronomy intended to use "reason" in the "worship" of the "cult of gastronomy elevated to religion" in the Classical sense of communality. Flanked by his best buddy, sidekick, novelist, and gluttonous fellow gastro-hack Marcel Rouff, Curnonsky created Brillat-Savarin's brainchild academy in 1930, so preserving for perpetuity the memory of the hallowed physiologist of taste. It's no coincidence Brillat-Savarin cheese received its name that same year. Curnonsky did better than Brillat-Savarin in the long run, with a dozen *à la* dishes named after him.

Mostly, though, Curnonsky detested the "Snobbery of anonymous cosmopolitan cuisine . . . and the fuddy-duddy flavors of that complicated, gimcrack cooking that tended to disguise tastes and smells and present under bizarre and pretentious names dishes where chemistry merges with prestidigitation."

This was a frontal attack on Escoffier and his remodeled *ancien* edible artworks. "Bizarre and pretentious," did you say? "Chemistry merging with prestidigitation?" Click refresh, remove "fuddy-duddy" replacing it with "dissonant" or "outlandish" and the jibe applies to the 32-karat creations of many of today's self-styled artists of haute and maestros of molecular.

CURNONSKY QUIPSTER EXTRAORDINAIRE

A follower of Brillat-Savarin, Curnonsky was famed for his wit and witticisms. Not all were entirely original. The eccentric pianist and professional bohemian Erik Satie said, "In art, I like simplicity, ditto with cooking." Curnonsky's most-quoted quip was "In cooking as in all other arts simplicity is the sign of perfection." Here are a few others.

"Cuisine is when things taste like what they are."

"With the best it's always difficult to do better but with the worst it's always easy to do worse."

"If the potage had been as hot as the wine, the wine as old as the chicken and the chicken as plump as the mistress of the house things would've been almost all right!"

". . . The reasonable practice of all excesses and the nonchalant abstention from all sports . . ."

"Paris may wear the crown of *grande cuisine* but the provinces hold the scepter."

To appreciate just how revolutionary was Curnonsky's mantra of simplicity, wander up to where the hoity 8th meets the toity 17th arrondissement in the neighborhood wrapped around the exquisite Parc Monceau and visit the astonishing Musée Nissim de Camondo and its miraculously intact, magnificent kitchen, pantry, and dining rooms from 1912.

The mansion is a citified, modernized replica of the Petit Trianon—in fact you could skip Versailles and come straight here. We don't have time to visit the suites of handsome rooms stuffed with authentic Louis-something antiques and six- or seven-figure artworks, the floorplan gorgeously and curvaceously unfolding across three floors with views over Paris' prettiest pocket-sized park. Just make sure to glance at the portrait of Louis Philippe alias Philippe Égalité in the cozy upstairs Blue Drawing Room, and the small oil showing naughty nibbles at a "flying table" supper, the portraitist eager to snack on his subject, in the master bedroom. The dining room used by the family and quality guests is another Petit Trianon replica, with a lovely Louis XVI–period wall fountain made for handwashing (remember how reluctant the French were to use forks?) and a fishing scene tapestry better than anything at Versailles today.

The kitchen, on the ground floor, is tiled top to bottom, even the ceiling. The stove is the size of a compact car, the oven a delivery truck, and their cast-iron blackness contrasts with the brilliance of a ton of polished copper pots. The dumbwaiter; maître d's office with proto-telephone, the white gloves, and step-'n'-fetch-it white lackey jacket; the bells and lights to summon the servants—all are here in perfect nick, ready to be revived by a contemporary oligarch. There's even a prototypical icebox (no, not a fridge, not yet) and an ozone water sterilizer to render polluted Paris water potable. Compared to the infernal kitchens of the Ritz this is *Paradiso*.

Close your eyes, imagine the heat, the smells, the noise, the bells ringing, and lights flashing—time to send up the Baron d'agneau de Pauillac aux Morilles and canards de Rouen à l'Archiduc. Now follow those Escoffier specialties and several dozen other monumental delicacies, all of them looking like the Paris Opera on platters, dig into the rich, creamy, meaty, saucy, floury, sweet lusciousness of it all and you'll understand why "simplicity" was a shocking bohemian notion when Curnonsky championed it. The *Titanic* hadn't sunk. The Great War hadn't come along upending the hierarchies in Europe. Revived by the arrivistes, the world of Louis and Marie-Antoinette, of emperors Napoléon I and III, lived on.

LARGER THAN

A gargantuan by the measure of his day Curnonsky-Bibendum stood over six feet tall, peaking at 277 pounds. He achieved these prodigious dimensions by Rabelaisian gourmandizing and abstention from exercise. Instead of walking, he drove—hundreds of thousands of miles. Instead of breaking a sweat, he wielded knives, forks, and spoons. Strangely for a gourmand he had no kitchen or dining room in his apartment and like Grimod and Brillat-Savarin, not to mention most distinguished food critics today, didn't know how to boil an egg, eating out twice daily, trying every spot in Paris before hitting the provinces. Amazingly two of his Paris favorites from the 1920s—La Tour d'Argent and Lapérouse—eagerly await your business today.

Curnonsky was a phenomenon of nature, another Louis XIV, the Man Who Ate France—and joyously invited others to follow, publishing nearly thirty food and travel books featuring the gastronomy of his native realm. Squint like the myopic Curnonsky and in your mind's eye see a Futurist Citroën, Marcel Rouff at the wheel burning up the tarmac at 35 mph, overloaded with human flesh, hams, and wheels of cheese.

The yearning for rural roots, terroir, and real, regional food was rife by the new century's early decades. Parisians were rushed, seeking to eat "fast and well," according to one menu Curnonsky spotted, "as if the two adverbs could be reconciled." He added, "Time does not respect anything done without him." Commentators of all stripes complained about the "bastardized, industrialized, muddled" cooking of Paris, the craziness of modern times, the decline of cuisine, the end of the three-hour lunch and siesta.

Broken clocks and purebred slow cuisine still thrived outside the big city. That's where the gastronauts headed. After Rouff's premature death from overeating, the grief-stricken Curnonsky halted the multivolume travel and cooking series they were writing together. But *Cuisine et Vins de France,* the magazine spin-off he founded in 1947, is still published and the same-name cookbook is a classic. No retrograde nostalgic, the Prince appreciated certain aspects of modernity—from the steam ovens and gas ranges to the greater freshness of fish and produce thanks to improved transportation. He especially loved the novel world of cars, comfy hotels, and mod cons. The first edition of what we now call the *Michelin Red Guide* appeared in 1900 its writ to identify gas stations, garages, beds without bedbugs, and eateries sans ptomaine or salmonella. The stars, luxury, and cultish nonsense came decades later. As France's culinary oracle, Curnonsky became a Michelin contributor and consultant. Proud of his culture without being jingoistic he also endorsed "exotic" cuisines notably Chinese. One forgotten fact is, Curnonsky only got into the gastro-journalism racket after a taste-bud-stimulating voyage to China.

All good things come to an end. The Prince popped off in the mid-1950s. I readily admit to kindred feelings and would have gladly broken a baguette with him.

Speaking of which, did anyone notice the bread at our table? The modern, crisp, porous baguette was probably first baked in Paris around the turn of the century, but got its name in 1919 or 1920, the Prince's heyday, a year or two before the strangely similar Wonder Bread was excogitated in America. By the time I first bit into a real Parisian baguette in 1976, the slender crispy long loaf was an industrially produced travesty shipped frozen (in dough form) then baked on site in *boulangeries* and guaranteed stale within an hour. How was I to know? I loved baguettes. Some things get better—when enough people in the know fight like hell to make changes.

I'm less sure about breaking bread with Marcel Rouff, a hero today to certain Frenchmen for his narcolepsy-inducing novel *La Vie et la Passion de*

Dodin-Bouffant, gourmet. This unveiled homage to Brillat-Savarin is based on an updated fictionalized version of the physiologist's life, its pages bathing France in a nostalgic buttery light. The book's most remarkable passages relate to Dodin Bouffant's travels in the "land of barbarians," i.e., Germany. A thoroughgoing culinary chauvinist Rouff boldly claimed the taste for gastronomy was "innate" in the French but absent from other "races," especially the Germans, English, and Americans. Like Curnonsky's silly nom de guerre, Rouff's claim stuck and still resonates with the resentful. There may have been some truth to the claim a century ago, but slippage in France and progress elsewhere has leveled the field. There's no time like the present to raise the level transnationally.

SOFT-POWER CUISINE

Promoters of the nouvelle cuisine of the 1970s onward have flayed Curnonsky and beat him with various sticks, citing his defense of old-fashioned bourgeois cooking and simplicity, and his rejection of haute and cosmopolitan novelty. The kind of food he liked, they argue, was toxic, made him fat and killed him. Balzac keeled over from coffee because he drank too much of it, but I'm not sure that's a reason to condemn coffee. Curnonsky gobbled antebellum delicacies, falling from a window to his death aged eighty after a life of extreme overindulgence, but that's no reason to condemn antebellum *cuisine bourgeoise.* Why not condemn the excess, not the coffee and cuisine, and marvel that anyone who led Curnonsky's life could reach eighty?

Living through exciting, scary times, witnessing upheavals in Europe and irreversible changes in France including the country's loss of its colonies and relegation to second-rate power, there's a reason gastronomy seemed a refuge, a haven of reassuring peace and plenty in the twentieth century. The First

World War was barely over when preparations for renewed hostilities began. Bizarrely the 1920s and '30s resemble the barbarian-encircled decadence of Rome and the heyday of Apicius. Strangely so does the Belle Époque, segueing from the end of the Second Empire, the disastrous Franco-Prussian War, and the Commune. Weirdly all these periods look a lot like the 1830s and '40s that followed the end of the Bourbon Restoration, and the First Empire that followed the failed Revolution of 1789–1799, and the Regency that followed the end of Louis XIV's long reign. And so forth ad infinitum backward and forward. Decline, decadence, the unknown, rapid change, the loss of political power, economic collapse—is there a pattern and does this sound anything like France in the 2000s and 2010s?

Rewind for two short paragraphs to the dark days of the interwar years because those years of folly and financial implosion and the years of humiliating Nazi Occupation and postwar declassification that followed, shed light on the French and their food today.

As Mussolini takes over Italy and Fascism spreads in Spain and Germany, Hemingway discovers herrings in olive oil at Brasserie Lipp, Parisians bake the first baguette, the Twenties Roar, Curnonsky and Rouff devour Paris then take to the road to rhapsodize regional cuisines. In 1927 three thousand chefs in white toques dub Curnonsky "Prince des Gastronomes," the Prince founds the Académie des Gastronomes three years later and, the year Hitler takes power, 1933, creates the Académie du Vin de France. The first Michelin stars twinkle. Food, wine, and song lighten the lightless Great Depression and mute the drumbeat of a coming, unwinnable war.

Meanwhile the French, feeling threatened by Germany, begin building the Maginot Line. The inward-looking mania for native gastronomy and deep-navel exploration produce the first *Larousse gastronomique* and Sartre's manifesto of existentialism, *La Nausée,* in the same banner year, 1938, the year Hitler annexes Austria in the Anschluss. The nasty new world won't go away, the Maginot Line won't hold, Hitler gazes at the Eiffel Tower from the Trocadéro Esplanade, feasting on French vegetables and sipping French Champagne. Parisians taste defeat, degradation, Collaborationism, and ancestral hunger again. The postwar period is a succession of inglorious retreats and shadowboxing matches in the shade cast by the towering new hamburger-fueled barbarian superpower. Why be surprised when French food and the French language are fashioned into soft-power shields and cultural identity cards? Why smirk when the myths of past greatness and the longing for simple joys tug in one direction and the thirst for novelty and a future unbound tug in another?

PART TEN

Digestif:
Neo-Retro-Post-Postmodern
Nouvelle d'Auteur, 1970s–the Present

PASSÉ PRESENT

Strange to say, as the city reached its natural intramural limit during the Second Empire, halted by the bastions of Adolphe Thiers that now mark the beltway, the last growth of the oyster shell, French cuisine also reached a gastronomic frontier broken only by the advent of the new nouvelle cuisine of the late 1960s and '70s.

Curnonsky, Rouff, Raymond Oliver, and the other great gourmets, gourmands, and gluttons of the first half of the twentieth century looked backward, glorifying the past the way their early nineteenth-century forebears glorified Louis XIV, the Regency, and the reign of Louis XV. The Ancient Romans had a name for such a person: *laudator temporis acti,* one who praises the past. *Passéisme* was, has always been, is, and probably will always be a distinguishing feature of Paris and Parisians. The nineteenth century and its cooking live on despite the savaging they've received over the last forty-five years. Actually they've been improved by the savaging, much of it deserved. Today's new-old cooking is doubtless tastier, more healthful, and delicious than it was in its heavy-handed heyday.

And why shouldn't the past live on? Without it there's no present and no future, not in France. Paris is not New York. I've never understood why certain people want to turn an orange into an apple—the Big Apple.

I'm also not sure how many serious Parisian food lovers are passionate about molecular or the ephemeral haute *cuisine d'auteur* de rigueur in the Michelin multiple-starred temples of gastronomic hauteur in Paris and elsewhere. Nowadays most of them are filled by migratory Yanks, Brits, Japanese, Chinese, and Russians—not many French. Like post-neo-academism that renders literature sterile or the institutionalized avant-garde that nearly killed the fine arts last century, *cuisine d'auteur* has become surprisingly predictable and global despite being artistic, extremely technical and difficult, and unique to each practitioner. It's unreproducible by even the most talented home-cook, rarely comforting, and often discomforting and disconcerting—but so was Cubism a century ago. Acolytes see these as positives, challenges for cool initiates, the new dining elite possessed of artistic sensibilities.

Are they elite? Foodistas and fashionistas seem to blur and merge when they gush about the emperor's new nouvelle cooking or the latest clothing trend. "Hoodwink," "smoke and mirrors," "flimflam," "snake oil," "play with your food," "shock and thrill the bobos," and other unkind expressions are sometimes used by the uninitiated in the French mainstream press to describe the current style of infantilized top-end restaurant dining. History is a great foil, reminding anyone who studies it that poseurs and pseuds are nothing new. By other names, foodistas and fashionistas have been part of the Paris scene since at least the seventeenth century.

DECLINE AND FALL

Nothing comes from nowhere. Nouvelle cuisine got started in the late 1960s as college students and factory workers were uprooting cobbles and upending the world. It took off like the supersonic Concorde in the mid-1970s, ironically just as the French economy was ending its three-decade postwar bull market. New imported foods and revolutionary cooking technologies were also coming on tap: blenders, mixers, processors, juicers, microwaves, nonreactive pans, frozen foods, and that other genial invention of industrial food preservers, sous vide. Liberated Frenchwomen were casting off their aprons and going to work by the millions, and the first wave of global fast food and convenience crap started hitting Gallic shores. The term *malbouffe*—lousy, unwholesome junky food—was coined over forty years ago by French writer Joël de Rosnay.

And along came Gault & Millau . . .

THE TEN COMMANDMENTS OF GAULT & MILLAU
OR THE MANIFESTO OF NOUVELLE

1. Thou Shalt Not Overcook
2. Thou Shalt Use Fresh, High-Quality Ingredients
3. Thou Shalt Lighten Thine Menu
4. Thou Shalt Not Be a Dogmatic Modernist
5. Thou Shalt However Try New Techniques and Technologies
6. Thou Shalt Avoid Marinades, Long-Hanging of Meats, and Fermentations
7. Thou Shalt Eliminate Heavy Sauces
8. Thou Shalt Not Ignore Dietetics
9. Thou Shalt Not Disguise Thine Foods
10. Thou Shalt Be Inventive

The televangelists of nouvelle included the chameleon Paul Bocuse, made Knight of the Legion of Honour in 1975, Michel Guérard, the Troisgros brothers, Alain Chapel, Alain Senderens, Joël Robuchon, Guy Savoy, Marc Veyrat, Pierre Gagnaire, Michel Rostang, and others. All were hailed by Gault & Millau and then Michelin, which saw the way the tires of novelty were rolling.

True to historical patterns, with teeter-totter predictability nouvelle became toxically earnest, preachy, joyless, miniaturized, and unfulfilling. Its emaciated eaters lost interest. A counterinsurgency began: terroir, the return to traditionalism.

By the time I climbed onto the Gault & Millau running boards in the late 1980s, the publication had become neo-baroque and uncharacteristically accommodating, using a laurel-leaf symbol and black toques to designate traditional, regional terroir cuisine. Strangely the places resting on their laurels, so to speak, were the ones I liked best. As a class they've survived the supposed decline and fall of French cuisine and many thrive in the twenty-first century.

Bellyaching and self-laceration is big business in France. Martyrdom has been a great blood sport for years—Saint Denis walked a long way from

Montmartre to his suburban sanctuary with his head in his hands. Since nouvelle cuisine and the private initiative of chefs proved incapable of saving French haute, rejected by most French food lovers, a phalanx of restaurateurs, all from the political right and beloved of free enterprise, began to lobby for help and subsidies. No matter the government was left wing. The battle to preserve endangered French gastronomy got underway in 1989 with Socialist Culture Minister Jack Lang's creation of the CNAC (Conseil National des Arts Culinaires). It flopped. Undaunted, the mega chefs, each a branded industry, tried again with UNESCO. The jury is still out on whether protecting the French way of eating will do any good.

Faced by unruly twenty-first-century guidebook editors and an unresponsive digital-age public, it was time to invent the French government-sanctioned ranking system called "La Liste" (www.laliste.com), brainchild of a former CEO of Gault & Millau. It launched in 2015 with a writ to project the excellence of French haute and its chefs into the internet age. La Liste's convoluted methodology uses an algorithm and weighting mechanism about as arcane and reliable as the U.S. electoral system. Among its private sponsors are French food and luxury industries and global conglomerates like Nestlé. Whether anyone beyond those on the payroll, and those listed, cares, is the big question.

French cuisine is endangered, is it? In need of subsidies, labeling, algorithms, and UNESCO to survive? Somehow I don't think so. Restaurateurs, like farmers, rarely celebrate bumper crops and bounteous harvests of table guests, but always spot the drought and downturn miles and months ahead. Declinist pathology is endemic in France and has spread to the New World where American critics have raised their cudgles and beaten French food to a pulp. To emulsify a few more metaphors, a certain style of quivering, vertical dry ice, smoke-and-mirrors French haute needs a respirator but *not* French cuisine *tout court*.

If a national monopoly was the goal, the empire of French gastronomy proved too successful for its own good. It spawned a global network of talented colonial barbarians every bit as skillful, inventive, and energetic as their former masters at lightening wallets while making the emperor's new omelet. Much the same could be said of the New World's makers of wine, bread, pastries, and cheeses. The neo-barbarians are no longer besieging Paris' gastronomical citadel. They've learned lessons, gone home, gone elsewhere, and are doing a fine job, sometimes a great job, and they're no longer paying tribute to France.

This is only part of the story. Perception is the root problem, if there is a problem, meaning the problem probably resides in the minds of a limited number of perceivers. The current Manichaean view of French gastronomy decries tradition and classics seeing only haute and forgetting that the best, most soul satisfying, real, and enduring cuisine is, and always has been, simple, the vernacular distillation of centuries of passion, wisdom, and skill. Even that paragon of perverse narcissism the Sun King preferred bouillon and roasts to the glam food "drowned in apathy and grease," meant to wow the aristos and arrivistes.

"We all are born gourmand," said the "fine *gourmette*" Colette. "The true gourmet is as delighted by buttered bread as grilled lobster, if the butter is good and the bread made right."

Bread, butter, *and* grilled lobster are still pretty good in Paris.

In 2005 *Gourmet* magazine claimed London was the best place to eat in the world—a mouthful. Soon after it was the great arbiter Michelin anointing Tokyo foodie mecca by lavishing more stars on it than those twinkling in the City of Light. Of course everyone knows New York is the true *Stomachus Mundi,* at least it is to the culinary opinion makers in New York. Where to next? Las Vegas, Shanghai, Sydney? If bull markets, oligarchy, voodoo economics, and relentless innovation are the motors of gastronomic excellence, as many Manicheans and glossy magazine writers insist, what about Moscow, Dubai, and Riyadh?

To understand the neo-surreal-post-nouvelle-late-imperial haute of Paris and other global food capitals first read the chapters in this book about Versailles. Then settle into your home entertainment center and watch the cult movie *King of Hearts.* It is set at the end of World War I in Senlis not far from the château where Vatel died in Chantilly. The town is empty except for a bunch of loony-bin escapees. The movie's soldier-hero played by Alan Bates unforgettably describes these fancy-free wanderers as a *population bizarre.* They're as nutty as Marie-Antoinette in fancy dress at the hamlet eating brioche. Welcome to the universe of Michelin, Gault & Millau, La Liste, etc. . . .

It's a bizarre universe of starstruck, betoqued chefs, critics, and sycophants.

They inhabit spaces suspended somewhere between Ancien Régime Versailles and the realm of cinema, a curiously humorless place with scripted "fun" on tap and plenty of seductive luxury. Elagabalus, Apicius, and Louis XIV are the ancestors of today's fashionistas, wineistas, and other gastronomic hedonistas but most haven't read history so don't know it.

Today the mainstream French food guides—there are many—face competition from websites such as TripAdvisor, blogs, and upstarts notably Le Fooding and Omnivore, the self-conscious trendsetters of the 2010s rewarding outlandishness in the style of the apostles of long-dead nouvelle cuisine or fusion. Does anyone remember fusion?

BONNE NOUVELLE

Far from Playland Paris in the humdrum village I've been frequenting for years in southern Burgundy's cattle country, there are currently two excellent organic vegetable farms, an organic bakery, an organic raw-milk cheesemaker, and another who does things naturally without certification and also raises free-range chickens and heirloom porkers. It's true the local café-restaurant went bust and won't come back, but there's a new grocery selling all of the above. The itinerant local farmers' markets haven't been as dynamic in decades. I rarely get anything that isn't very good to outstanding. I have never known the wines of the abutting Mâconnais and Côte Chalonnaise to be better—yet still fine value, incomparably more affordable than anything drinkable made in California. Multiply this equation by dozens or hundreds of similar rural districts in France and you realize that Curnonsky's quip "Paris may wear the crown of *grande cuisine* but the provinces hold the scepter" is still true. Much of the bounty winds up in the capital.

There remains the undeniable problem of Paris' neo-schlock cooking, what I have dubbed "karaoke cuisine" and "cuisine horrible." Most of the late-rising improvised adepts of this microwaved, synthesized tourist fare get their deep frozen, powdered, canned, bottled, premixed, premade, semi-processed, ready-to-serve meals from strategically sited big-box wholesalers near the Paris beltway.

The karaoke cuisine crisis had become so acute that in 2014 the French government created "Fait Maison," a quality-labeling scheme. Its logo is a saucepan topped by a roof and chimney as in housemade. Though the definition of "fait-maison" was tightened in 2015 raising standards, unscrupulous restaurateurs find workarounds, knowing the chances of punishment by anti-fraud squads are next to nil. The logo is at best a useful icebreaker for a serious conversation with your waiter or chef about the cooking.

How do you recognize schlock eateries? I enjoy cruising the streets and back alleys of Paris, checking kitchens and nearby garbage cans for wholesale frozen food packages, empty tubs of industrial sauce, drums of trans fats and other indigestible cooking oils. Here are my ten tips for avoiding karaoke: 1) If a kitchen isn't busy early, it often means the "chef" doesn't work from scratch. 2) If you hear microwaves peeping, head elsewhere. 3) Long menus and small, understaffed kitchens suggest schlock. 4) Roast suckling pig at your local corner café, served at bargain prices, is a giveaway. 5) When the set-price menu includes multiple courses for under $20 beware: the nicer the nice, the higher the price. 6) If the menu boasts a few "fait-maison" dishes, ask why all the dishes aren't housemade. 7) If *"cuisine traditionelle"* or *"cuisine française,"* are writ large on the marquee you're almost guaranteed to find counterfeits. 8) If the décor is pink and familiar, you probably saw it in other pseudo-romantic franchises. 9) If the coffee isn't French bona fide artisan-roasted or imported from Italy, watch out, you're entering Auvergne territory, land of ready-mades. 10) If the chef or waitstaff can't swear there are no glutamates in the food, especially the sauces, you know the sauces are premade and MSG abounds, ready to disguise mediocrity.

My strategy is straightforward: I avoid tourist traps and am prepared to spend real money for real food.

Several impassioned American reporters whose works I've read in the last decade compile impressive statistics proving France's foods and wines are in terminal free fall. As the twentieth-century Roman poet Trilussa quipped,

"There are two of us and one chicken. You take the whole chicken. Per capita we each have half." Caveat statistics.

For what they're worth, some recent figures are encouraging. Less plonk and more good organic wine is being made. Raw milk cheeses are holding their own at 10 to 15 percent of production. It's less than it was fifty years ago in part because total production has skyrocketed, most of it pasteurized, rubberized, conglomerate supermarket cheese similar to the stuff found in inventive foodista heaven, i.e., America and the United Kingdom.

In France, hundreds of small, uncertified fine cheesemakers like the ones in my village are off the radar, out of the stats. Is pasteurized Camembert a national tragedy? That's France 101, a cheese undone by its own success, trying to meet worldwide demand and answer food-scare hysteria at a profit. Pasteur was French. Yet three in four quality French cheeses are still made with raw milk. What percentage of U.S. or UK cheese is? Answer: a tiny, fractional amount.

Here's a statistic from the horse's mouth: METRO Cash & Carry, a chain favored by karaoke cooks for its ready-mades, has 21 million customers in 25 countries, with 94 outlets in France, 107 in Germany, 48 in Italy, and 37 in Spain, motherland of molecular. The United States and United Kingdom have native networks, hundreds of sprawling wholesale restaurant and institutional food megastores and to-your-door suppliers of ready-mades like Sysco. They provide everything from the fresh sublime to the frozen and processed ridiculous—the same kinds of products used by French operators that American investigative reporters now decry. That's a story just waiting to be reported.

How long have critics bewailed the death of the novel? Hint: about as long as others have lamented the death of French cooking. Last I checked novels were doing okay despite digitalization and homogenized, pasteurized MFA writing, and the food, wine, bread, cheese, and produce in France were surviving, too, sometimes against the odds.

It's a funny thing. I keep going out to shop or eat in my Paris neighborhood expecting disasters as prognosticated by the parachute reporters. Instead I have great meals, drink fabulous wines, buy delicious terrines and charcuterie, pungent raw milk cheeses, and wonder whether I've developed sensory senility or suffer from Pangloss Syndrome. Maybe the gloom-and-doom paratroopers have a hidden agenda? Certainly all is not for the best in this, the best of all possible culinary worlds, to paraphrase Voltaire. It's as easy to eat badly in Paris as it is in every other big city in Europe and America. But Parisian gastronomy isn't in its death throes, far from it.

On Paris streets the banquet of wildly different foods served in different ways by different kinds of restaurants, brasseries, bistros, cafés, caterers, sidewalk or market stands, takeout operations, and even food trucks tempts passersby as never before, two thousand years' worth of culinary culture fermenting, bubbling, overflowing, a superimposition of Trimalchio's Feast, Nicolas de Bonnefons' Versailles tables, of Carême, Escoffier, Oliver, and a thousand practitioners of haute and post-nouvelle. Beyond the inevitable big-box retailers and mega-wholesalers scores of neighborhood street markets and specialty food shops, artisan ice cream makers, chocolate and pastry makers, butchers, bakers, and even intramural winemakers ply their trades—profusion found in few other places. Like street fashion, grunge, haute couture, and everything sartorial in between, the food and wine of Paris are more varied and better than at any other time in the last forty years, since I've known the city. I'm not looking back to some mythical golden age when I was young. I'm enjoying the gold flecks in our current, complicated, challenging, fascinatingly alloyed age.

As I write these lines, my eyes are tearing up in pleasant anticipation. The luscious veal blanquette and the firm wild rice from the Camargue are

À bientôt à Paris! (from Brillat-Savarin's Physiologie du goût, *illustrated by Bertall, date unknown)*

simmering on my stovetop. A platter of ripe, raw milk cheeses bought on rue Saint-Antoine at one of the world's least known but best cheese shops is taking the air. Ditto my local wine merchant's organic Menetou-Salon, a subtle, light-bodied Pinot Noir from the Upper Loire Valley happily unsuited for adepts of "bold" wines. I've made a crisp salad of organic arugula and sweet cherry tomatoes from my favorite organic stand at the Boulevard Richard-Lenoir market ten minutes on foot from my door. The sourdough loaf and *tartes fines* of apricot and plum were fashioned this afternoon by an unsung baker on the Île Saint-Louis. Sure, I could've shopped at the foodie designer boutiques and spent a fortune on a *mille-feuille* from Pierre Hermé. But you don't have to if you know where to go. Speaking of which, just look at the time. I must run—dinner beckons. My wife has set the table and poured the wine. This isn't a self-satisfied *au revoir*; it's an open invitation to join me at table in Paris sometime soon.

KEY DATES

300–52 BC: Parisii tribe of Celts colonize Paris area
53–52 BC: Conquest of Parisii by Julius Caesar
1st century BC–fifth century AD: Gallo-Roman period
481–751: Merovingian Dynasty
752–987: Carolingian Dynasty
987–1328: Capetian Dynasty
1328–1589: Valois Dynasty
1589–1789: Bourbon Dynasty
1789–1799: The French Revolution
1793–1794: The Terror
1799: The Consulate; Napoléon Bonaparte is First Consul
1803–1815: The Napoleonic Wars
1804: Napoléon Bonaparte crowned Emperor Napoléon I
1815: Waterloo, final defeat of Napoléon I
1814–1830: The Restoration of the Bourbon Monarchy, Louis XVIII (reigns 1814–1824) and Charles X (reigns 1824–1830)
1830–1848: Reign of "Citizen King" Louis Philippe I
1848: February Revolution, Second Republic, Louis Napoléon Bonaparte elected president
1851–1852: Coup d'état, Louis Napoléon Bonaparte crowned Emperor Napoléon III
1852–1870: Second Empire
1870–1871: Franco-Prussian War, Siege of Paris, Commune

1870–1940: Third Republic
1940–1944: Nazi Occupation of Paris
1946–1959: Fourth Republic
1959–present: Fifth Republic

KEY CHARACTERS

Anne of Austria (1601–1666)

Queen of France, wife of Louis XIII, mother of Louis XIV, reigns 1643–1651.

Marcus Gavius Apicius (first century AD)

One of the great gourmets of antiquity; the plutocratic merchant and sometimes-diplomat authored parts of the early recipe collection *De re coquinaria* (*The Art of Cooking*).

Jacques Arago (1790–1855)

Explorer, contrarian, and muckracking writer; author of *Comme on dîne à Paris*; brother of celebrated scientist and politician François Arago.

Honoré de Balzac (1799–1850)

Gourmand, novelist, playwright, authored a hundred novels, most grouped into *The Human Comedy* (*La Comédie humaine*).

Antoine Beauvilliers (1754–1817)

Maître d' of the Count of Provence later Louis XVIIII; chef and pioneering restaurateur who in 1782 founded La Grande Taverne de Londres; author of seminal cookbook *L'Art du cuisinier*.

Jean Anthelme Brillat-Savarin (1755–1826)

Lawyer, magistrate, and gastronome; author of *La Physiologie du goût* (*The Physiology of Taste*), cornerstone of France's intellectual appreciation of food and wine.

Antonin (Marie-Antoine) Carême (1784–1833)

France's first celebrity chef and cookbook writer, dubbed the "chef of kings and king of chefs."

Charlemagne (742–814)

King of France, Holy Roman Emperor, lover of salads and vegetables, reigns 768–814.

Curnonsky (1872–1956)

Restaurant critic, guidebook and cookbook author (*La France gastronomique*); real name Maurice Edmond Sailland (or Saillant), aka Bibendum; evangelist of simplicity, cuisine bourgeoise, and regional cooking.

Urban Dubois (1818–1901)

Among the most talented French chefs of the nineteenth century, author of many cookbooks, his fame has been eclipsed by that of Carême and Escoffier.

Alexandre Dumas (1802–1870)

Gourmet, novelist, and playwright; authored *The Count of Monte Cristo, The Three Musketeers,* and seminal *Le Grand Dictionnaire de Cuisine.*

Auguste Escoffier (1846–1935)

France's most famous chef and cookbook writer; author of *Le Guide culinaire* (*The Complete Guide to the Art of Modern Cookery*); heir of Antonin Carême, whose device "chef of kings and king of chefs" he adopted.

François I (1494–1547)

French king, transforms Paris into New Rome, reigns 1515–1547.

Alexandre Balthazar Laurent Grimod de la Reynière (1758–1837)

Lawyer and theater critic, best known as France's first food writer and theorist of gastronomy, author of the long-running guidebook series *Almanach des Gourmands.*

Georges-Eugène Haussmann (1809–1891)

Aka Baron Haussmann; prefect of the Seine responsible for Second Empire remake of Paris.

Henri IV (1553–1610)

French king, first known as Henri II of Navarre, father of Louis XIII, promised populace "a chicken in every pot," reigns 1589–1610.

Julian the Apostate (331?–363)

Roman Prefect of Gaul; declared Roman Emperor in Lutetia Parisiorum; first to use the modern name of the city, Paris.

Julius Caesar (100–44 BC)

Roman Emperor, dictator 49–44 BC, conqueror of Gaul (58–52 BC).

François Pierre de La Varenne (1615–1678)

Chef, author of groundbreaking French cookbooks *Le Cuisinier françois* (1651) and *Le Pâtissier françois* (1653).

Louis XIII (1601–1643)

French king, son of Henri IV and Maria de' Medici, reigns 1610–1643.

Louis XIV (1638–1715)

French king, aka the Sun King, son of Louis XIII (paternity disputed) and Anne of Austria, reigns 1643–1715.

Louis XV (1710–1774)

French king, the great-grandson of Louis XIV, reigns 1715–1774.

Louis XVI (1754–1793)

French king, grandson of Louis XV, reigns 1774–1792.

Louis XVIII (1755–1824)

Younger brother of Louis XVI; alias the Count of Provence; becomes French king, reigns 1814–1824.

Louis Philippe I d'Orléans (1773–1850)

Alias the Citizen King; reigns 1830–1848.

Cardinal Mazarin (1602–1661)

Real name, Giulio Raimondo Mazzarino; governs France 1643–1661 during Regency of Anne of Austria (1643–1651), mother of King Louis XIV. Possible genetic father of Louis XIV.

Catherine de Médicis (1519–1589)

Wife of Henri II; real name Caterina Maria Romula di Lorenzo de' Medici; mother of kings François II, Charles IX, Henri III, and Queen Marguerite de Valois (wife of Henri II de Navarre, later Henri IV of France).

Marie de Médicis (1575–1642)

Wife of Henri IV, a Florentine, real name Maria de' Medici, mother of Louis XIII, famed for her gourmandizing.

Napoléon I, Emperor (Napoléon Bonaparte, 1769–1821)

Revolutionary general; first consul, emperor of First French Empire 1804–1814.

Napoléon III, Emperor (Louis Napoléon Bonaparte, 1808–1873)

Nephew of Napoléon I; dictator, emperor of Second French Empire 1852–1870.

Antoine-Augustin Parmentier (1737–1813)

Agronomist, author, popularized the potato in France. Many dishes featuring mashed potatoes are named for him.

Madame de Pompadour (1721–1764)

Jeanne-Antoinette Poisson, aka Madame de Pompadour; King Louis XV's most celebrated official mistress, starting in 1745.

François Rabelais (1494?–1553)

Roistering monk, physician, scholar, author of *Gargantua and Pantagruel*; considered France's great Renaissance writer.

Taillevent (1310–1395)

Real name Guillaume Tirel; chef of kings Charles V and VI, author of early French cookbook *Le Viandier*.

Voltaire (1694–1778)

Real name François-Marie Arouet; Enlightenment essayist, playwright, philosopher, historian.

IMAGE CREDITS

All historic images are from the author's private collection or in the public domain courtesy of Wikimedia Commons or The Library of Congress (Louis XIV dining with Molière at court LOC 2003662191; Louis XVI arrested while dining LOC 2015646584).

Contemporary image of sign showing Grimod de la Reynière by the author.

ABOUT THE AUTHOR

Author and journalist David Downie is a native San Franciscan who moved to Paris in the mid-1980s. He divides his time between France and Italy. His travel, food, and arts features have appeared in dozens of leading print and online publications worldwide. Downie and his wife, photographer Alison Harris, create custom walking tours of Paris and other European destinations. Please visit David Downie's websites: www.davidddownie.com and www.parisparistours.com.